IRISH FEMINISMS:

Past, Present and Future

Dr Mary Cullen

Dr Margaret Mac Curtain

IRISH FEMINISMS:
Past, Present and Future

Essays in Honour of
Mary Cullen and Margaret Mac Curtain

Edited by Clara Fischer and Mary McAuliffe

ARLEN
HOUSE

IRISH FEMINISMS: PAST, PRESENT AND FUTURE

is published in 2015 by
ARLEN HOUSE
42 Grange Abbey Road
Baldoyle
Dublin 13
Ireland
Phone: +353 86 8207617
Email: arlenhouse@gmail.com

978–1–85132–118–6, paperback
978–1–85132–124–7, hardback

International distribution by
SYRACUSE UNIVERSITY PRESS
621 Skytop Road, Suite 110
Syracuse, New York
USA 13244–5290
Phone: 315–443–5534/Fax: 315–443–5545
Email: supress@syr.edu
www.syracuseuniversitypress.syr.edu

Typesetting by Arlen House
Cover Artwork: 'Composition' (1930) by Mainie Jellett
Collection: Dublin City Gallery The Hugh Lane

CONTENTS

Acknowledgements

Our sincere thanks are due to the authors of the work presented here, as well as to those who contributed in other ways. A volume of this sort requires many helping hands, from photographers allowing us to reprint their work, to readers providing feedback on chapters. We are grateful for all of their support, and acknowledge the generosity with which *Irish Feminisms: Past, Present and Future*, has been met. We also extend our gratitude to the co-ordinators and supporters of the Irish Feminist Network, for volunteering time and labour to the 2012 conference from which these essays emanated. Thanks are due to Dublin City Gallery The Hugh Lane for their help with the cover image, and to the publishers, Arlen House, for seeing this project through with us. We would also like to thank our colleagues in UCD Women's Studies and the Gender Institute, London School of Economics and Political Science. Finally, we are grateful to the two feminist scholars and activists, Mary Cullen and Margaret Mac Curtain, to whom this book is dedicated. Their practice and thought have formed significant contributions to feminisms in Ireland, which we will continue to draw on for years to come.

FOREWORD

Ann Louise Gilligan and Katherine Zappone

When Mary Robinson was inaugurated as President of Ireland in 1990 she said that she would be representing a new Ireland – one that is open, tolerant and inclusive. She wanted her Presidency to promote the telling of stories – 'stories of celebration through the arts and stories of conscience and of social justice'. She spoke of the need for women 'who have felt themselves outside history to be written back into history, in the words of Eavan Boland, "finding a voice where they found a vision"'. We remember the extraordinary inspiration and impetus that these words provided.

Nearly twenty-five years later, this book tells some of these stories. Spanning a hundred year period twelve diverse contributors from the academy, politics, and community present a wide ranging introduction to Irish feminisms in fourteen chapters, each bringing aspects of the story and the journey to light, often speaking from the margins about this very exclusion of women from history that has arisen from gender ideologies that promote sexist, patriarchal and hierarchical thinking and imagining.

The result is a lively, questioning, well researched and very accessible book dealing with Irish feminist movements from the early debates and dilemmas of women seeking a voice in the affairs of State, to contemporary feminists finding outlets for their voice and vision through journalism, blogs and social media.

The themes and topics reflect a very varied terrain. Whether it's the question of suffrage, or political representation, abortion or reproductive rights, or the newer landscapes of lesbian, gay and trans gender rights, the areas of violence against women, prostitution and sex trafficking, or the problems posed for migrant women, Irish feminists have attempted to negotiate pathways where, as Adrienne Rich observed, 'the maps they gave us were out of date/by years'. This is done with honesty, integrity and genuine commitment by each of the contributors who are experts in their own field. Each brings an angle of vision and interpretation to their inquiry that is refreshing, educational and enlightening.

This is not an abstract, disembodied book. On the contrary, there is a huge commitment to activism and transformation, both in the stories and themes explored and in the lives of the contributors themselves. Whether that is expressed through community activism on the national or international stage, or whether it is lobbying, campaigning, protesting or mobilising, there is a good blend of theory and practice. A number of chapters take as their focus individual women's lives and voices, like Mamo McDonald (President of the ICA and long-time activist who says that life made her a feminist) or Mary Dorcey and Marie McMahon of Irishwomen United, who continue to contribute as feminists and activists in Ireland. Equally contributors who write from their own lifetime commitment to feminism – for example academic, Ailbhe Smyth and community activist, Grainne Healy – all offer an invaluable contribution to any discourse on Irish feminism, as they provide a glimpse of the trajectory of a life and how one's ideas are developed and embodied over time.

Healy uses Mary Dorcey's metaphor 'moving into the space cleared by our mothers' to frame the movement of feminisms from the 1970s up to the present day. The constant questioning, discussion and ground-breaking hard work that happens over nearly fifty years for those seeking equality is certainly no ivory tower pursuit. It is a story that must be told both for this generation and for those who come after us. The spaces that have been cleared by our foremothers allow the next generation to find a standing place.

Ailbhe Smyth's entry is written as a diary of a feminist academic 'shuffling between mainstream and margins of one kind or another'. Her title (adapted from Muriel Rukeyser), 'Resist, fall, fail, resist', while specific to her own journey, could also describe the trajectory of Irish feminism over the past one hundred years. We wonder why is it that so much seems to have been forgotten or needs to be re-learned by each succeeding generation?

Many of the contributors refer to feminisms as occurring in waves. Using this metaphor as Fischer does (in her chapter on feminist storytelling) we can consider the whole period from the 1900s to the present day as a 'continuous ever-present movement that sometimes eddies and intensifies, and sometimes constitutes stiller waters'. This ever-present movement of Irish feminists is gradually changing the landscape over time, refusing myths and stereotypes of domesticity, resisting silencing and exclusion, and blunting the edges of gendered legislation. From the early days of Hanna Sheehy Skeffington writing in *The Irish Citizen* in 1919, 'we stand for the rights of all Irish women as women, independent of part or sect', to the founding of AkiDwA by Salome Mbugua and other Irish-African women in 2001 to address isolation, racism and gender-based violence against migrant women, there is continuity in the struggle for justice and freedom from oppression. The issues that Irish feminists struggle with in a pluralist and multi-cultural Ireland may be different to those our foremothers encountered but they still revolve around questions of power, inclusion, and visibility. The vision or goal has always been that of a more inclusive and just society that accepts and celebrates difference. As one wave of feminism ebbs, we celebrate that the next one is flowing in its wake.

Moving like a shadow through the book are many references to the tragic story of Savita Halappanavar's untimely and apparently preventable death in Galway University Hospital in 2012. Highlighting the inadequacy of Ireland's abortion laws, many thousands took to the streets in protest with demands to change the legislation. Ivana Bacik's feminist review of the law on abortion is a lucid sequenced analysis of legal, social and political developments on the reproductive rights campaign in Ireland from 1983 onwards. There has been a clear shift in public opinion and positive signs ahead in relation to a period of Constitutional reform. The kind of outrage experienced at the tragic death of this young woman raises awareness of the kind of systemic injustice embedded in patriarchal systems and highlights the urgency for reform. The surge of emotion recalls Seamus Heaney's words on justice and history:

> History says, Don't hope
> on this side of the grave.
> But then, once in a lifetime
> the longed for tidal wave
> of justice can rise up,
> and hope and history rhyme.

When you take a time span of a hundred plus years and ask a dozen people to write about different aspects of the trajectory of Irish feminisms over that time, you get a wide variety of standpoints and opinions. Coming from diverse fields of history, politics, sociology, law or women's studies, speaking from a lifetime of community and social activism, and writing from the vantage point of the journalist, brings an abundance of riches and the reader is left with the task of resolving many of the contradictions and questions that arise within the text as a whole.

Only one definition of feminism is offered throughout the book. While many authors imply what feminism is, or speak of themselves as feminist, the only definition found is 'advocacy of equal rights for women coupled with organised and sustained action for the purpose of achieving them' (Marilyn Boxer cited in Margaret Ward's chapter), and, even this is seen as inadequate by Ward herself or not expansive enough to cover Irish feminism when coupled with the issue of nationalism. We look forward to the ways in which this book will inspire further explorations of the meanings and understandings of Irish feminisms. We think that the systemic injustices alluded to throughout the essays provide a platform to question the whole way a culture makes meaning or as Irigaray once said to 'jam theoretical machinery' with the interruptive narratives of repressed subjectivities.

The book is entitled *Irish Feminisms: Past, Present and Future*, it could equally be read as a study of Irish feminist movements and some of the *feminist activists* that shaped and sustained those movements. Kellie Turtle in her chapter on contemporary feminism in Northern Ireland is an example of questions raised that excite and call for further explorations as movements go forward. Examples include: the uncompromising vision of radical feminism – is this the only true feminism? Or liberal feminism – is its conciliatory approach selling feminism short? Is there continuity, or is the emerging third or fourth wave feminism a different feminism altogether? How does one build on what has gone before? What is the place of men in the future of feminism? Is there still a time and place for women-only gatherings? Turtle provides a comprehensive treatment of these issues as she studies a new period of feminist mobilisation while also building on the legacy of earlier activists, and raises very pertinent questions around the sexual objectification of women, the challenge to young women to reconcile gender equality and sexual liberation, and the importance of linking issues of reproductive health and rights to other social justice issues.

How does one put in place a critically reflective praxis methodology in relation to one's feminism? Many authors raise questions about conflict, bullying and differences of opinion within feminist organisations. They speak about the problems of remaining radical when State funding is in place. Others write about how the employment of men in some feminist organisations changes the way the work happens on the ground. A sustained theoretical analysis of these issues will make a significant contribution in our understanding the evolution of feminism. Fischer offers initial reflections in her piece on feminist storytelling and Sherlock offers a theoretical analysis on the Irish trans gender landscape, Turtle offers the most sustained analysis of how feminist movements evolve. Her commitment to intersectionality that pays attention to the interactions of multiple systems of oppression, including gender, race, class, disability, is suggested as a safeguard mechanism against which one must become aware of one's blind spots in relation to the marginalisation of women whose identities and experiences we have failed to represent. This is sound advice for any feminist organisation.

Looking to the future of feminism in Ireland, Mary Robinson once said, that 'a society that is without the voice and vision of a woman is not less feminine. It is less human' (quoted in McTeirnan). Throughout the book the question of the new legislation in relation to electoral quotas repeatedly arises. That 30% of candidates must be women by 2016, rising to 40% in seven years offers some possibility of better visibility and representation of women across the political parties. However, this immediately brings us into the realm of power and raises the issue of whether, and how, men will share it. Perhaps it also indicates that it is time to redefine masculinities. How might this come about? What would it look like in practice?

How feminism evolves in Ireland, as the second wave gives way to the third or even the fourth, and co-mingles for a time, is considered throughout the book. It is important to acknowledge the tireless contribution of women from the 1960s onwards to sustaining a vision of equality and inclusiveness that contemporary feminists can build upon. It is also important, as many of the contributors stress, that there is a graciousness in how the mantle is passed on to the next generation, and equally important that each generation listen, see and value the other as she really is and not through projection, judgement and dismissal. Ailbhe Smyth's advice from this volume is appropriate to any generation of feminists:

> Realise we have to be rigorous, steadfast and brave in what we do: our scholarship, writing, teaching, organising. Recognise we have to be clear-sighted about the toll this takes on our lives. Think about the solidarity that comes from working together with others. Think how we have to be careful of ourselves and of each other because hearts and souls are always fragile.

Throughout this book the words of June Jordan ring (as quoted by Smyth), reminding us that feminisms' primary 'orientation is activism'. In staying true in different ways to a 'deeply subversive vision' (McCarthy quoted in McKay) women have challenged the hegemony of patriarchal thinking and the unjust structures it has created. For over a hundred years Irish women have insisted on being written back into history. They have insisted that their voices be heard, that their vision for a more inclusive and just society become a reality.

The legacy of Irish feminists, whether past or present, always streams into the possible space of the future. We recommend *Irish Feminisms: Past, Present and Future* as a worthy and timely contribution to this debate.

> When you have buried us   told your story
> Ours does not end   we stream
> into the unfinished   the unbegun
> the possible
>
> – Adrienne Rich

IRISH FEMINISMS:
Past, Present and Future

IRISH FEMINISMS: PAST, PRESENT AND FUTURE
AN INTRODUCTION

Clara Fischer

Irish Feminisms: Past, Present and Future arose from a conference organised by the Irish Feminist Network in 2012, the purpose of which was to facilitate 'discussion on successive feminist 'waves' in Ireland, and what they contributed and continue to contribute to gender equality in this country'.[1] Ambitious as this remit is, the conference, and indeed the resultant volume, soon revealed the complexities involved in undertaking such a wide-ranging analysis of feminisms in Ireland. For, an attempt to chart and assess a social movement as diverse as Irish feminism over the better part of a century, will necessarily be partial, incomplete and perspectival. *Irish Feminisms: Past, Present, and Future* therefore makes no claim to constitute a finished overview or final reading of feminist thought and practice in Ireland. Rather, the aim of the book is to provide a 'snapshot', or series of images, taken during the period of summer 2012–2013, with a variety of contributors offering their particular views on feminisms in Ireland – past, present and future.

Such feminist depictions of past events, of contemporary issues, or of future trajectories, though, need not be neatly separable, if at all. The benefit of presenting diverse feminist agents and topics across sometimes vast timespans lies precisely in the opportunity it affords readers to seek out continuities, as well as discontinuities. What were the concerns of suffrage campaigners (Ward)? Were these concerns met during their lifetime, or do they persist in contemporary feminist subjects, and possibly form future feminist preoccupations? What were the feminist tools and knowledge reservoirs passed on (or not) through successive generations of feminists in Ireland? What do the generational dynamics among feminists themselves look like in a context that now boasts not just the third, but increasingly the fourth wave of feminism (Turtle, Fischer)? On the other hand, what are the unique, and perhaps defining political events and issues of a specific time period? Which achievements have feminists been able to celebrate, and which losses and injustices do we still struggle with?

Throughout the book such questions surface, and resurface, as the text's subtitle is implicitly or more directly interrogated by feminist analyses that focus on the temporal specificity of historical, social, and political contexts, while also offering opportunities for addressing contradictions or confluences across distinct moments of time. The contributions collated here, then, can be seen as reflective of feminist engagement of the wave metaphor, which has itself been problematised, but continues to be used as a marker of feminist temporality. Indeed, early talk of 'waves' or 'tides' to describe social movements is often credited to Irish feminist activist, Frances Power Cobbe. Of feminism she said in 1884:

> This movement has stirred an entire sex, even half the human race. Like the incoming tide, also, it has rolled in separate waves, and each one has obeyed the same law, and has done its part in carrying forward all the rest.[2]

Just how and to what extent each feminist wave has 'carr[ied] forward all the rest', is often explored in this book. Relations among feminists across generational lines, but also across ideological lines, are examined by contributors, who provide reflexive insights on feminist movement building and solidarity, as well as on in-fighting and differentiation (McKay). Indeed, as the metaphor of the feminist 'snapshot' indicates, there is a particular need for introspection and reflexivity if one is to assess one's own role in the construction of feminisms past, present and future. Many of the chapters presented here, then, betray a certain self-awareness of the pictures they paint, and are not just outwardly-directed examinations of particular policy problems, but frequently look inward to the private, and to the affective life of feminism itself.

Throughout the book, tensions between conservatism and radicalism arise (Fischer on McDonald, McAuliffe on Irishwomen United), and certain gendered injustices sometimes reappear. The issue of reproductive rights, for instance, is addressed repeatedly, albeit in different contexts (Bacik, McTeirnan), as is women's representation and agency in the formal political institutions of the state (McGing, McAuliffe). There are also personal reflections on feminist life in academia (Smyth) or in the community and NGO sector (Healy), and contributions on migrant women's rights (Mbugua) and on feminism's relationship to Irish trans activism (Sherlock). The book includes chapters on Ireland north and south, and crosses geographical and political boundaries, as well as disciplinary and stylistic demarcations. It is made up of the voices of journalists, NGO practitioners, volunteers, students, policymakers, and academics. In collating these essays, it was always clear that a book on Irish feminisms must at least attempt to be as multi-faceted as feminism itself.

With that said, given the above noted perspectival and necessarily partial nature of the work, *Irish Feminisms* should be used as a source to spark further debate and feminist exploration of feminisms past, present and future. Although each chapter is unique, and each of the contributors adds to a very diverse series of feminist pictures, on-going recording and examination of feminist ideas and practice is essential to collating and retaining knowledge about feminisms in Ireland, to help us work toward achieving our respective and collective feminist projects. I am grateful to each of the writers for sharing their thoughts and experiences in *Irish Feminisms* in service to 'the movement that has sparked an entire sex', and hope that the book will contribute to 'carrying forward' Irish feminisms in future years.

NOTES

1   Irish Feminist Network, 'IFN Conference: "Feminist Activism in Ireland: Past, Present and Future"', http://www.irishfeminist network.org/news--events/ifn-conference-feminist-activism-in-ireland-past-present-and-future, accessed 12/08/2013.

2   Karen Offen, *European Feminisms, 1700–1950: A Political History* (Stanford CA, Stanford University Press, 2000), p. 153.

'A VOICE IN THE AFFAIRS OF THE NATION'?
DEBATES AND DILEMMAS WITHIN FIRST WAVE FEMINISM IN IRELAND

Margaret Ward

If we define feminism as 'advocacy of equal rights for women coupled with organised and sustained action for the purpose of achieving them',[1] then Ireland, both north and south, was not wanting in feminist advocates during what is considered to be the 'first wave' of feminism. The campaigns of first wave feminists in nineteenth- and early twentieth-century Britain and Ireland resulted in the opening of higher education for women; reform of the girls' secondary-school system, including participation in examinations; widening of access to the professions; married women's property rights; and the gradual realisation that possession of the parliamentary vote was the only way to ensure equality of citizenship for women. Irish reformers, although not as well known, were the equivalent of their British sisters in terms of their achievements. We have, for example, Anne Jellicoe in Dublin and Margaret Byers in Belfast, campaigning for advancements in the education of girls; the work of Isabella Tod in Belfast and Anna Haslam in Dublin, for the abolition of the Contagious Diseases Acts (1864, 1866 and 1869) and for temperance and social reform. Isabella Tod was also responsible for the first suffrage society in Ireland, establishing in 1873 the North of Ireland Women's Suffrage Society. This was followed in 1876 by the Dublin Women's Suffrage Association (later to become the Irish Women's Suffrage and Local Government Association – IWSLGA), formed by Anna and Thomas Haslam, and the stepping stone for many suffragists who later moved to other organisations and campaigns. Many suffrage campaigners espoused a large number of causes – they were vegetarians, anti-vivisection, sometimes humanist rather than supporters of organised religion – in other words, similar to their counterparts across the Irish Sea, but perhaps even more admirable, given the more conservative nature of Irish society.

As Maria Luddy has shown, from the 1860s Irish women were 'strongly influenced' by suffrage groups in the rest of the United Kingdom, with Irish suffragists copying their campaigning tactics and Irish and British women also campaigning together on many women's rights issues.[2] While British and Irish feminists had a common aim – to persuade the British government to support votes for women legislation – the imperial parliament at Westminster was not necessarily an acceptable political arena for all Irish women. Although the early first wave feminists were largely unionist in orientation and opposed to Ireland leaving the United Kingdom, as the movement developed there were considerable numbers of suffragist campaigners who hoped for a Home Rule parliament in Dublin in which to exercise their vote.

While it is undoubtedly the case that much anti-Home Rule sentiment was motivated by an antipathy towards the Catholic Church, Isabella Tod's opposition to the first Home Rule Bill of 1886 was based on a belief that continued rule from Britain was a better option for women, given the dominance of the Catholic Church in Ireland: 'knowing Ireland thoroughly, I knew that all the social work in which I had taken so prominent a part for twenty years was in danger'.[3] Tod, Anna Haslam, Margaret Byers and other feminists maintained a principled stand that appeared to centre largely upon feminist convictions. Haslam's biographer believes her antipathy to Home Rule was based on the belief that it 'would result in a diminution of personal liberty'.[4] This feminism was, however, aligned 'with the more conservative English groups'.[5] Millicent Fawcett, the leader of the National Union of Women's Suffrage Societies in England, was a noted anti-Home Rule advocate who visited Ireland during the 1880s and 1890s.

Few women in Ireland spoke in public at this period and feminist campaigning was mainly confined to drawing room meetings and the signing of petitions. Isabella Tod was the only female member of a delegation from the Ulster Liberal Unionist Association in Belfast to address protest meetings throughout England. When the second Home Rule Bill was introduced in 1892, Tod organised a committee of sixteen women, including her close friend Margaret Byers, founder of the first girls' secondary school in the north, to speak before a large Unionist gathering. Tod's address emphasised again the right of the unionist community 'to preserve our own civil and religious liberty'.[6] Her anti-Home Rule campaigns lost her support amongst British feminists, who were mostly in support of Irish Home Rule. Josephine Butler, founder of the Ladies' National Association and prominent campaigner against the implementation of the Contagious Diseases Acts, when speaking at a conference in Dublin in the 1880s, also praised the political campaigning of Home Rule advocates.[7]

Given this context, in considering first wave feminism from an Irish perspective, there needs to be a more expansive definition than a movement framed solely around 'advocacy of equal rights for women'. Framing first wave feminism in Ireland only as a movement centred around campaigns for educational reform, property rights and the vote obscures what is distinctive about the Irish situation and marginalises movements that involved nationalist women, which also require consideration. There is a strong case to be made for the inclusion of the Ladies' Land League, who fought so bravely for the rights of the tenant farmers of Ireland in the 1880s. They were the first women's organisation in Ireland and under the leadership of Anna Parnell they made it clear that women intended to determine the political goals of the campaign in much more radical fashion than their male colleagues. Anna Parnell was keenly aware of women's politically subordinate position, the consequence of their lack of voting rights: 'if the men of that country have made up their minds it shall not be done, the women cannot bring it about'.[8] There were close links between radicals in the British suffrage movement and the Ladies' Land League.

Jessie Craigen, who worked for the Ladies' National Association on the repeal of the Contagious Diseases Acts, gave up that position in order to campaign for the League. Helen Taylor, stepdaughter of John Stuart Mill, was president of the Ladies' Land League of Great Britain. She came over to Ireland to attend evictions and she organised the Political Prisoners' Aid Society.[9] In 1885 Anna Parnell demonstrated her feminist credentials by supporting Helen Taylor during her unsuccessful challenge to women's political exclusion while attempting to be selected as Liberal-radical parliamentary candidate for North Camberwell.[10]

A persuasive case can also be made for the inclusion of Inghinidhe na hÉireann (Daughters of Erin), formed in 1900 as the first nationalist women's organisation. This was an outcome of women's exclusion from other nationalist organisations, a legacy of the acrimonious demise of the Ladies' Land League and subsequent male determination to maintain political control, even at the expense of a sex that had no political power. Inghinidhe na hÉireann were determined advocates of women's rights: 'our right to have a voice in directing the affairs of Ireland is … the inherent right of women as loyal citizens and intelligent human beings'.[11] Their objective was the complete independence of Ireland: 'freedom for our nation and the complete removal of all disabilities to our sex' was, they said, their 'battle cry'[12] and their journal declared support for 'complete separatism, the rising cause of feminism and the interest of Irishwomen generally'.[13]

As nationalists, Inghinidhe women refused to look for the 'imprimatur of a hostile government'[14] and did not support the movement for women's suffrage because, they protested, they did not want a vote for an 'alien' parliament. They argued that their role was to achieve equality for women within Irish nationalism. *Bean na hÉireann*, their journal, is an invaluable source for first wave Irish feminism. As Karen Steele has concluded, 'if it lacked an explicit commitment to the suffragist cause' it 'nonetheless expressed advanced feminist and labour views for its time'.[15] Reading its pages, one is struck by how modern the views of contributors were. They were active in the workforce, active in political life and advocates of physical force as the way to achieve political independence. They rejected the notion of 'separate spheres' for women and men – for them the sphere of women was not bounded by 'frying pans and fashion plates'. They complained about the 'early Victorian views' of the Dublin Gas Company who refused to accept a woman as guarantor: 'naturally we think the word of a woman quite as good as the word of a man'.[16]

While *Bean na hÉireann* engaged in spirited debate with suffragists, there is strong evidence that individual Inghinidhe members were supportive of suffrage. Helena Moloney, editor of *Bean*, supported the suffrage movement 'both politically and personally' and approved of the militant campaign in England,[17] while Constance Markievicz, one of their best known members, acknowledged that suffrage gave her a 'first bite ... at the apple of freedom' when she joined the Sligo branch of the Irishwomen's Suffrage and Local Government Association in 1896.[18] The best summary of the nationalist rationale against fighting for the vote was a lecture delivered in 1909 by Markievicz to the Students' National Literary Society in Dublin and subsequently published as a pamphlet by Inghinidhe. While she was full of hope for the future:

> a strong tide of liberty seems to be coming towards us, swelling and growing and carrying before it all the outposts that had women enslaved and bearing them triumphantly into the life of the nation to which they belong.

She also counselled against involvement in the suffrage movement:

> so many Unionist women would fain have us work together with them for the emancipation of their sex and votes – obviously to send a member to Westminster. But I would ask every nationalist woman to pause before she joined a Suffrage Society or Franchise League that did not include in their programme the Freedom of their Nation. A Free Ireland with No Sex Disabilities in her Constitution should be the motto of all Nationalist Women. And a grand motto it is.

Markievicz urged nationalist women to:

remind their men ... to examine any legislation ... not from a party point of view, not from the point of view of a sex, a trade or a class, but simply and only from the standpoint of their nation.[19]

In significant contrast, Hanna Sheehy Skeffington (who would become the best known of the Irish militant suffragists) used the pages of *Bean na hEireann* to challenge the Inghinidhe women to examine how their male colleagues treated them. She argued that they were not considered equals, but only recognised for their roles as mothers and housekeepers. Sheehy Skeffington had, from her earliest writings, continually linked the goals of feminism and nationalism, while criticising nationalists for their failure to support the feminist cause. 'Until the women of Ireland are free, the men will not achieve emancipation', she argued, adding that Irish women of every political persuasion should

refuse any longer to be the camp followers and parasites of public life, dependent on caprice and expediency for recognition. It is for Irishwomen to set about working out their political salvation.[20]

She always retained the conviction that women should participate only in organisations that included equality between the sexes as a defining principle. She also felt strongly that women needed their own independent organisation, which provided them with the necessary intellectual and political independence to challenge patriarchy in whatever form it took. Inghinidhe's existence, despite this critique, led to women's participation in what became Sinn Féin, the first nationalist organisation to have both women and men on its executive. Many Inghinidhe women later ended up in the Irish Citizen Army, participating in the Easter Rising on an equal basis with their male comrades.

The formation in 1903, in Manchester, of the Women's Social and Political Union (WSPU) as a militant organisation not afraid to risk prison for their activities was a huge inspiration for Irish feminists. As the suffrage campaign developed momentum with the constitutional crisis around Home Rule, women in Ireland increasingly had to define whether they put 'nation' or 'suffrage' first. As a younger generation 'in a hurry with reform'[21] took up the suffrage cause, the political orientation of Irish feminism changed considerably. Carmel Quinlan succinctly sums up differences between the Irish Women's Franchise League (the IWFL – founded in 1908 in Dublin) and the Irish Women's Suffrage and Local Government Association (IWSLGA) as being 'social, generational and ideological'.[22] While the relationship between the IWSGLA and the 'neophyte, young, militant IWFL, was essentially a mirror image of the English situation and the Fawcett's National Union of Women's Suffrage Societies and the Pankhurst's Women's Social and Political Union',[23] there was an additional difference that had its roots in the distinctive nature of the Irish movement. This was illustrated by the 1906 resignation of Hanna Sheehy Skeffington from the IWSGLA. She disagreed over the wording of its annual report, having wanted 'British' to be substituted for 'our own' in the phrase 'our own enterprising colonies'.[24] It was a significant difference.

In 1908 Hanna Sheehy Skeffington and Margaret Cousins co-founded the Irish Women's Franchise League as a militant organisation, determined to achieve 'Suffrage First – Before All Else'. It was an independent, Irish-defined organisation, recognising that the colonial relationship between Britain and Ireland would determine the strategy of the Irish militants. They needed to develop a programme of action which would be 'suitable to the different political situation of Ireland as between a subject-country seeking freedom from England, and England, a free country'.[25] Crucially, they declared they wanted 'home rule for Irish women as well as Irish men'. While the primary focus was trying to force the Westminster government to pass a bill granting women the vote, women from many different groups were also attempting to persuade an increasingly hostile Irish Parliamentary Party (who, with a minority Liberal government, now held the balance of power at Westminster) not only to support all suffrage bills coming before Parliament, but also to support the inclusion of female suffrage within the forthcoming Home Rule Bill.

Irish suffragists attended suffrage meetings in London, for example participating in mass suffrage demonstrations when the Conciliation Bill was going through parliament in 1910, conspicuous as 'a blaze of orange and green'. Some also received training from English groups: from Dublin six members of the Irish Women's Franchise League, including Margaret Cousins, and from Belfast, Dr Elizabeth Bell and Margaret Robinson, all volunteered with the Women's Social and Political Union, serving prison sentences in Holloway as a result. Cousins noted, 'it was a helpful apprenticeship for our campaign later in Ireland'.[26] The IWFL was never particularly welcome in Belfast, despite the efforts of a few prominent members of the Irish Women's Suffrage Society, such as Margaret McCoubrey, who shared the Sheehy Skeffington sympathy with labour politics. Elizabeth Bell was unionist in political sympathies (as were possibly the majority of members of the Irish Women's Suffrage Society, given the political composition of Belfast). Feminists who also had unionist inclinations do not seem to have devoted time to persuading Ulster Unionists into support for their cause. Isabella Tod had died in 1896 and there was no prominent unionist feminist to take her place. Edith, the 7th Marchioness of Londonderry, an ardent suffragist, lived in London, where she was a member of the National Union of Suffrage Societies. In this she was, in Diane Urquhart's phrase, an 'aristocratic oddity'.[27] Much more typical of upper class unionist women was her mother-in-law, Theresa, the 6th Marchioness, who was vociferously anti-Home Rule and anti-suffrage.[28]

Many suffrage campaigners who sympathised with the unionist cause, aware of the potential of the wider political issue to fracture the movement, tried to retain the emphasis upon franchise, rather than constitutional issues. The contribution of Mary Edith Cope of the Armagh Suffrage Society is one of the best exemplars of this. In 1912, contributing to women's protest at their exclusion from the Third Home Rule bill, she declared:

> I write from the purely Unionist point of view, But it seems to me imperative that all women, of whatever political party, should now stand for a great principle – the principle that no democratic Government can be considered complete which ignores not only a class but a whole sex.[29]

However, Cope was not a typical Ulster unionist, coming as she did from Surrey following her marriage to John Garland Cope of Drummilly, Loughgall. She had previously been a member of the Women's Freedom League (whose President was the socialist Charlotte Despard).[30]

Initial militancy by Irish women, such as heckling, had had some impact, in that suffrage delegations were subsequently received by previously unresponsive politicians, but the demand for inclusion of women within Home Rule was ignored. Women's frustration resulted in the start of 'militant militancy', as Hanna Sheehy Skeffington termed it, with six members of the IWFL on 13 June 1912 smashing windows in Dublin Castle, the GPO, the Custom House and other prime targets. Sheehy Skeffington chose Dublin Castle, seat of British rule in Ireland, and talked about avenging the wrongs of fifty years.[31] In the words of IWFL member Meg Connery, the women were 'outlaws' because they were excluded from the rights of citizenship.[32] The analysis of Sheehy Skeffington on the eve of her first imprisonment was explicit in its insistence that this was the beginning of a militant feminist revolution aimed at bringing to an end the social, political and economic subordination of Irish women. Women were resorting to violence, not in furtherance of 'male liberties' but for themselves. They were fighting to end the injustices and abuse suffered by so many women, ranging from the sweatshops of Belfast, prostitution on Dublin streets and the sordid institution of the 'bargain marriage', which was contracted to keep farms together and had banished love from the Irish countryside.[33] In a speech in Phoenix Park she linked the women's militancy with the physical force tradition of Irish nationalism:

> If Wolfe Tone, Emmet and Davitt had not stood in the dock and suffered death and imprisonment, those at the meeting might not be present today but very likely would be in the colonies.[34]

Margaret McCoubrey of Belfast's IWSS also drew links between the suffrage militants and the Irish tradition of violent protest.[35]

We know from the personal lives of the Sheehy Skeffingtons and the Cousins the extent to which they rejected traditional gender roles. The *Irish Citizen*, initially edited by both Frank Sheehy Skeffington and James Cousins until the Cousins left Ireland, was explicit in its conception of the ultimate goal of the feminist revolution. Its masthead declared: 'for men and women equally the rights of citizenship. From men and women equally the duties of citizenship'. Thomas Haslam, though of an older generation, was another strong advocate of men and women jointly influencing the making of laws. In 1917, shortly before his death, aged 92, he had called for women's participation in campaigning on a wide range of issues, notably prostitution, because 'it is we, men, who are mainly responsible for its existence'.[36]

It was evident that the suffragists of first wave feminism wanted much more than simple reform of the franchise. Carmel Quinlan's study of the *Irish Citizen* concludes that the evidence points to 'no difference of approach' on sexual matters between the militant and non-militant suffrage societies.[37] Dana Hearne's summary of the discourse on sexuality within the *Irish Citizen* was that it demonstrated:

> women's voices and power were needed in the public realm in order to transform a world ... in this new world, male sexuality would be controlled, and the female standard of chastity would become the norm.[38]

Much of the evidence for this comes from the 'Women Watching the Courts' column. Here, articles on child sexual abuse, rape, incest and domestic violence revealed a side of Irish society not previously revealed by the press.[39]

This framing of sexual discourse and suffrage assumes a heterosexuality which was not necessarily the case. Some women activists of this period also led very woman-centred lives and possessed strong companionate relationships. June Purvis discusses the difficulties in defining 'lesbianism' and whether it has to include eroticism, or whether it can relate more generally to women refusing to organise their lives around men.[40] Without being prurient, one can conclude that many politically active women of the period prioritised women in both their personal and political lives. There was the life-long relationship between Dr Kathleen Lynn, a non-militant suffragist and Irish Citizen Army officer, and Madeleine ffrench-Mullen, formerly of Inghinidhe na hEireann and the Irish Citizen Army.[41] The two women founded St Ultan's hospital and worked and lived together for the rest of their lives. Helena Moloney, also of Inghinidhe and the Irish Citizen Army, lived for thirty years with Evelyn O'Brien. Louie Bennett of the Irish Women's Reform League and Irish Women's Suffrage Federation lived with Helen Chenevix; both were also prominent trade unionists. Elizabeth O'Farrell from Cumann na mBan, who carried out the flag of surrender in 1916, is buried in Glasnevin beside her friend Julia Grenan – both women having been active together in the Easter Rising. In England, there was possibly less constraint in describing the nature of relationships: Constance Markievicz's sister Eva Gore-Booth lived in Manchester with Esther Roper and helped to publish a journal *Urania,* which presented 'same-sex female life unions … as a preferable alternative to heterosexual marriage'.[42] Christabel and Emmeline Pankhurst, as well as many prominent leaders of the Women's Social and Political Union (WSPU), had lesbian relationships with other activists.

English-style militancy came to the north of Ireland in late 1913, although members of the IWSS had been engaging in militant activities for some time. Windows in Belfast's post office were smashed in November 1912 when an amendment to the Home Rule Bill that would have given women the vote was defeated and pillar boxes were attacked in early 1913.[43] However, in a move which startled the entire suffrage movement, the Ulster Unionists announced that the draft constitution for a provisional government which would break away from any Home Rule arrangement included votes for women. Belfast suffragist Elizabeth Priestly McCracken expressed 'jubilation at the marriage of unionism and women's suffrage'.[44] However, Sir Edward Carson, the Unionist leader, was an opponent of female suffrage and he refused to confirm this offer. The WSPU had already established an 'Ulster Centre'. Dorothy Evans, a full-time organiser, who had served jail sentences in England, was sent to Belfast by Christabel Pankhurst, together with Florence McFarlane (who used the pseudonym Madge Muir and had previously been WSPU secretary in Birmingham), and Mary Larmour from Scotland.

At first Irish women were indignant that an English organisation had come over. Mrs Chambers said she considered their presence in Belfast to be 'wholly superfluous' and people worried that the delicate political situation would be made worse. Dorothy Evans revealed a series of letters between herself and Carson, reminding him of his 'solemn pledge' to the women of Ulster and she demanded an assurance that no matter what the final constitutional settlement, be it maintenance of the union or a separate Ulster government, women must have the vote. Carson told a deputation of northern suffrage groups that he could give no assurance. When Dorothy Evans led a deputation of women to London where they camped in the rain outside Carson's house for four and a half days, he refused to meet them. This prompted Evans to state 'they ... declared war on Sir Edward Carson ... the civil war that was absolutely certain was the one between the women and the powers that be'.[45]

Their first action occurred on 27 March 1914 when there was an arson attack on Abbeylands House in Whiteabbey, in the grounds of which the UVF had been drilling. Damage was estimated at £20,000. The IWSS members worked closely with the WSPU women, welcoming the fact that their presence in Belfast had increased public interest in women's suffrage. Initially there were joint meetings between the two organisations, but so many joined the ranks of the WSPU that by April the IWSS had disbanded. It was different in Dublin, where the WSPU was received with hostility, closing down after a short while because of lack of support. In total, seven women in the north were imprisoned for suffrage militancy between March and August 1914.[46] There were thirty five arrests altogether during the course of the Irish suffrage campaign, but only twenty seven women imprisoned, as several were jailed more than once.[47]

The impact of the First World War was devastating for both British and Irish suffrage movements, which divided into pro- and anti-war camps. The WSPU was the most vocal supporter of the war effort, as Christabel Pankhurst immediately called off militancy, re-named the *Suffragette* newspaper *Britannia* and pledged women's support for the war effort. On the whole, Irish women were less bellicose, with the IWSLGA collecting funds for a bed in the Red Cross Hospital in Dublin Castle and the Munster Women's Franchise League collecting funds for an ambulance for France. Belfast suffragist Elizabeth Priestly McCracken complained to Hanna Sheehy Skeffington, 'dreadfully difficult to get women to be interested in anything beyond knitting socks or sewing shirts for soldiers' when she was trying to develop a winter programme of activities for Belfast women. However, she did host a meeting with Sylvia Pankhurst in March 1915.[48] Pankhurst had broken with her mother and sister and, as a socialist and feminist, came to Ireland as part of her campaign to ensure women would not be exploited but be given equal pay for equal work and representation on tribunals being set up to regulate the war industries. For its part, the IWFL was vehemently anti-war, with the *Irish Citizen* declaring 'Votes for Women – Damn Your War'.

In contrast to the polemics of a few years previously there was now a certain convergence between some political activists. In 1915 Constance Markievicz, speaking about women's political activity, praised the suffragettes for being the only women to still have a fighting spirit.

With the formation of Cumann na mBan[49] as an auxiliary organisation to the male Irish Volunteers,[50] she now agreed with Hanna Sheehy Skeffington that the women attached to national movements were there chiefly to collect funds for the men to spend, and admitted 'these ladies auxiliaries demoralise women, set them up in separate camps and deprive them of all initiative and independence'. In her inimitable style she advised women to 'leave their jewels in the bank, wear short skirts and buy a revolver'.[51] This was hardly advice applicable to many, but it symbolises how Irish first wave feminism has to be differentiated from its counterpart in countries where imperial rule was not a concern.

In the period before the Easter Rising 1916 there was also dialogue between feminists in the IWFL and some republicans. A significant meeting took place in April 1915. It was prompted by the British government preventing British and Irish women from attending a Women's Peace Congress in The Hague. When a protest meeting was called in Dublin it was attended not only by many suffrage groups but was also addressed by Thomas MacDonagh, a friend of the Sheehy Skeffingtons and by then also the Director of Training for the Irish Volunteer movement. Leading Irish Republican Patrick Pearse sent a letter of support, stating that suffrage women being banned by the British government from reaching The Hague should have the effect of ranging women on the side of the national forces. This was immediately condemned by Meg Connery of the IWFL, chair of the meeting, as a 'masculine inversion'. She retorted that the incident should have the effect of bringing the nationalists to the side of the women. MacDonagh agreed, stating in reply to his colleague that this incident did show that they should range the forces of nationalism on the side of women. He went on to say he hoped 'as a Volunteer, that he would have a better opportunity than voting to show that by "people" he meant the women as well as the men of Ireland'.[52] This meeting took place less than a year before the Easter Rising. It is notable that a discourse on gender equality was becoming commonplace in advanced political circles. Cliona Murphy, considering the links between nationalism and suffrage, argues that 'the very existence and urgency of the nationalist issue strengthened the suffrage movement. It made the suffragists determined that whatever type of new Ireland would emerge Irish women would be a part of it'.[53]

In private correspondence Hanna Sheehy Skeffington wrote to Louie Bennett (who had objected to the nationalist sentiments expressed in the meeting as it was supposed to have been a feminist meeting about peace):

> If I saw a hope of Ireland being freed for ever from British rule by a swift uprising, I would consider Irishmen justified resorting to arms in order that we might be free.[54]

For her part, Bennett was very clear on her opposition to war, writing in the *Irish Citizen* in May 1915:

> Militarism in the most subtly dangerous form has its hold upon Ireland. Those women who take up the crusade against militarism must not tolerate the 'fight for freedom' and 'defence of rights' excuses for militarism.[55]

These two very different positions within Irish feminism regarding the use of physical force sum up the dilemmas facing feminists whose fight for emancipation took place in a context of imperial rule. It was a debate familiar also to women in India.

After the Easter Rising Hanna Sheehy Skeffington summarised its achievement as 'the only instance I know of in history where men fighting for freedom voluntarily included women'.[56] James Connolly's influence in ensuring that the Proclamation of the Republic promised equal rights and opportunities to women and a government voted on an equal franchise basis cannot be overestimated.

He had been a consistent supporter of the suffrage cause, declaring at a meeting in 1913, when militancy had lost them considerable support, 'he had never yet heard of a militant action which he was not prepared fully and heartily to endorse'.[57] In later years Hanna praised him as 'one of those all too rare revolutionaries whose doctrines of freedom apply all round'.[58] She had been told by Connolly that she had been selected as a member of a civil provisional government which would be formed if the Rising managed to hold out for a significant length of time. However, notwithstanding the importance of Connolly, I would argue that it was an achievement of Irish first wave feminism to win equal rights in the Proclamation, because it was the unrelenting pressure of feminist campaigners that ensured a discourse on gender equality was part of that great wave of intellectual ferment in the period leading up to the Rising. During the Rising, while women from Cumann na mBan defied every kind of prejudice as they carried messages, tended the wounded and organised food and provisions, Connolly's influence meant that women within the Irish Citizen Army experienced less resistance from male comrades. Margaret Skinnider argued successfully that she had the right to take a sniper's role because the Proclamation promised her equal rights and opportunities.[59]

In the period after the defeat of the Rising women from a number of different groupings (Cumann na mBan, the Irish Citizen Army, the trade unions, some of the bereaved wives of the leaders of the Rising) and also, following her return from America (where she had been seeking justice for the brutal murder by a British army officer of her husband Frank), Hanna Sheehy Skeffington joined forces to put pressure on Sinn Féin to ensure that women would be treated with equality in that organisation. They formed the League of Women Delegates, marched in delegation to the Sinn Fein office, argued for equal representation for women but, being totally outnumbered at the seminal Sinn Féin Convention of 1917, were unable to achieve more than four women on a twenty-four person executive. The following year Constance Markievicz would make history as the first woman in Britain or Ireland to be elected to parliament, when women over thirty, subject to certain qualifications, won the right to vote and to stand for parliament. That historic event is generally considered to mark the end of first wave feminism – or at least its crest – as other gains, for example, in the workplace, were soon lost as a backlash against women began. However, for Irish women, more needs to be said, because women in Ireland continued their fight for political equality and national independence.

Only two women (significantly, both participated in the Rising as Irish Citizen Army members) were selected as Sinn Féin candidates for the 1918 elections: Constance Markievicz in Dublin and Winifred Carney in Belfast. Hanna Sheehy Skeffington had wanted to be a candidate, but rejected the offer of an unwinnable seat and Kathleen Clarke, widow of Tom Clarke, was highly disappointed when she failed to be selected. Women from the IWFL worked hard to ensure the election of Markievicz. Meg Connery maintained that she had been 'thrown as a sop to the women of the country' and Hanna Sheehy Skeffington, despite having joined Sinn Féin, complained to Nancy Wyse Power of Cumann na mBan that it was 'the worst managed constituency in Dublin'. As a women's organisation she believed the IWFL had a 'duty in this manner and [I] think it is a disgrace ... if Madame Markievicz is let down by an inefficient committee'.[60] In Belfast, Carney, standing for a worker's republic, had even less support, complaining:

I had neither personation agents, committee rooms, canvassers or vehicles and as these are the chief features in an election it was amazing to me to find that 395 people went to the ballot on their own initiative.[61]

On voting day in the Rathmines constituency, Mary Kettle (Hanna's sister and a former IWFL member) and Professor Mary Hayden backed the Irish Party; Anna Haslam voted for the Conservative, Sir Maurice Dockrell, and Hanna Sheehy Skeffington supported Sinn Féin. All candidates were declared suffrage supporters. It was an occasion for rejoicing and pageantry. The *Irish Citizen* commented:

> It speaks well for the broadmindedness of the new women voters that women of all parties – Unionist, Irish Party and Sinn Fein – joined heartily to honour Mrs Haslam and suffrage.[62]

During much of this period the *Irish Citizen* endured as a paper and as an invaluable record of Irish feminism. It was now edited by Louie Bennett and Hanna Sheehy Skeffington, in a sometimes difficult alliance. An editorial in October 1919, despite the mayhem of the War of Independence, made a bold statement on the importance of retaining an independent women's voice:

> We stand for the rights of all Irish women as women, independent of party of sect … No party, unhappily, is yet quite free from sin where women are concerned. It is to hold the mirror up to the failings and shortcomings of each in turn that the Irish Citizen exists, and we reckon it a sign of grace that we are blamed in turn by each party for not becoming mere camp-followers of this or the other side.[63]

The last issue was dated September-December 1920, when Hanna wrote she hoped the paper would survive, but to do so it needed a women's movement and readers and thinkers. The following year the *Irish Citizen* ceased production after its typeface had been smashed during a raid by the Black and Tans. That seems a symbolic date to mark the end of first wave feminism in Ireland. In 1921

Ireland was partitioned. Women over twenty one in twenty six counties of Ireland would win the right to vote in 1922 – their last victory for many decades. Feminists continued to oppose the Free State backlash against women, but they had now entered another era, with Irish feminism forced into a temporary abeyance.

NOTES

1   Marilyn Boxer, 'First-Wave Feminism in 19th Century France', *Women's Studies International Forum*, 5/6, 1982, p. 552.

2   Maria Luddy, 'Separate but Equal', *Irish Times*, 17 October 2012, p. 16.

3   Diane Urquhart, *Women in Ulster Politics* (Dublin, Irish Academic Press, 2000), p. 47.

4   Carmel Quinlan, *Genteel Revolutionaries: Anna and Thomas Haslam and the Irish Women's Movement* (Cork, Cork University Press, 2002), p. 133.

5   Luddy, 'Separate but Equal', p. 16.

6   Urquhart, *Women in Ulster Politics*, p. 48.

7   Margaret Ward, 'The Ladies' Land League and the Irish Land War: Defining the Relationship Between Women and Nation', in Ida Blom, Karen Hageman and Catherine Hal (eds), *Gendered Nations* (Oxford, Berg, 2000), p. 232.

8   Anna Parnell, *The Tale of a Great Sham*, edited by Dana Hearne (Dublin, Arlen House, 1986), p. 173.

9   Ward, 'The Ladies' Land League', p. 232.

10   *Ibid.*, p. 233.

11   *Bean na hÉireann*, January 1909.

12   *Bean na hÉireann*, April 1909.

13   Karen Steele, *Women, Press and Politics during the Irish Revival* (Syracuse, New York, Syracuse University Press, 2007), p. 109.

14   Mary McLarren, in reply to an IWFL paper read to Sinn Fein, *Bean na hÉireann*, April 1909, reprinted in Margaret Ward, *In Their Own Voice: Women and Irish Nationalism* (Dublin: Attic Press, 1995), p. 29.

15   Steele, *Women, Press and Politics*, 111.

16   *Bean na hÉireann*, October, 1909, reprinted in Ward, *In Their Own Voice*, p. 29.

17 Nell Regan, 'Helena Moloney', in Mary Cullen and Maria Luddy (eds), *Female Activists: Irish Women and Change 1900–1960* (Dublin, Woodfield Press, 2001), p. 145.

18 Constance de Markievicz, Debate on Irish Women and the Extension of the Franchise, *Dáil Eireann*, 2 March 1922, reprinted in Ward, *In Their Own Voice*, p. 120.

19 Markievicz, 'Women, Ideals and the Nation', *Ibid.*, pp 30–32.

20 Hanna Sheehy Skeffington, *Bean na hEireann*, November 1909, *Ibid.*, 32–34.

21 Hanna Sheehy Skeffington, 'Reminiscences of an Irish Suffragette', 1941, unpublished, in Andrée Sheehy Skeffington and Rosemary Owens, *Votes for Women – Irishwomen's Struggle for the Vote* (Dublin, 1975), p. 11.

22 Quinlan, *Genteel Revolutionaries,* p. 168.

23 *Ibid.*, p. 167.

24 *Ibid.*, p. 167.

25 James and Margaret Cousins, *We Two Together* (Madras, Ganash, 1950), p. 162.

26 *Ibid.*, p. 175.

27 Diane Urquhart, *The Ladies of Londonderry* (New York, Palgrave, 2007), p. 138.

28 *Ibid.*, pp 110–11.

29 *Irish Citizen*, 15 June 1912.

30 Mary McVeigh, 'Votes for Women: the Armagh campaign', Armagh History Group, http://www.armaghhistorygroup.com/uploads/cms_file/210420111152.pdf

31 Sheehy Skeffington, 'Reminiscences of an Irish Suffragette', p. 20.

32 *Irish Citizen*, 16 November 1912.

33 Sheehy Skeffington, 'The Women's Movement – Ireland', *Irish Review*, July 1912, pp 225–7.

34 Ward, *Hanna Sheehy Skeffington: A Life* (Cork, Attic Press), p .84.

35 Urquhart, *Women in Ulster Politics*, p. 33.

36 Quinlan, *Genteel Revolutionaries*, p. 185

37 *Ibid.*, p. 182.

38 Dana Hearne, 'The Development of Irish Feminist Thought: A Critical Historical Analysis of the Irish Citizen, 1912–1920'. Ottawa: National Library of Canada, 1993. Quoted in Quinlan, p. 183.

39 Louise Ryan, 'Publicising the Private: suffragists' critique of sexual abuse and domestic violence' in L. Ryan and M. Ward

(eds), *Irish Women and the Vote: Becoming Citizens* (Dublin, Irish Academic Press, 2007), pp 75–89.

40   June Purvis, *Emmeline Pankhurst. A Biography* (London: Routledge, 2002), p. 391.

41   The Irish Citizen Army was originally formed by James Larkin and James Connolly as a workers' defence organisation during the 1913 Lock Out, by 1914 it was re-organised by Connolly and pledged to fight for a Workers' Republic. Women were accepted as full members and Constance Markievicz and Kathleen Lynn were officers within the ICA, both taking active roles during the Easter Rising as part of the ICA contingent, together with a number of other female activists

42   Sonja Tiernan, *Eva Gore-Booth: An Image of Such Politics* (Manchester, Manchester University Press, 2012), p. 227.

43   Urquhart, *Women in Ulster Politics*, p. 30.

44   *Irish Citizen*, 20 September 1913.

45   Urquhart, *Women in Ulster Politics, p.* 30.

46   For more on the north, see Myrtle Hill, 'Ulster: debates, demands and divisions', in Ryan and Ward, *Irish Women and the Vote*, pp 209–230.

47   William Murphy, 'Suffragettes and the Transformation of Political Imprisonment in Ireland, 1912–1914' in Ryan and Ward, *Irish Women and the Vote*, p. 131.

48   Margaret Ward '"Rolling Up the Map of Suffrage": Irish Suffrage and the First World War, in Ryan and Ward, *Irish Women and the Vote*, p. 140.

49   Cumann na mBan nationalist women's organisation, formed in November 1913 as the female auxiliary to the Irish Volunteers, its perceived subordinate status was a contentious issue for some feminists. Members of Cumann na mBan served in various outposts during the Easter Rising. The Proclamation of the Republic enabled them – after the Rising – to declare the organisation to be an independent body of Irish women pledged to work for an Irish Republic.

50   Founded in November 1913, initially as a nationalist riposte to the formation in the north of the anti-nationalist Ulster Volunteer Force, the Volunteer movement split in 1914, when a minority opposed to Irish involvement in the First World War reorganised and began preparations for what would become armed uprising to British rule in Ireland.

51 Constance Markievicz, *Irish Citizen*, 23 October 1915, reprinted in Ward, *In Their Own Voice*, pp 46–47.

52 *Irish Citizen*, 17 April 1915.

53 Cliona Murphy, *The Women's Suffrage Movement and Irish Society* (Hertfordshire, Harvester, 1989), p. 46.

54 Hanna Sheehy Skeffington to Louie Bennett, n.d. 1915, for more on this issue, see Margaret Ward, 'Nationalism, Pacifism, Internationalism: Louie Bennett, Hanna Sheehy Skeffington and the problems of "Defining Feminism"', in A. Bradley and M. Valiulis (eds), *Gender and Sexuality in Modern Ireland* (Amherst, University of Massachusetts Press, 1997), pp 60–84; Rosemary Cullen Owens, 'Women and Pacifism in Ireland 1915–1932', in M. Valiulis and M. O'Dowd (eds), *Women & Irish History* (Dublin, Wolfhound Press, 1997), pp 220–238.

55 Louie Bennett, *Irish Citizen*, May 1915.

56 Sheehy Skeffington, 'Memories of the Suffrage Campaign in Ireland', *The Vote*, 30 August 1929.

57 Ward, *Hanna Sheehy Skeffington*, p. 115.

58 Sheehy Skeffington, 'Memories of the Suffrage Campaign in Ireland', *The Vote*, 30 August 1929.

59 Margaret Skinnider, *Doing My Bit for Ireland* (New York, Century, 1917), pp 132–148. Issued on Easter Monday and read out by Patrick Pearse outside the General Post Office, the headquarters of the insurgents, the Proclamation guaranteed 'equal rights and equal opportunities to all its citizens' and promised a national government 'elected by the suffrages of all her men and women'.

60 Hanna Sheehy Skeffington to Nancy Wyse Power, 1919, reprinted in Ward, *In Their Own Voice*, p. 83.

61 Winifred Carney to Joe McGrath, January 1919, reprinted in Ward, *In Their Own Voice*, p. 82.

62 Quinlan, *Genteel Revolutionaries*, p. 187.

63 *Irish Citizen*, October 1919.

'THE UNQUIET SISTERS':
WOMEN, POLITICS AND THE IRISH FREE STATE SENATE 1922–1936

Mary McAuliffe

In December 1935 Senator Kathleen Clarke rose in the Irish Senate to oppose the introduction of the Conditions of Employment Act, in particular, Section 16 of the Act, which would place restrictions on how and where women workers could participate in the workforce. This Act can be seen as a continuation of the type of gendered legislation the Cumann na nGaedhael government had introduced from the inception of the Irish Free State. In 1922 the fundamental principles of the 1916 Proclamation, which guaranteed religious and civil liberty, equal rights and equal opportunities to all citizens, were echoed in the Irish Free State Constitution, guaranteeing that every person 'without distinction of sex ... [shall enjoy] ... the privileges and be subject to the obligations of such citizenship'.[1] Despite this promise of full and equal citizenship, it soon became apparent that, ideologically, the new state found the activities of women in the public realm problematic.

The promise of equality in 1916, reiterated in 1922, was, as Luddy writes, a benchmark 'by which women's groups measured the performance of various governments with regard to women's rights … [but] was a standard rarely met by any government in the period'.[2] The anti-women legislation introduced through the 1920s and into the 1930s can be understood in several ways. Firstly, it can be seen as a response to the fact that many politicised Irish women, especially women in Cumann na mBan, had rejected the 1922 Anglo-Irish Treaty and were considered to be anti-government. Statements in the first Dáil often revealed a real lack of acceptance of female participation in the public realm of politics and work. Indeed, this participation was seen as injurious to both women (it unsexed them) and to the political arena itself; it was felt by some that the presence of women brought a bitterness, hysteria and emotionalism which had no place in civilised, rational public (male) debate.[3] As Knirck has noted, contemporary secular and religious commentators agreed that women were bringing a disagreeable, unfeminine, corrupting influence to the public arena and 'the natural response was to cast them out'. Nor, as Kevin O'Higgins, TD and Minister for Justice, stated, did a few words in the constitution about equality 'wipe out the difference between the sexes, either physical or mental or temperamental or emotional'.[4]

Secondly, this social conservatism can be broadly understood as a response to the chaos of the War of Independence (1919–1921) and the bitter conflicts of the Civil War (1922–1923) and, as an attempt to restore a traditional order and hierarchy.[5] The first two decades of the 20th century had seen women emerge, in greater numbers, from the domestic sphere and participate in the hitherto male-dominated spheres of Irish politics. For many of these women, influenced by the ideologies of feminism and nationalism, the expectation was that a free

Ireland would guarantee them full and equal citizenship. However, the new State felt that the contribution of women would be most acceptable in the domestic sphere. The ideal Irishwoman was, above all, a wife and mother; the home and the hearth was to be her sphere of influence. Irish women's citizenship became, as Valiulis has noted, 'rooted in the private sphere ... [and] directly related to motherhood within marriage'.[6] Thirdly, this dominance of the ideology of domesticity reflected the growing influence of the Catholic Church which, in its sermons and literature through the 1920s, railed against the moral deterioration of the world in general and of Irish women in particular. The concept of an Irish woman as a full and equal citizen was problematic to the church as it distracted from her 'natural' role. As Edward Cahill, S.J. wrote in 1925, granting the vote to women was an error which was 'inconsistent with the Christian ideal of the intimate union between husband and wife that they should exercise the political franchise as distinct units', leading to disputes in the home about political issues, which would bring disharmony to the domestic sphere and undermine the duty of care a women owed to her husband and family.[7] With the right to vote came the rights and duties of citizenship which might distract the ideal woman from her domestic duties. This positioning of women in the home was, according to Church literature, to serve as the moral cornerstone of the new Catholic nation, without which the nation would and could not develop. Furthermore, this discourse dictated that the moral purity of the ideal Irishwoman was essential for the wellbeing of the Irish family and the Irish nation. Therefore, female morality was to be regulated by Church and State, and enforced and preserved at all costs.

By 1922, most Irish women had the vote and many legal barriers to full citizenship were removed. However, from the beginning of the Irish Free State there was a concentrated attempt to block women's continued advance into the public arena. Indeed, as many historians of Irish women's political and social history have shown, not only were attempts made to stop further advances for women, there was also a backlash, with serious legislative attempts being made to undermine rights already gained. The decade 1922 to 1932 would see the stabilising of the democratic principles of government under a Cumann na nGaedhael-led government, but it would also see the constant chipping away at the civil rights of women and the promotion of the dominant discourses of women in the home/private sphere, where the right to work outside the home, the right to control fertility and reproduction, the right to self-determined female sexuality and access to political power by women was regulated and restricted. One of the first pieces of gendered legislation introduced was the 1924 Juries Bill which would allow women to opt out of serving on juries. This was alarming to feminist activists who viewed it as a retrograde step in their campaign for full and equal citizenship within the new State. The Irish Women Citizens' and Local Government Association pointed out that this legislation was 'unfair to the men citizens and derogatory to the women'.[8]

Other pieces of restrictive, gendered legislation introduced included, in 1925, the Civil Service Amendment Act which gave the government the power to ban women from certain civil service exams. This Act was, effectively, an attempt to bar women from the higher ranks of the civil service, a right of access to work that women had already won. Then came the 1927 Juries Bill which was an attempt to deny women the right to sit on juries altogether. There was also the 1929 Censorship of Publications Act which banned advertising on contraception. After a period of abstention Fianna Fáil entered the Oireachtas in 1927. By 1932 it constituted the largest political party in the State and, with the Labour Party, was able to form the new government. If women had any hopeful expectations of change, they were soon disabused. Soon after the new government took power Senator Kathleen Clarke remarked that 'things which they (Fianna Fáil) condemned as wrong for W.T. Cosgrave's government to do became right for them'.[9] Clarke was correct – Fianna Fáil continued what the first Irish Free State governments had begun. They also introduced anti-women legislation, including the Criminal Law Amendment Act 1935 and the 1936 Conditions of Employment Act.

Despite this maginalisation of women's political influence and the effort by the State to erode women's political, economic and social rights, there was a fight back against the anti-women backlash of Church and State. Outside the political centres of power feminist activists were busy opposing legislation which chipped away at their rights as citizens and these activists were not without allies at the centre of power. In the Dáil female TDs followed party line on legislation, and, as Clancy has argued, the contribution of female Dáil deputies 'lay in their solid enduring support for the political parties to which they belonged'.[10] It is noticeable, however, that many of the women elected or appointed to the Senate in the period 1922 to 1936 tended to show much more sympathy for campaigns on women's rights, children's rights, protection of women workers and other issues of equality. These Senate women also proved to be more able politicians and speakers, more disinclined to follow party politics, and more vocal in their attempts to stem the erosion of women's rights by the successive Free State governments.

From 1922 to 1936 there were six women Senators, five of whom, to a greater or lesser degree, were active in opposing anti-women legislation. These women senators were Kathleen Browne, who served between 1929 and

1936, Kathleen Clarke (1928–1936), Eileen Costello (1922–1934), Ellen Odette Cuffe, Countess of Desart (1922–1933), Alice Stopford-Green (1922–1929), and Jenny Wyse-Power (1922–1936). These women were from very varied backgrounds, socially, politically and ideologically.

The Countess of Desart was an English-born member of the British aristocracy who married into the Anglo-Irish Ascendancy, and was appointed, as a Unionist candidate, to the first Senate. She was, also, the first Jewish Senator. She had been a patron of the Gaelic League and an avid supporter of and campaigner for the promotion of Irish industries and the protection of low-paid workers. For example, she opposed any taxation on domestic servants and advocated for the protection of laborers and agricultural workers. However, she had vehemently opposed women's suffrage and in May 1913 presided over the annual general meeting of the National League for Opposing Woman Suffrage held in Dublin. On the other hand, Kathleen Browne, Kathleen Clarke, Jenny Wyse-Power were all committed nationalists and Wyse-Power and Clarke were committed feminists.

Browne was from a land-owning family, of Anglo-Norman extraction, in Wexford. As well as being an organiser for the Gaelic League and an early member of Sinn Féin, Browne was a member of United Irishwomen and of Cumann na mBan. From 1922 she campaigned tirelessly for the rights of labourers, small farmers and farmers' wives. While not a feminist, believing that women could 'get what they want by standing on their own two feet', she worked with United Irishwomen, and after 1929, in the Senate, to improve the lives of lower middle class, working class, small farm and labouring women.[11] She ran for the Senate in the 1925 election, on a women's issue platform, but failed to gain a seat. She was subsequently appointed to the Senate in 1929 on the death of Alice

Stopford Green. In 1933, she castigated the government for destroying the poultry industry, particularly as this industry was so important to the incomes of farmers' wives; arguing that without the income generated from poultry raising, small farm families would be short of food and clothing.[12] She had become disillusioned with the Irish Free State, stating that 'if the men ... who visioned a national and free Ireland could have grasped what would have come about in a free Ireland ... they would never have lifted a finger to make this a self-governing country'.[13] She became an organiser in the Blueshirt movement, gaining notoriety by wearing a blue blouse to signal her allegiances in the Senate in 1934.[14] She became a member of Fine Gael and served in the Senate until its abolition in 1936. She died in 1943.

Jennie Wyse-Power came from a substantial farming background in Wicklow and she and her husband owned and ran shops and a café in Dublin. Politicised early, she had joined Anna Parnell's Ladies Land League in 1880 while still a teenager. She devoted her life to nationalist and feminist causes. She was a co-founder, with Maud Gonne, of the cultural nationalist organisation, Inghinidhe na hÉireann, she was on the executive of Sinn Féin, becoming vice-president in 1911, and was a member of the Irish Women's Franchise League and a founder member of Cumann na mBan. Her formal political career included election to the North Dublin Union Board of Guardians (1903–1912), election to Dublin Corporation in 1920 and she was nominated to the Senate in 1922, where she served until it was dissolved in 1936. Like Browne, but for differing ideological reasons, a sense of disillusionment set in at the course of politics in the Free State. In 1925 she resigned from Cumann na nGaedheal and served as an independent until 1934 when she joined Fianna Fáil. She was a persistent and outspoken critic of the anti-women legislation introduced during the 1920s and 1930s. Her last major involvement was as a campaigner against the 1937 Constitution. She died in 1941.

Kathleen Clarke, born in Limerick, had been a dressmaker and shopkeeper, and was the wife and sister of Tom Clarke and Edward Daly respectively, both executed for their roles in the 1916 Rising. Prior to that, Clarke was immersed in the republican cause and was at the first meeting held to form Cumann na mBan in April 1914. As vice president of Cumann na mBan she, and her colleague, Jennie Wyse Power, ensured that equal rights for women became official policy of that organisation in 1917. Like Wyse Power she was elected to Dublin City Council and, in 1939, she became the first female Lord Mayor of Dublin. She was elected to the Dáil in 1921 and was vehement in her opposition to the treaty, although she did chair unsuccessful negotiations to try and avoid civil war. She lost her Dáil seat in 1922 but continued her political career as an early member of Fianna Fáil. She was elected to the Dáil in June 1927, only to lose her seat again in September of that year. She accepted a nomination for the Senate in 1928 and served there until its abolition in 1936. She was a vocal defender of women's rights, and despite her membership of Fianna Fáil she opposed the anti-women legislation introduced once that party took power in 1932. Both Clarke and Wyse Power openly campaigned against the 1937 constitution. The inclusion of articles regulating the rights of women workers and articles 41.1 and 41.2, which placed women firmly in the domestic sphere were, they argued, a betrayal of the promises of the 1916 Proclamation, and principles of equality promised therein. Clarke continued her political career well into the 20th century, and, when she died in 1972 she received the rare honour of a state funeral.

The final two female senators, Alice Stopford-Green and Eileen Costello, were educators and supporters of Irish culture and nationalism. Alice Stopford was born in Kells, Co Meath and married the historian John Richard Green in 1877. Financially independent following his death in 1883 she was free to indulge her interest in history. In those years she began to question the impact of imperialism on Africa and this anti-imperialist stance was encouraged by her friendship with Sir Roger Casement. She began to research and write Irish history, and like many others involved in cultural nationalism she viewed independence as a path towards regaining an imagined nation based on a romanticised past. Her contributions to Irish nationalism were also practical; she was the major funder of the Howth gun-running, although she was not a supporter of armed rebellion. The arrest and subsequent trial of Roger Casement led her to lobby hard, if unsuccessfully, to prevent his execution. She moved to Ireland in 1918 and her house on St Stephen's Green became a meeting place for leading nationalists and was often raided by the British. She was appointed to the Senate in 1922 where she sat on several committees. She rarely spoke in the Senate but did join with Senator W.B. Yeats in arguing, unsuccessfully, for the retention of divorce. She had a heart attack in 1925 and died in 1929; her seat in the Senate was taken by Senator Kathleen Browne.

Senator Eileen Costello was from the opposite end of the social strata to Stopford-Green. She was born in the Strand St. workhouse in St Pancras, London, purportedly to a poor Irish emigrant father and a Welsh mother; her ancestral roots are unclear. She did, however, manage to get an education as she qualified as a teacher and joined the Irish Literary Society in London where she met the Yeats sisters. She joined the London branch of the Gaelic League and became an avid folksong collector and Irish language enthusiast. In 1903 she married Thomas Bodkin Costello, and by 1905 she had converted to Catholicism, changed her name to Eibhlín Uí Choisdeailbh, and moved to Tuam, Co. Galway. A committed nationalist, she stood for Sinn Féin in the 1920 local elections, was elected a district councillor for north Galway and a Tuam town commissioner and was subsequently elected its chairman. In 1922 she was elected as a Cuamnn na nGaedhael member of the Senate and remained a Senator until her defeat in the 1934 election. She was consistently pro-woman in her engagement with Bills in the Senate, often arguing with Wyse-Power and Clarke against the effect of gendered legislation. She was of the opinion that rather than chipping away at the rights of the female citizen, that women 'needed to be educated into responsible citizenship ... since they had not realised their power yet'.[15]

From 1922 most of the female senators opposed the anti-women legislation introduced by the government, and unlike their female Dáil colleagues, they did not need to adhere to any party line. One of the earliest pieces of anti-women legislation introduced was the 1925 Civil Service Regulation (Amendment) Bill, which was an attempt by Cumann na nGaedhael to prevent women gaining jobs in certain areas of the civil service. The legislation would have given the government power to ban women from taking certain competitive civil service exams and, in effect, bar them from the higher echelons of the civil service. Opposition to the Bill in the Dáil did not come from the only female TD, Margaret Collins-O'Driscoll, who despite 'being canvassed by very influential members of my sex to vote against this Bill' failed to see how it infringed on women's rights.[16] She supported the Minister of Finance (Ernest Blythe), who felt the legislation was needed to give the Civil Service Commission the right to 'confine examinations to members of one particular sex'.[17] Collins-O'Driscoll accepted that the Bill would limit the number of female appointments to the Civil Service, but argued that the 'number of appointments women would be excluded from would be very small', as not many women would be seeking these positions.[18] Women were, it was felt, more suited to the lower grades in the civil service, as typists, stenographers and telephonists. In the Dáil one of its main opponents was Professor William Magennis TD, although he was at pains to emphasise that he had 'never been a bit of a feminist in any sense'.[19] Magennis noted that as education was opening up for women in Ireland, sex barriers to work for these educated women were being introduced 'with the result that we shall educate, at the cost of the nation, scores, hundreds in fact, of women and export them'.[20]

Outside the Oireachtas feminist organisations campaigned against the Bill while in the Senate female Senators and some of their male colleagues were quite hostile to the Bill. The Bill was brought to the Senate in December 1925, to immediate opposition from Senators Eileen Costello and Jennie Wyse Power. Wyse Power began her statement by saying that she 'objected to the principle of the Bill ... so strongly that [she] intended to vote against it ... [and that she] considered that the Bill is unconstitutional'.[21] For Wyse Power, the Bill went against the right of equal citizenship guaranteed to women in the 1922 Constitution, and, in addition, it was not in the interests of women workers.

In the Dáil those who proposed the Bill argued that it was legislating for occupations which were physically unsuitable for women. Wyse Power argued that while she did 'not think that women want to do things that they are physically unfit for', she regretted that the argument in favour of the Bill came 'from the men who were associated in the fight with women who played the part at a time when sex and money were not considerations'.[22] Indeed, while Wyse Power agreed that many women might be physically unfit for certain types of work, so too were some men, stating that there was 'no use in saying to women: "You are not fit for the Army and the police", while they themselves may not be either. I think it fits both ways'.[23] Her colleague Senator Costello was as angry as Wyse-Power about the content of the Bill, calling the government unjust in seeking to introduce such a morally wrong and monstrously unfair piece of legislation.[24] She argued that while the Minister might say that women were unsuitable for some posts in the civil service, what he really meant is that women were unwanted. She also said that

> Women are still to be subject to the obligation of citizenship, but their privileges are to be curtailed and restricted. I think the qualifications for the various posts in the Civil Service are quite sufficient already. These are the qualifications as to age, health, character and ability, and I do not think any other qualifications are needed.[25]

The Bill, she felt, was against the spirit of Article 3 of the 1922 Constitution which she quoted in her speech, 'every person, without distinction of sex ... shall enjoy the privileges and be subject to the obligations of such citizenship'.[26] Costello also argued that women themselves were, to an extent, to blame that legislation like this was introduced. While there were many groups outside of the Oireachtas such as the Irish Women Citizens' and Local Government Association, the Irish Women Workers Union, the National University Graduates Association and individuals like the veteran feminists Hanna Sheehy Skeffington and Mary Kettle who campaigned against this and other gendered legislation, Costello felt that

> it [was] to a certain extent the fault of the women themselves that such a thing as this should be allowed. They had very high privileges conferred on them, but they have not lived up to these privileges. This has been shown during the recent Seanad elections and at other elections as well. I do hope that if actions such as the present one in bringing in this Bill are continued, that the women will very soon wake up.[27]

She felt that women had not yet taken advantage of the citizenship conferred on them and if they didn't soon that equality might disappear. Costello recognised that this legislation was not just about women in the civil service, but about the right of women to participate fully in the political and economic life of the country, to go where they were 'unwanted'. In this instance the arguments of those opposed to the Bill carried the day and the Civil Service Amendment Bill was defeated in the Senate, by twenty votes to nine. One of those who supported the Bill to curtail women's access to civil service posts was the veteran anti-suffrage campaigner, the Countess of Desart, although she did not speak on the subject in the Senate.

Despite this setback in the Senate, successive governments brought forward a raft of legislation which would seek to regulate, control and constrain the rights of Irish women. In 1927 a Bill was introduced which would remove a right already given Irish women; in 1919 women were allowed, by a British Parliamentary Act, to sit on juries. In 1924 a Bill had been introduced which did keep women's right to serve on juries but gave them the choice to opt out of that service if they so wished. For the ideal, respectable Irish woman jury service was not regarded as proper and, as Hanna Sheehy Skeffington pointed out in 1927, despite their right to sit on juries, women, on being called to jury service, were being 'ordered en masses to "stand aside", when they answered their names in court'.[28] Feminist groups mounted a vigorous campaign against this legislation, which was seen as regressive and unconstitutional, pointing to Article 3 of the 1922 Constitution which guaranteed equal citizenship for all 'without distinction of sex'. In the Senate, Costello and Wyse Power were again to the forefront in the debates against the introduction of this legislation. Wyse-Power protested that if this Bill became law 'the civic spirit that is developing in women' would be arrested.[29] She argued that the growing participation of women in political issues of the 'last 50 years' had gradually allowed and encouraged women into the public sphere. She saw this cooperation of men and women in the public arena as an 'asset', not just to Ireland but to any nation where it was encouraged.[30] The Minister, with a 'bold stroke', would eliminate women from jury panels and undermine all that had been achieved in terms of female participation in the public realm. Senator Costello returned to her argument that if 'women are to take their part as citizens, these duties should be put upon them and enforced, because that is the only way they can be educated into good citizenship'.[31] She felt that allowing women to opt in or out of citizenship duties did them no favours as women were slow to respond to the duties of citizenship and, unless obliged to undertake these duties, would generally opt out. Male senators were more inclined to agree with the Minster for Justice, Kevin O'Higgins, that a woman performing the 'normal' functions of womanhood would not desire service on juries. Senator William Barrington stated that:

> Women have a great many private duties to perform. They have to look after their houses, and in many cases have to cook their husband's dinner and look after their children. Why these women should be taken away from these duties which are essential to the welfare of the State, to serve on juries which they hate, and simply at the bidding of a few of the prominent women who are engaged on the militant side of the question, is more than I can see.[32]

Costello admitted that she had voted for the 1924 Juries Act which allowed women to opt out of juries, something she realised was a mistake as the '1919 position, [of the right of women to be on juries] was whittled down by the 1924 Act'.[33] Because of the intense opposition to the Bill, a compromise was sought and the government accepted an amendment to the Bill, which, while exempting women from jury service, would allow individual women to opt in for jury service if they so wished. Costello, reluctantly, accepted the amendment as it was 'a step back towards the 1919 position'.[34] Senator Wyse-Power felt that the amendment would do little to make it easy for women to serve on juries. Women, she said, would be:

> in the most invidious position as jurors that they could possibly be placed in … the woman who comes forward and places her name upon the voluntary panel … her position will be a most difficult one indeed. Jibes and sneers are very often flung about upon this question and if a woman, I repeat, who had the courage or the strength to put her name down for the voluntary panel, should come and claim exemption on proper and right grounds we can all realise the taunts that may be flung at her and her sex.[35]

When it came to a vote Senators Costello, Wyse-Power and Stopford-Green voted for the amendment, while the Countess of Desart voted against it. Despite the arguments from the Senate and the campaigns of feminist groups outside the Oireachtas, the 1927 Juries Bill was passed, with the amendment that women could opt in for jury service by putting their name on a voluntary panel.

The governments of the Irish Free State were to continue to enact anti-women legislation throughout the later 1920s and into the 1930s. However, as Valiulis has shown, the experience that feminist activists, women's groups and the women senators gained in opposing the early anti-women legislation did have some positive effect; 'it enabled women to build a broad-based coalition which would be important in fighting the restrictive legislation in the 1930s'.[36] The Free State developed the traditional assumptions of Irish womanhood based on marriage and domesticity, reinforced by the Irish government, by the Catholic Church and by society. Feminists, on the other hand, demanded a more complex role for Irish women, one which could combine marriage, motherhood and a space in the public realm. Indeed, as wives and mothers, feminists felt women had something special and unique to bring to the duties of citizenship and, as such, should not be prevented from serving public roles. However, the dominant ideal of Irish femininity, defined by social conservatism and traditional Catholic thinking, relegated the contribution of women in the new State to the sphere of the home. Irish society generally accepted that women's place was in the home, while the man, as head of the household, was industrious at work providing for his wife and family. This social conservatism continued and deepened into the 1930s when further legislation was introduced to restrict the rights of the female citizen. In 1932, shortly before the Cumann na nGaedheal government left power, it was proposed that women national teachers would retire on marriage, the justification being that married women teachers would not give their full attention either to their job or to their family. This marriage bar, despite resistance from the Irish National Teachers' Organisation (INTO), was introduced and was not revoked until 1957.

While previous Bills were a function to control women's political and economic citizenship, measures such as the 1928 Censorship Act and the 1929 Illegitimate Children (Affiliation Orders) Bill, were part of a process of controlling women's bodies, regulating female sexuality and reproduction, defining the ideal of a moral and pure Irishwoman and providing for the punishment of those women whose behaviour was considered less than acceptable or respectable. As gender historians have shown, the Irish Government blamed Irish women for falling short of that ideal, of failing to 'observe traditional Irish morality' and of exhibiting 'a lack of modesty, purity and deference'; so much of the legislation of the later 1920s and into the 1930s was an attempt to curtail the sexual autonomy of women.[37] The Censorship Act forbade, amongst other provisions, the importation into the State of any books, magazines, newspapers which advocated contraception and also banned distribution of books regarded as indecent or obscene. Regulating female access to the workplace and denying female access to contraceptives reinforced the idea of reproduction as the primary work of the ideal Irish woman. However, where and when reproduction could legitimately take place was also regulated. The ideal Irish mother had to be married as sex outside marriage was taboo and illegitimate children were not acceptable. While the 1929 Illegitimate Children (Affiliation Order) Bill was introduced in order to do something about the plight of unmarried mothers and their children, in the Senate male Senators spoke of the fear of 'hardened females' who deliberately became pregnant and who would blackmail 'innocent' men with affiliation orders. Both Jennie Wyse-Power and Kathleen Browne came to the defence of women, with Browne saying that

> the vast majority of these unfortunate girls are comparatively innocent of the crime they commit. They are trapped into this unfortunate state … I am absolutely certain that not one in a thousand would go into a public court [to claim maintenance from the father], though they might go into a court where the evidence would be heard in camera.[38]

Despite some vocal opposition from male senators and from the Minister, who stated that senators should remember that 'all mothers are not completely virtuous women',[39] the 'in camera' amendment was accepted and the Bill passed in 1930.

In 1932 the Cumann na nGaedheal party which had held power since 1922, and which had consistently chipped away at the equal rights of Irish women, was defeated in a general election and a new government formed. If the women Senators and feminist activists had hope of better treatment from this new government they were soon disabused of the notion. Hanna Sheehy Skeffington was sceptical of any change, writing that she had 'no belief in de Valera. Well meaning of course, better than Cosgrave, but really essentially conservative and Church bound, anti-feminist, bourgeois and the like'.[40] As well she might have expected, the 'well meaning' de Valera and his government continued to restrict the rights of Irish women through legislation. In 1934, the Criminal Law Amendment Act was introduced. This Bill caused much debate and controversy, not least in the Senate where an attempt to rush through the legislation without amendment was not accepted. Outside the Senate, the Joint Committee of Women's Societies and Social Workers opposed this Act because the government wanted to set the age of consent at fifteen and introduce a six-month prison sentence for prostitution. There was also opposition from Senators Browne, Clarke and Wyse-Power. Senator Browne wanted the age of consent set at eighteen, which had been agreed at Committee stage, but as a compromise was willing to settle for seventeen. She accused the government of 'giving less protection to our young girls than the governments of Great Britain and Northern Ireland' where the age of consent was sixteen.[41] Browne and her allies were successful in defeating this Government amendment to have the age of consent lowered from eighteen to fifteen.

In 1935, the Conditions of Employment Bill was brought before the Senate. One of the most contentious issues in the new Bill was Section 16 which stated that:

> The Minister may in respect of any form of industrial work, after consultation with representatives of employers interested in such form of industrial work and with representatives of workers so interested, by order make regulations either (a) prohibiting the employment of female workers to do such form of industrial work, or (b) fixing a proportion which the number of female workers employed by any employer to do

such form of industrial work may bear to the number of other workers so employed.[42]

Outside the Oireachtas the opposition to the Bill was vigorous, especially from the Irish Women Workers' Union and, in the Senate, opposition was led by Senators Jennie Wyse-Power and Kathleen Clarke, supported by Senator Kathleen Browne. The Bill received general support from the male senators who accepted the argument that Section 16 was 'put into this Bill to try to preserve some little employment for the male workers'.[43] Senator Wyse-Power stated that she found it 'regrettable that this Government should have followed the example of the last Government in imposing restrictions on women in industry'.[44] As in other debates on gendered legislation, Wyse-Power referred to the revolutionary expectations of women: the 'girls' who believe that 'when our own men are in power, we shall have equal rights'.[45] Faced with legislation which restricted their rights she did not know how they now felt, but she did hope that if the legislation was carried women already in employment in industry would not be interfered with. Senator Kathleen Clarke was also vehemently opposed to Section 16 based on:

the principle of equal rights and equal opportunities for all the citizens of this State. How you can agree to a section such as this, giving the Minister power to legislate against one section of the community while claiming that you have established equal rights is a thing I cannot see.[46]

As the Bill moved into the committee stage Clarke and Wyse-Power, joined by Senator Kathleen Browne, continued their arguments against Section 16. Wyse-Power saw this section of the Bill as a direct attack on the poorest women in Irish society. Poor families, even with a working father, were often dependant on the wage brought home by their working daughters, who 'do not drink it or play "house" with it ... what they earn goes directly into the home'.[47] She also spoke about the plight of the unmarried woman in Irish society. There were, she acknowledged, thousands of more females than males in the country, so 'where were the homes' they were to marry into, where were the husbands to support them?[48] Senator Clarke based her opposition to the Section of Bill dealing with women firmly on the grounds that this section went against the spirit of the Proclamation of 1916:

> that proclamation gave to every citizen equal rights and equal opportunities, and it seems to me that if you legislate against one section of the community, if you are going to curtail them in the way they are to earn their living, where are the equal opportunities provided for in that proclamation?[49]

Senator Kathleen Browne also opposed the section dealing with women workers. She argued that while the ideal place for a woman was in the home there were cases where 'if the woman were prevented from doing certain work, it would mean great hardship and, possibly, the starvation of the family'.[50] Despite the best efforts of Senators Wyse-Power, Clarke and Browne, the reality was that Irish women, both working class and middle class, had been and continued to be discriminated against by the State. The ideology of the domestic sphere for women and the public/political/work sphere for men runs through the contemporary arguments about the introduction of Section 16 of the Bill. The plight of both the single woman worker and the married woman worker was ignored in favour of the male worker, who may or may not have dependents. The Bill was carried in both the Dáil and Senate and passed in 1936.

This was the last opportunity that the female Senators had to oppose anti-women legislation as the Irish Free State Senate was abolished in 1936. However, the speeches and activities of these women reveal that most of them, especially Wyse-Power, Browne, Clarke and Costello, had considerable sympathy for the concept of women's rights. Individually or in concert with one another they argued against much of the gendered legislation which was introduced throughout the 1920s and 1930s, culminating, as activists outside the Oireachtas, in their opposition to the 1937 Constitution, or more specifically, to the articles dealing with the position of women in Irish society which were included in that Constitution. Cullen Owens has noted that, while women in the Dáil were much less vocal in support of women's rights, 'women members of the 1922–1936 Senate, in particular Jennie Wyse-Power, Kathleen Clarke, Eileen Costello and Kathleen Browne, who – across party lines – consistently opposed legislation which sought to restrict the role of women'.[51] The female Senators were not radicals; indeed their speeches often demonstrate that they did hold some traditional viewpoints, especially in relation to the female body, reproduction and sexuality. For example, in 1934, Kathleen Clarke opposed the ban on contraceptives in the Criminal Law Amendment Act, not because she supported access to contraceptives (she was at great pains to point out that she was 'in perfect agreement with the Church and the State in the condemnation of the use of these things'), but because she felt prohibition was unworkable.[52] Having seen the ill effects of prohibition of alcohol on American society she felt that a prohibition on the sale of contraceptives would 'drive the trading in and the use of these things into secret and illicit channels in which you will not be able to get after them'.[53]

What motivated these women was a belief in the right of Irish women to be full and equal citizens in this new Irish State. This was the promise made in the 1916 Proclamation and reiterated in the 1922 Constitution. It was this promise that formed a constant clarion call to their opposition to legislation that denied women this right. Wyse-Power, Clarke and Costello emerge as the most committed to the cause of equality for women in Irish society, although Browne, and earlier Stopford-Green, also supported campaigns to counteract or change legislation which they perceived as unjust to women, workers, landless labourers or the poor. At the centre of power in the Irish Free State, these women articulated, to their male colleagues, the campaigns of civil society feminist groups who were active outside the Oireachtas. Often allied with women's groups they brought the concerns of these groups, about the constant legislative subversion of women's rights as citizens, to the upper echelons of political power. Much of the legislation passed between 1922 and 1936 reaffirmed conservative views on women, traditional Catholic social thinking and the dominance of the discourse of domesticity for women.

Although its meaning and intent had been steadily eroded in the 1920s and 1930s, the importance of the promise of equal citizenship in the Proclamation of 1916, which was enshrined in the Constitution of 1922, cannot be underestimated. Even as de Valera introduced a new Constitution that would place the female citizen firmly in the home, women like Wyse-Power and Clarke still clung to the 1916 Proclamation and continued the battle for full and equal citizenship. While the female senators had been unable to fully subvert this dominance, they did consistently promote the idea that a woman had a right, as a citizen, to contribute to politics and the economy.

NOTES
1   http://www.ucc.ie/celt/online/E900003-004/ accessed 21/01/11.
2   Maria Luddy 'The Problem of Equality: Women's Activist Campaigns in Ireland, 1920–40', in Thomas E Hachey (ed), *Turning Points in Twentieth-Century Irish History* (Dublin, Irish Academic Press, 2011) p. 61.
3   See Jason Knirck, *Women of the Dáil: Gender, Republicanism and the Anglo-Irish Treaty* (Dublin, Irish Academic Press, 2006) pp. 160–162.

4   Knirck, *Women of the Dáil*, pp 165–166.
5   See Maryann Valiulis, 'Power, Gender, and Identity in the Irish Free State', in *Journal of Women's History*, Vol. 6, No. 4, 1995, pp. 117–136.
6   Maryann Gialanella Valiulis, 'Virtuous Mothers and Dutiful Wives; the Politics of Sexuality in the Irish Free State', in Maryann Gialanella Valiulis (ed), *Gender and Power in Irish History* (Dublin, Irish Academic Press, 2009).
7   Valiulis, 'Power, Gender and Identity', p. 134.
8   Maryann Gialanella Valiulis, 'Defining the Role in the New State: Irishwomen's Protest against the Juries Act of 1927', in *The Canadian Journal of Irish Studies*, Vol. 18, No. 1, July 1992, p. 44.
9   Carol Coulter, *The Hidden Tradition: Feminism, Women, and Nationalism in Ireland* (Cork, Cork University Press, 1993), p. 26.
10   Mary Clancy, 'Aspects of Women's Contribution to the Oireachtas Debate in the Irish Free State, 1922–1937', in Maria Luddy and Cliona Murphy (eds), *Women Surviving: Studies in Irish Women's History in the 19th and 20th Centuries* (Dublin, Poolbeg, 1990) p. 207.
11   *The Wexford People*, Saturday 5 July 1934.
12   *Seanad Debates*, Vol 17, 25 October 1933, cols 1634–1635.
13   *Seanad Debates*, Vol 17, 25 October 1933, cols 1634–1635.
14   The 1934 Wearing of Uniform (Restriction) Bill, sought to prevent the wearing of uniforms in the House of the Oireachtas. Browne made an impassioned speech in defence of the Blueshirt organisation. This Bill was in part occasioned by the fact that Browne wore the uniform in the Senate. The female members of the Blueshirts were known as the Blueblouses, as they wore a blue blouse as part of their uniform.
15   Sylvia Walby, 'Women and Nation', in *International Journal of Comparative Sociology*, Vol. 33, No. 1–2, 1992, p. 222.
16   Clancy, 'Aspects of Women's Contribution to the Oireachtas Debate', p. 217.
17   *Dáil Debates*, Vol. 13, 18 November 1925, cols 515.
18   *Dáil Debates*, Vol. 13, 18 November 1925, cols 515.
19   *Dáil Debates*, Vol. 13, 2 December 1925, cols 44.
20   *Dáil Debates*, Vol. 13, 2 December 1925, cols. 44.
21   *Seanad Debates*, Vol 6, 17 December 1925, cols 7.

22 *Seanad Debates*, Vol 6, 17 December 1925, cols 255–257. 'The fight' Wyse Power is referring to here is the War of Independence.

23 *Seanad Debates*, Vol 6, 17 December 1925 cols 255–257.

24 *Seanad Debates*, Vol 6, 17 December 1925, cols 255–257.

25 *Seanad Debates*, Vol 6, 17 December 1925, cols 255–257.

26 *Seanad Debates*, Vol 6, 17 December 1925, cols 255–257.

27 *Seanad Debates*, Vol 6, Thursday 17 December 1925, cols 246–247.

28 Valiulis, 'Defining the role in the new State', p. 48.

29 *Seanad Debates*, Vol. 8, 30 March 1927, cols 682–683.

30 *Seanad Debates*, Vol. 8, 30 March 1927, cols 682–685.

31 *Seanad Debates*, Vol 8, 8 April 1927, cols 808–809.

32 *Seanad Debates*, Vol 8, 30 March, 1927.

33 *Seanad Debates*, Vol 8, 8 April, 1927, cols 808–809.

34 *Seanad Debates*, Vol 8, 8 April, 1927, cols 808–809.

35 *Seanad Debates*, Vol 8, 8 April, 1927, cols 803–804.

36 Valiulis, 'Defining the role in the new State', p. 55.

37 See Valiulis, 'Virtuous Mothers and Dutiful Wives', p. 105 and Maria Luddy, 'Sex and the Single Girl in 1920s and 1930s Ireland', *The Irish Review*, 2007 (No. 35) p. 89.

38 *Seanad Debates*, Vol 13, March, 1930, col 703–704.

39 *Seanad Debates*, Vol 13, 1930, cols 708–709.

40 Caitriona Beaumont, 'Women, Citizenship and Catholicism in the Irish Free State, 1922–1948', *Women's History Review*, 1997, 6:4, p. 571.

41 *Seanad Debates*, Vol 19, February 1934, cols 1230.

42 Conditions of Employment Act, 1936. http://www.irishstatutebook.ie/1936/en/act/pub/0002/sec0016.html#sec16 accessed 24/01/2013.

43 *Seanad Debates*, Vol. 20, 27 November, 1935, cols 1244–1245.

44 *Seanad Debates*, Vol. 20, 27 November, 1935, cols 1247–1248.

45 *Seanad Debates*, Vol. 20, 27 November, 1935, cols 1247–1248.

46 *Seanad Debates*, Vol. 20, 27 November, 1935, cols 1256–1257.

47 *Seanad Debates*, Vol. 20, 11 December, 1935, cols 1400.

48 *Seanad Debates*, Vol. 20, 11 December, 1935, cols 1400.

49 *Seanad Debates*, Vol. 20, 11 December, 1935, cols 1398–1399.

50 *Seanad Debates*, Vol. 20, 12 December, 1935, cols 1404–1405.

51 Rosemary Cullen Owens, *A Social History of Women in Ireland, 1870–1970* (Dublin, Gill and Macmillan, 2005) p. 322.

52 *Seanad Debates*, Vol 19, February 1934, cols 1247.

53 *Seanad Debates*, Vol 19, February 1934, cols 1247.

SECOND WAVE FEMINISM IN IRELAND:
REFLECTIONS ON THEN AND CHALLENGES FOR NOW
– ONE ACTIVIST'S PERSPECTIVE

Grainne Healy

In the 1970s I was still in school when feminists first
appeared on the *Late Late Show*. As a young working class
trade unionist involved in bringing trade union
recognition to McDonalds restaurants in Dublin, I was
introduced to the many women who were then organising
for women's rights and I just fell under the spell of this
intoxicating, energising movement. It was a movement
which helped me make sense of the world as I had
experienced it, in my then young life. Almost 40 years on, I
still feel this way about feminism. On the back of major
social change and clamour by earlier feminists, my
feminist activism in the 1980s and 1990s was, as Mary
Dorcey's poetry reminded us, only possible because we
were 'moving into the space cleared by our mothers',[1] just
as the current feminist movement is moving into the
spaces we have cleared. These clearings which women are

about in 2012 also clear spaces, I hope, for feminist successes of tomorrow.

1970s Spaces Cleared

Feminists in the 1970s in Ireland had fought hard and won much from a church-controlled, patriarchal, political hegemony. Through street protest and political lobbying great practical changes leading to individual rights for women were achieved. By the early 1970s the Council for the Status of Women (CSW) had been established (1970), and AIM and Cherish were founded (1972).[2] The marriage bar was gone. Deserted Wives and Unmarried Mothers' allowances were introduced. The first refuge for battered women was opened, and the campaigning support group Association for Deserted and Alone Parents (ADAPT) was founded in 1973. The McGee case was won, and the ban on importation of contraceptives for private use was found unconstitutional.[3] The Anti-discrimination (Pay) Act was passed. Children's Allowance payments were granted to mothers. Maintenance orders for deserted wives were introduced. Women's Aid opened their refuge. Irish Women United (IWU) had formed and launched the Contraceptive Action Programme (1974). As Ireland campaigned to join the European Economic Community (EEC, now the EU) it had rejected the Irish government's request for a derogation from the Commission's Directive on Equal Pay. The Juries Act was amended (following the deBurca/Anderson case) and women were included for jury service (exclusion having been deemed unconstitutional).[4] IWU invaded the 'male only' Forty Foot bathing area in Sandycove. The Family Home Protection Act (1976) was passed and meant that prior to the sale of a family home written consent by both spouses was required, thus giving women security of their homes which up until then could be sold by a husband without a wife's consent. The First Rape Crisis Centre opened in Dublin. The Employment Equality Act passed and the Employment Equality Authority was set up. The Unfair Dismissals Act came into being (1977). Women Against Violence Against Women marches had taken place. Máire Geoghegan-Quinn was appointed to Cabinet (the first woman in Cabinet since Constance Markievicz was appointed Minister for Labour in the First Dáil of 1919). The 1979 Family Planning Act was passed, although it did restrict the sale of contraceptives to 'bona fide' couples only (when I was a student in UCD in 1977, the college authorities removed the condom vending machines from the Student's Union offices). The Women's Right to Choose Group was formed. The Campaign for an Irish Women's Centre was launched (1979). What spaces and what progress! But not perfect and not equal, and not all feminists had a common agenda or analysis of what was to be done or how. Sounds familiar?

1980s SPACES CLEARED

The 1980s was the decade of the backlash. Against a background of growing emigration and high unemployment, even those of us with third level education found it very hard to find employment. The feminist issues of this decade were reproductive rights and violence against women. There was a regeneration of energy and feminist vision and activism towards the end of that 80s decade when women's local community development and the discipline of women's studies in universities and in the community provided spaces and places for analysis and solidarity and vision-building. But the early '80s were depressing times for those of us who did not emigrate. In 1980 we saw the first Irish Pregnancy Counselling centre established. Status conference and *Status* magazine were launched and the Dublin Women's Centre opened to provide a physical space in Dublin for groups like Women in Learning (WIL), the women's studies group to which I belonged (1980). WIL was a self-directed women's group which created and delivered women's studies classes with and for women in the Dame Street centre above Nico's restaurant every Thursday for many years. It was a place where we laughed when doing 'Exploring Sexuality' classes and Joni Crone brought in black and white coffee table books of very close-up art photographs of vaginas for us to study, not telling us what they were. The gathered group all thought they were lovely pictures of forests and ski slopes in the black and white world of the Swiss Alps!

We laughed and we cried. The Pro-Life Amendment Campaign (PLAC) began their campaign for an abortion referendum (1981) and we held reclaim the night marches (1982). Open Door Counselling was established and the Anti-Amendment Campaign (AAC) never quite managed to organise the necessary local structures nationwide which would have been required to defeat PLAC (1983). We had neither the money nor the organisation. The abortion referendum result guaranteed, in Article 40.3.3., 'the right to life of the unborn' and made it equal to the life of the mother (1983).

But counter discourses were afoot and among those disseminating these voices were Irish Feminist Information (IFI) and those publishing other feminist magazines. WIL published our own *Wimmin Magazine* for about two years and actually went around pubs selling it to cover the costs – and we did! That was in the days of sticking down galleys of proofs onto A3 sheets with Pritt Stick and bringing the galleys to the printers in the Dublin Co-op. Women's education and the drive to provide our own was gathering steam and it was during these years that organisations like Kilbarrack Local Education and Renewal (KLEAR) were established and the Aontas women's group worked in feminist ways to support fledgling feminist communities around the country (1983). We published a 'how to set up a group' and 'basic rules for establishing education groups or women's groups'. Meanwhile, the Women for Disarmament group held the anti-Reagan demonstration in the Phoenix Park, and while most of us joined the picnic and brought food, the disarmament women with the red paint on their hands were arrested and badly treated in various prisons around Dublin (1984).

Three really important events happened in 1984: Attic Press was established by Roisin Conroy and Mary Paul Keane, UCD Women's Studies Forum was established by Ailbhe Smyth (the forerunner to the Women's Education Research and Resource Centre, WERRC), and in that same year Anne Lovett's death took place during childbirth in Granard in a lonely churchyard.[5] And we asked 'what sort of a country is this?'

The same year, the Kerry babies case and the hounding of Joanne Hayes was really a mobilising event of horrors, but it was also a blooming of solidarity amongst Irish feminists.[6] One beacon of fun and feminist focus was the International Interdisciplinary Conference held in Trinity College Dublin in 1987. The feminist non-academic women came in their droves once the costs of entry had been negotiated down from two hundred pounds to a pound a session! We joined activists and world-renowned feminists like the theologian and academic Mary Daly to explore and explain how our world was operating and how we understood the processes at work.[7]

The first divorce referendum was defeated (1986), and various court cases and student and clinic actions led to the Supreme Court Hamilton ruling on abortion in 1987 and on abortion information (1988). The activists in all these campaigns were a great mix of women from rural and urban parts. They were working class, middle class, students, professional women, journalists, medics, academics, lawyers, teachers, clerical workers, health care professionals, anarchists, unemployed and under-employed, traveller women, trades unionists, members of the left parties and members of no party, straight and lesbian.

The hunger strikes and the war in the North, and groups like Women Against Imperialism, broke the silence in the southern feminist movement on the North. The fear of what was happening north of the border silenced many, but also mobilised women and brought many northern women south searching for refuge, but never forgetting the need to address the war, and its cause, in their home towns.

THE 1990s

Unless you lived it, you can have no idea what it was like when the '80s ended and the 1990s began with the election of Mary Robinson as President of Ireland (1990). The same year saw the formation of WERRC at UCD, which opened up women's studies to many thousands of women. It was the end of a very bruising and exhausting decade with legal battles lost and won, and referenda lost, but with a feminist movement that was very much alive and well. Since the 90s my own feminist activism has taken me from the community women's studies sector into the National Women's Council of Ireland (NWCI, previously the Council for the Status for Women) where, for about a decade, a number of feminist activists agreed to put ourselves forward to be elected to leadership roles in this organisation and sought to make it the representative body for women's groups in Ireland. With women like Noreen

Byrne, Monica O'Connor and Carol Fawsett we were committed to move the CSW away from being seen as the council for the status of some women, and toward its place as a significant national body with representative status to national Government and EU structures. Via links to the European Women's Lobby, the NWCI was hugely influential in growing that EU-oriented space during the 1990s.

This grouping also sought to open the NWCI space itself to be a wider, more inclusive set of women's groups representing a wider set of women's concerns. We got members to agree to rename CSW, the National Women's Council of Ireland. The organisation became active on issues like childcare, violence against women, and women's education. I am also proud to say we did get a motion passed that saw NWCI reach a position on abortion that meant the organisation could begin for the first time to call for abortion services in Ireland. It also housed the important EU funding mechanism for women in Ireland, NOW (New Opportunities for Women). I represented, with great pride, NWCI at the committees which selected Lesbians Organising Together/Lesbian Education Awareness (LOT/LEA) as the first lesbian group in the EU to receive funding for its work for lesbians in Ireland.

NWCI was central to the social partnership process of the 1990s and early 2000s. This process entailed trade unions, government, employers and social NGOs negotiating a series of social agreements which avoided industrial unrest, and agreeing wages and social welfare rates. Thousands of hours were put into working with other social change partners on feminist issues. We saw the biggest trade union in the country, SIPTU, join NWCI, along with lesbian groups, and all the while the larger representative groups like Irish Countrywomen's

Association and Catholic Women's Federation stayed on board and kept faith with their feminist sisters, for as long as we could stay in social partnership. Representative spaces of NWCI allowed us to be instrumental in key decisions made in the National Economic and Social Forum (NESF), a body set up to examine policy issues of concern to society. The NESF was constituted into committees, which had representatives from the various social partners, and published reports advising Government on strategic economic and social matters. I was part of the management body of that forum for a number of years and oversaw the publication of significant reports on lone parents and lesbian and gay rights. We could also influence decisions in the Equality Authority, which began to take up lesbian and gay issues in its early reports. During this time with feminist CEOs (Katherine Zappone, Joanna McMinn) the organisation took on many of the activist strategies developed in the 1980s – using the media, having marches and actions, focus groups, education projects, local development initiatives – while also using the 'insider space' of governmental lobbying to ensure the women's agenda was always on the cabinet table. Whether in the NESF or the Equality Authority or the Equality unit of various departments, the NWCI worked well with allied social partner organisations.

It wasn't perfect and there were clashes of priorities and rows, and just as the wider global women's movement was attempting to be more intersectional, more inclusive of class and race, so too was the NWCI. It did not always keep everyone happy, but the democratic processes of a national body with over 160 representative women's groups takes time. For me, learning how to bring the membership along with the leadership, who have taken their priorities from the membership, was a priority and a huge learning personally, and one which I carry with me today as we continue to create new structures to continue with the feminist vision of a world of true equality for all.

FEMINISM INTO THE 21ST CENTURY: VIOLENCE AGAINST WOMEN

The issue of violence against women has always been a passion for me, representing as it does, the coalface of the outcomes of gender inequality for women. My decade with the European Women's Lobby Observatory on Violence against Women (1995–2008), which took a position on prostitution as a form of violence against women, has also been hugely influential on my own thinking. The Observatory was an EU space where I chaired a team of 15, then 27, national experts on violence against women in Brussels. We explored how, as feminists in a growing EU, we could push national governments to better protect women from gender-based violence. This was an important site where national and EU political lobbying skills were developed. Using these structures and processes we got text agreed at UN conferences, and worked on policy documents submitted to Government departments. All the while we held the clear analysis that violence against women in all its forms is one of the key barriers to women's liberation and continues to be a major barrier to gender equality. We insisted that states must be held to account for the protection of women from male violence. This was the decade where violence against women organisations in Ireland were funded and built capacity – something which is truly under threat today in 2012.

Drawing down important EU funds to embed this work in Ireland under the Dignity Daphne project was a hugely energising and mobilising experience in the mid 2000s. This work, which in Ireland has now become the 'Turn off the Red Light Campaign', is being driven by Immigrant

Council of Ireland (ICI), Ruhama and others, and is a crucial contemporary action on violence against women. At its base are the experiences of women who are sexually exploited. These women come in through the doors of ICI and Ruhama services.[8] Their experience as survivors informs the work of that campaign. The processes that the campaign uses are a mixture of traditional discussion group mobilisation, ally building with the trades union movement and civil society, getting men to act as champions for the cause, and the use of media, including excellent use of the new social media, film, and art exhibitions to raise awareness of the horrors of sex trafficking. The campaign is currently pushing for Irish legislation to criminalise the purchase of sex. Such exploitation is not a valid form of labour, and its regulation and legalisation is but an attempt by neo-liberal market states to turn even our sexual exploitation into a profit-making industry: an industry where the owners make profits and the women get exploited. It's not a matter of better working conditions – it is a matter of tackling demand and criminalising the purchase of sex. The only acceptable form of sexual interaction is the negotiated one. Any exchange of sex for money or goods is exploitative. There is no sub-category of women which feminism will make available to men for sexual exploitation.

FEMINISM IN THE 21ST CENTURY: LESBIAN AND GAY RIGHTS

A current area of activity to further the feminist vision lies in marriage equality rights for same-sex couples. This is an area which is not uncontested. The inclusion of class and race perspectives in feminist gender analysis over the course of the last three decades has been transformational and has really moved us from being a movement of white, middle-class, able-bodied women to being a more globally useful, locally appropriate and relevant movement. However, when we come to look at the issue of gay and lesbian rights, I would like to suggest we add a fourth lens – that of heteronormativity. Just as a failure to include 'race' or 'class' alongside 'gender' left the feminist project wanting, does failure to address head-on the issue of 'heteronormativity' (which relates to the systematic preferencing of heterosexuality and hetero ways of being in the world) mean that no amount of gender equality will ever deliver gay and lesbian liberation, unless this lens is adopted by the feminist movement in our analysis to further the feminist project?

For lesbian and gay people in many parts of the world, who live lives of invisibility from public policy, the State fails to recognise us as citizens, fails to respect our relationship choices, fails to acknowledge our family life. Heterosexuality is so normative that it is practically invisible, and enforced, as Adrienne Rich said.[9] For her it is compulsory. I believe that it is heterosexuality that requires the enforced binary of male – female as the model for all our intimate relationships. It uses gender roles with their power differentials, to show us the limited ways in which we must live out our lives as men and women. The systems which uphold heteronormativity displace gay and lesbian people from both the public and private spheres of life.[10] The exclusion of same-sex families from family policies, the same-sex marriage ban, the ban on same-sex adoption, or child custody, displace us from the protected private sphere (protected for heterosexuals, that is) while institutional discrimination, and in some places criminal laws of heterosexual coercion, displace us from a position in the public sphere.

The gay/lesbian citizen has been constructed as 'citizen deviant' and the current debates and campaigns for marriage equality are priorities because they relate to a most important liberty: liberty of equal definitional authority to say what counts as a marriage and what counts as family. The marriage equality campaign does not champion 'the married relationship' as the one and only valid relationship form, but sees it as one among many requiring acknowledgement and respect – one which should be open to all who would choose it. The creation of a separate institution called Civil Partnership – just for gays – can be seen as an incremental step towards lesbian and gay equality with heterosexuals. But separate is rarely equal. It could also be seen as accepting the right of the heteronormative state to define who has a recognisable family or who 'does' family in an acceptable (heterosexual) way and which relationships have state recognition (again the heterosexual ones). To expect same-sex couples entering marriage (when it is open to them) not to continue to challenge heteronormativity and gendered roles is to underestimate them in an amazingly patronising way. The entry of same-sex couples into marriage may well be a huge win for deconstructing the heteronormative, which holds heterosexuals and non-heterosexuals so closely to the limiting gender norms we so want to smash. Marriage equality for same-sex couples is part of this struggle and is part of the feminist agenda.

Concluding Comments

Living the life of a feminist activist over the decades of the second wave and into the third and now fourth wave has been and continues to be exciting. They were also times when I was a partner, a parent, a daughter and a sister. I was making waves and forging paths for myself and others to follow or strike off from. While many of the challenges of the second wave remain and new ones have emerged, solidarity with each other and with others across the social justice spectrum is a must if our common vision of a just and equal society is to be achieved. I still believe we can.

NOTES

1   Mary Dorcey *Moving Into the Space Cleared by Our Mothers* (Galway, Salmon, 1991).
2   Aim (Action, Information, Motivation) was founded in 1972 as a pressure group providing information and legal advice for women. It campaigned for protection and maintenance for women and family law reform. Cherish was an action group formed by single mothers to give advice and support to single parents. It campaigned for an end to 'illegitimate' status of children of unmarried parents.
3   In 1974 the Supreme Court ruled in favour of Mary McGee and found that the existing ban on importation of contraceptives for private use was unconstitutional. The result was the recognition of a marital right to privacy by the court.
4   The Juries Act 1927 had laid down that women could not sit on juries. In 1974 Mairin de Burca and Mary Anderson, members of IWU, took a case to the Supreme Court which resulted in the court finding the Juries Act of 1927 unconstitutional and the ban on women sitting on juries was overturned.
5   Ann Lovett was found beside her dead newborn child in a churchyard in Granard, Co. Longford in 1984. She died later in hospital. She was a 15 year old schoolgirl and her death, following so soon on the passage of the Eighth Amendment to the Constitution, which gave equal rights to the woman and the unborn foetus, highlighted the lived reality of many women in Ireland and how they dealt with and concealed unwanted pregnancies. This tragic case showed how young, rural, isolated women with unwanted pregnancies were vulnerable and effectively lacked any protection or solution to their situation unless they could have access to support services and abortion in the UK. Ann Lovett did not have such access.
6   1984: Joanne Hayes in Tralee, Co. Kerry was at the centre of what came to be known as the 'Kerry Babies' case. Just three

months after Ann Lovett's death the body of a baby with stab wounds sparked an investigation into women who were suspected of being sexually promiscuous in the locality. Joanne had already had a baby following a relationship with a married man and she and her family were interrogated. Joanne confessed to a further pregnancy and admitted to infanticide. She and her family insisted she had buried the baby on the farm. The investigation insisted that she had had twins, one of which was the dead baby found stabbed on a beach. Despite forensic evidence which held that she could not have been the mother of the stabbed baby, a tribunal of investigation and a court case attempted to press murder charges on Joanne for a crime that forensically was not possible. The charges were finally dropped but the demonstrations and outcry at her treatment by the authorities and the media was ferocious and marked a move away from Catholic conservatism and the total control of women's sexuality by the church and state in Ireland.

7   Daly's publications include *Beyond God the Father* (Boston, Beacon Press, 1974); *Gyn/ecology: The Metaethics of Radical Feminism* (Boston, Beacon Press, 1973); *Pure Lust* (Boston, Beacon Press, 1984); Webster's Intergalactic *Wickedary* (Boston, Beacon Press, 1987).

8   Ruhama was established in 1989 and is an NGO which works on a national level with women affected by prostitution and other forms of commercial sexual exploitation.

9   Adrienne Rich 'Compulsory Heterosexuality and Lesbian Existence' is a 1980 essay in *Blood, Bread, and Poetry* (New York, Norton, 1986).

10   Cheshire Calhoun, *Feminism, the Family and the Politics of the Closet* (Oxford, Oxford University Press, 2000).

'TO CHANGE SOCIETY':
IRISHWOMEN UNITED AND POLITICAL ACTIVISM, 1975–1979

Mary McAuliffe

In a letter to *The Irish Times*, dated 2 August 1975, in which she defended a protest by Irishwomen United (IWU) at the Fitzwilliam Lawn Tennis Club, IWU member, Rosine Auberting stated that IWU were fighting for a principle, 'the freedom of choice for all women'.[1] These were fighting words and they reflected the real growth of feminist activism in Ireland in the 1970s. Several decades separated these second wave feminists from their sisters in the first wave, even if there had been continuous, if less militant, feminist campaigning between the 1940s and the 1960s. The attempts by Irish governments to claw back on women's rights from the 1920s had eased during the 1950s, although many of the legal and societal bars to female participation in the workplace and to freedom of choice in their lives remained. Organisations like the Irish Countrywomen's Association (ICA) and the Irish Housewives Association (IHA) had continued to agitate for a better deal for the female citizen, urban and rural. Indeed, by 1946, the IHA had a specifically feminist goal in its constitution, stating that it aimed to 'secure all such reforms as are necessary to establish a real equality of liberties, status and opportunity for all persons'.[2] The type of maternalist feminism espoused by the ICA and IHA kept women's issues on the agenda in an Ireland where 'gendered political forces had limited women's access to political and economic power'.[3] While marriage and motherhood continued to be the dominant discourse for women, Ireland in the 1950s and 1960s was changing. With better education, falling childbirth rates, falling marriage rates and rising employment rates, women were making their presence in the public sphere and in the workforce felt. By the end of the 1960s a new energy was evident amongst those campaigning for equal rights. A lobbying campaign by an ad hoc committee of established women's groups succeeded in persuading the then Taoiseach, Jack Lynch, to set up the first Commission on the Status of Women in 1969, which reported to the Government in 1973. Issues identified by this Commission included the continued dominance of the discourse of domesticity in Irish society, discriminatory pay for women workers, no support for widows, deserted wives or unmarried mothers, gendered education and the fact that women did not serve on juries. However, even as this official body was reporting to the Government on the status of women in Irish society, younger women were beginning to find their own voice in a nascent second wave feminist movement.

Although the Council for the Status for Women (CSW) was gaining some traction with government to implement reforms in Ireland, some viewed the CSW and other long-standing women's groups as part of a traditional mainstream, a mainstream that did not speak about issues of real concern to younger women. Hilda Tweedy, co-founder of the IHA and a member of the CSA, stated that there 'was considerable tension between the two women's movements … [the] justifiably angry young women looked upon … the CWS as "establishment" and anything we did was suspect to them'.[4] This suspicion worked both ways as the older, more established activists felt that the disruptive, direct action activism of the Irish Women's Liberation Movement (IWLM) and IWU would provoke a backlash to any campaigns for women's rights. However, as Connolly noted conflict was part of the feminist movement in Ireland in the 1970s where arguments tended to take place 'within autonomous groups within the women's liberation sector over ideologies and radical politics and between women's rights and women's liberation [groups] over tactics'.[5] These differences between the long established activist women and the younger feminists who supported the more radical grassroots direct action campaigns were influential in the creation of the first women's liberation group in Ireland in 1970.

The first meeting of this new organisation, IWLM, was held in Bewleys Café, Dublin in 1970. Inspired by the civil rights movement in Northern Ireland and the Women's Liberation Movements in the UK and the USA, and informed by feminist publications from both the UK and the US, this small group of young Irish women were determined to campaign for Irish women's liberation in a markedly different way. Similar to other early second wave feminist groups elsewhere the IWLM was made up of left-leaning, educated, middle class and professional women, including several political women and female journalists. In 1971, the IWLM issued its manifesto, *Chains or Change? The Civil Wrongs of Irish Women*, which outlined the many areas of discrimination against women in Ireland. These included continuing inequalities under the law, the lack of equal pay for equal work, gendered and unfair taxation laws, lack of access to contraceptives, the continuing marriage bar, discrimination at work, gendered differences in education of boys and girls, unfair treatment of widows, deserted wives, unmarried mothers and single women and few or no childcare facilities.

In the short time that it existed the IWLM undertook some spectacular and very public activism, as well as introducing methods and ideas from US feminism, including 'consciousness raising about the ... reality of women's lived experience, still invisible and unexplored in the public discourse of the time'.[6] In 1971 a group of IWLM women appeared on the most popular television show in the country, *The Late Late Show*, where they spoke on women's issues which were hitherto taboo in respectable Irish society. June Levine recalled that 'a free for all screaming match' took place, but the effect was to galvanise many women around the country.[7] Soon after the IWLM held a public meeting in the Mansion House in Dublin, to which, to the surprise of many, over one thousand women turned up. The demands of the IWLM were discussed and debated; there was enormous energy to create a national movement, however leaderless, loosely organised and decentralised. The IWLM was not, ultimately, able to take full advantage of this growing interest in feminism and feminist activism.

Direct action did, however, garner much media attention for feminism in Ireland. The public campaigns of the IWLM included the famous contraceptive train, when, in May 1971, members took the train from Dublin's Connolly Station to Belfast and bought contraceptives and brought them back to Dublin. Of course, the purchase, importation and advertising of contraceptives had been banned in Ireland under the 1935 Censorship of Publications Act. As the IWLM openly displayed their purchases at Connolly Station they were directly challenging the accepted notions of respectability, morality, female sexuality and women's position in traditional Irish society, as well as breaking the law. This direct action activism, while reminiscent of the militancy of some first wave suffrage campaigners, was divisive, both within and outside of the movement. One woman resigned from the IWLM after the contraceptive train action because she felt the organisation was 'anti-clergy, anti-government, anti-ICA, anti-police, anti-men',[8] while others shouted that the IWLM had 'gone too far ... and there were calls for the IWLM to 'moderate its tone'.[9] Divergent views on the Northern Irish question and internal differences on ideology, directions and types of activism led to the fragmentation of the IWLM by 1972. However, the issues it had brought to public consciousness were to remain firmly on the agenda and many of the women who had been active with the IWLM were to be active in other feminist groups.

Despite ongoing activism by various individuals and organisations it was not until 1975 that another feminist group emerged which would gain as much of a grip on the public consciousness as the IWLM. Irishwomen United (IWU) was a loose grouping of several left wing groups which came together in April of that year. Among those involved in IWU were Movement for a Socialist Republic, People's Democracy, Revolutionary Struggle, the Revolutionary Marxist Group, the Communist Party of Ireland, the Irish Republican Socialist Group, the International Lesbian Caucus, the Sandymount Self-help group, and Women for Radical Change, as well as lesbian groups, trade union groups, and student groups. As IWU member Marie McMahon said

> women involved [in setting up IWU] were women who were
> very politically minded either in terms of their gender, like
> gay women or women who were involved in left wing groups
> ... a highly politicised group of people plus students who

would have been extremely articulate and educated even though they were very young.[10]

Anne Speed, who was one of the driving forces behind the setting up of the organisation, said that the

> IWU grew out of a feminist and lesbian feminist awareness and a commitment by those ... on the left to building an autonomous women's voice, and an autonomous women's movement. We could make common cause with male colleagues on the left ... but there were issues of feminism which only those who experienced the discrimination would be most determined to resist ... it was that convergence that led to the formation of IWU.[11]

Prior to their launch at Liberty Hall on 8 June 1975, a working group comprised of representatives of the organisations drew up a charter. Many of the demands in the IWU charter were similar to those of the IWLM's *Change or Chains* manifesto because as McMahon (a member of both IWLM and IWU) said

> We haven't yet achieved any of the aims that we set out in IWLM, we still hadn't got equal pay, we still didn't have legalised contraception. I think the law had been changed on Juries alright but the main things, the two big things were equal pay and contraception ... they were the two things that allowed women to control their own lives...economic independence and the right to control their own bodies and neither of them have been achieved despite the trojan work by the IWLM ... so the IWU was formed.[12]

However, the IWU, influenced by socialism, lesbian feminism and radical feminism, added more demands to their charter, including free contraception, self-determined sexuality and the establishment of women's centres. IWU member, the poet and writer, Mary Dorcey has often spoken about the difficult battle to get recognition for lesbian women and the right to self-determined sexuality included in the charter. In 1975, for conservative and respectable Irish society 'gay didn't yet exist, homosexual was hardly ever used and was only used about men and queer wasn't used either except as an insult, so women didn't even have a name'.[13] Including self-determined sexuality in the IWU charter was the opening salvo in what would be ongoing discussion in the group about sexuality. This was a radical idea in an Ireland where female sexuality had been regarded as of primary concern, not of the woman herself, but of the Catholic Church and the State.

Reproductive rights, access to contraceptives, concerns about rape and sexual violence were of primary concern to the young women in IWU. In particular reversing the continuing ban on the advertisement, importation or sale of contraceptives was a core demand and central to many of the direct action events organised by IWU. As well as contraceptives, equal pay was a major issue. Industrialisation and urbanisation were changing the relationship between Irish women and the workplace in the 1970s. Growth in business during this period led to a growth in demand for an expanded workforce, and the inclusion of women, married and single, in work outside the home, was one way of securing that necessary workforce. In addition, with the introduction of free secondary education, there were many young educated women who were looking for choices beyond the traditional 'wife/mother' binary. These women were often politicised, not afraid of insisting that their voice be heard and that their demands be met, that their right to full and equal citizenship be secured once and for all. The politicised, educated woman worker was not going to accept the unequal pay offered her. Her demands, as articulated by IWLM and later IWU, were for equal pay, getting rid of the marriage bar and any other legal barriers to inclusion in the workforce based on gender, and the introduction of an equitable taxation system. As Anne Speed has said:

this was the first generation coming from the free education to second level, so you had a layer of women from skilled working class families who had come through free education and who had expectations of opportunities and found that a conservative society had closed doors to them... there was a great deal of anger and frustration, particularly from young lesbian women. They were extremely angry but extremely brave and militant because they came to the realisation that, while they might have been educated equally as young children, when they came to try and express themselves as individuals politically or sexually, their rights were being denied in society.[14]

The IWU charter, which was printed in every copy of the IWU journal, *Banshee,* stated that 'we pledge ourselves to challenge and fight sexism in all forms and oppose all forms of exploitation of women which keep them oppressed'.[15] Demands in the IWU charter included the removal of all legal obstacles to equality, free legal contraception, the recognition of motherhood and fatherhood as a special function, equality in education, the male rate for the job where men and women are working together, state provision of funds and premises for women's centres to be run by women themselves, and the right of all women to self-determined sexuality.[16] The first edition of *Banshee* laid out the methods by which IWU would set about achieving these aims, working on a 'basis of general meetings (discussion and action planning ... every week), joint actions (pickets, public meetings and workshops, at present on women in the trade unions, contraception, social welfare and political theory) and consciousness raising groups'.[17] From the beginning there was an intensity which the members brought to organising on various issues. As Anne Speed recalls

IWU was an independent organisation and direct action was very important to us ... and we prided ourselves on being an organisation that would take direct action ... we occupied the office of the Federated Union of Employers, we went to

Fitzwilliam [a male only tennis club] we went out to the Forty Foot … and we went there because there was a practice, not a law, but a practice which intimidated women from going to swim in one of the most important places that you could swim on the east coast.[18]

These direct actions included pickets on all male clubs and pubs and swimming places, campaigns focused on contraception and equal pay as well as holding seminars, discussion groups and conferences. The group also prepared a discussion paper on 'How to build a women's movement'. This discussion paper emphasised the need, as articulated above by Anne Speed, to build an autonomous women's group, that the IWU charter, and activism on contraception and equal pay, were merely a starting point to a more profound radicalisation of all issues relating to women's oppression in Ireland.[19] Marie McMahon recalls that:

There were to be no leaders in the groups, everything was democratic and autonomous to women, to those in the group, so we decide to divide into groups which would work out different strategies for campaigning – for equal pay and contraception. I'd say the most radical step we took in that direction was the one for equal pay when we occupied the Federated Union of Employers (FUE) … at this stage equal pay had been made a law and we weren't getting it so we decided, those of us who weren't afraid of being arrested, to occupy their building in Fitzwilliam St.[20]

The direct action campaign at the headquarters of the FUE was part of their equal pay campaign. In early 1975 women workers had come together in a broadbased coalition, 'Save the Equal Pay Act', which the IWU were not invited to join because of their radical image. Despite not being formally part of the coalition, the IWU collected thousands of signatures for the petition organised by the Equal Pay Campaign. Impatient with the speed of the Equal Pay Campaign's activism, and the delays in introducing equal pay, the IWU decided on more direct and public action – they occupied the office of the FUE. As Anne Speed recalls

> all the young women involved in IWU were very frustrated as there was a lack of a kind of a campaign activity that they could engage with ... there was no point of connection with what the trade union movement was doing ... so what the IWU decided to do was take an action which highlighted something that was happening, which was the employers [the FUE] campaign to diminish the importance of equal pay, to defeat the implementation of the Directive in their own economic interests, to deny the right to equal pay ... the IWU decided that this was the niche that we could fit into and we could take some action on. And we were criticised by the trade union movement officially for that ... we stole a march on then, we got front page coverage.[21]

The FUE were chosen as they were opposed to equal pay and lobbied the government to get a derogation from the EEC Directive that equal pay be introduced in Ireland. As well as occupying the offices of the FUE, the IWU also interrupted Taoiseach Liam Cosgrave as he launched a book entitled, ironically, *Women in Ireland - a special issue for International Women's Year, 1975*. The Irish Times breathlessly reported on the chaotic scenes at the book launch as young women from IWU invaded the room. The Taoiseach made 'a brief speech in which he referred to the Government's commitment to reform in the field of women's rights. He mentioned legislation dealing with family law, equal pay and anti-discrimination laws for female workers which, he said, would be dealt with in the next session of the Oireachtas'.[22]

One of those IWU present, Patricia Cobey, informed the Taoiseach that the *Women in Ireland* booklet was redundant while the issues of inequality and full human rights for women had, still, to be dealt with. The IWU women demanded that equal pay, contraception and better social conditions be dealt with immediately. They also took the Taoiseach to task as he had helped defeat a Bill on contraception when he voted against his own government on the implementation of the Importation, Sale and Manufacture of Contraceptive Bill, in 1974.[23] The Taoiseach, apparently white-faced with anger, was hurriedly ushered from the room while some of the establishment women present applauded the actions of the IWU. As one attendee said, 'she [Patricia Cobey] had the courage to stand up and say what we believe ... I wish I could do it'.[24] As the campaign for equal pay gathered pace, the government applied for a derogation from the equal pay directive from Brussels which was refused, and the Anti-Discrimination (Pay) Act, which had been passed in 1974, came into effect.

Another of the core demands of the IWU was access to contraception and, in 1976, members launched the Contraception Action Programme (CAP). As Connolly notes the 'structure of the campaign [by the IWU] and the repertoire of strategies [used] broadened in scope in 1976', and received broad support from other organisations such as trade unions, students' groups, the CSW, other women's groups and individual activists.[25] The setting up of unique campaigning groups within the IWU was one of their strategies, as Mary Dorcey recalls:

> We divided into different groups and at different times we had different campaigns ... we had the contraception action programme [CAP] which was extremely fiercely fought ... and we had the FUE occupation, that was the equal pay demands ... and we had the invasion of the Forty Foot and the invasion of Fitzwilliam ... which were always ongoing, we had to keep doing them each year.[26]

CAP was another stand to these intense and radical campaigning strategies employed by IWU. Its objectives were an end to restrictive legislation on contraception, on the availability of all methods of contraception and the provision of information and counselling on contraception, as well as demanding the setting up of education programmes on sex, birth and contraception in schools, the training of doctors and medical professions on birth control and the distribution of contraceptives, free through Health Centres, and at cost from pharmacies and GPs. As with all their campaigns the IWU employed direct action with CAP. As Mary Dorcey recalls 'we used to sell condoms at the Dandelion Market (Dublin) at the weekend which was illegal' and members would go to housing estates to distribute contraceptives.[27]

Another action was taken against the banning of the British feminist magazine, *Spare Rib*, in February 1977, following a complaint to the Censorship Board, because it carried information on contraceptives. Marie McMahon was central to this action and recalls that

> we printed the page [with the banned information] of the *Spare Rib* into big posters and we went postering and I got arrested … I was brought to court and I got a week in prison … I refused to pay the fine of £2,000 … there were huge demonstrations outside the prison while I was there.[28]

McMahon was bound to the peace and on refusing to sign the peace bond she was threatened with imprisonment. Although it was not until March 1980, well after the end of IWU and, ironically when *Spare Rib* was by then legal, that she was imprisoned. Angry demonstrations were held in support of McMahon and she recalls hearing the women who were demonstrating outside Mountjoy Prison, 'I could hear my name being shouted from the road'.[29] McMahon herself recalls other direct actions relating to the campaign for contraception:

> I think the most radical thing we did, we tried to get into the Archbishop's Palace [in Drumcondra, Dublin] and we had torchlights with us. We got up on the wall of Archbishop's Palace which horrified passers-by … and cars stopped and people told us we were a disgrace … our slogans were 'if

bishops would get pregnant, contraception would be a sacrament' and 'not the church, not the state, women should decide their fate' ... so we sang both of them all evening in the pitch dark, with our firelighters in our tins, on top of the wall.[30]

Mary Dorcey also recalls more personal direct action against politicians who voted against the contraceptive bill. IWU women would always be ready to publically challenge politicians who were publically anti-contraceptives.

If IWU women came across these politicians in public and if their lifestyle was known to be contrary to what they were saying in public we regarded them as prime targets ... especially if they lived a liberal, permissive lifestyle but voted otherwise ... we would challenge them in public and shout at them ... our slogan to them was 'are you a virgin or a hypocrite'?[31]

Dorcey recalls doing this to a senior Labour politician in a pub in Dublin. She and her IWU friends were roughly hustled out of the pub for daring to challenge him.

As well as direct action, the IWU launched a journal which was a broad based feminist magazine and named *Banshee* 'not only because the being is feminine, but also because her appearance and behaviour do not correspond to conventional male ideas about what a woman should look like and be like'.[32] In the first edition, its rotating committee of editors wrote that *Banshee* was the IWU's answer to the media silence on women's issues. In their editorial they questioned if any reader could possibly know from the attention paid to women in the media that females made up 51% of the population? Where, they asked, were the howls of outrage when 'Irishwomen were denied contraception, divorce and abortion? That we work for half the wages men get?', no-one, they wrote, 'wants to hear what women think?'[33] *Banshee* was in the tradition of feminist magazines, like *Spare Rib* in the UK, which sought to provide an alternative viewpoint to traditional news media and women's magazines. Eight issues of *Banshee* were produced between 1976 and late 1977. In its pages one can find the wide range of issues which exercised the women of IWU including all the demands in the IWU charter, as well as issues such as abortion and divorce. Discussions on patriarchy, the family and wages for housework, the plight of the single woman, the Church (vol 2), feminism and lesbianism (vol 3), prostitution, contraception (and the different methods available), the lack of rights for the married women worker (vol 6), censorship, women and the law and body image (vol 8) filled its pages. It also included book reviews, literary pieces, news about women's rights and campaigns in other countries, snippets of women's history, reports on the various direct actions campaigns which IWU was undertaking and a humorous, satirical page entitled 'Red Biddy' which took pot-shots at the activities of various Irish politicians and others who were perceived as being anti-women. It also included a letters page where readers could engage with the activities and ideologies of IWU, including those who were opposed to some of its demands. In issue two among letters which were broadly supportive of the IWU was a letter from a Ms. Clare Hook who took the IWU to task, for, as she wrote, making the mistake of 'placing abortion so high on your list of priorities, before wives and mothers. Many people who would be in complete sympathy with your other aims won't read any further'.[34] For activists like Anne Speed:

> the magazine was important because it was somewhere where we could record what we were about, what our goals and aims were, what we were doing and provide a commentary on the society we were living in and we realised that the history of women's political involvement was not properly recorded ... it was down to us to write our own history.[35]

The ending of IWU in late 1977 and into 1978 was a gradual process. Ideological debates about republicanism, socialism, lesbianism and radical feminism proved divisive. Members were concerned about the 'lesbian bloc which felt that anything that wasn't directed at sexuality was creating division. Then you have the ones that thought the North was very much part of our conflict ... having ties with republican women and the Armagh women was very much part of that'.[36] As Connolly has noted 'conflict was inherent in IWU over ideological purity and between those who promoted what was termed the "revolutionary struggle" and adherents of the radical feminism'.[37] For others their professional and personal lives were taking precedence over the intense campaigning IWU members undertook and, for others, it was simply exhaustion; 'In the spring of '77 IWU did have a day workshop on where we were now, where we were going ... because everybody knew there were, not cracks, but exhaustion'.[38]

However, despite its short lifespan IWU had achieved much thanks to the intensity, energies, ideas and strategies of its members. Despite the sometimes negative responses to direct action IWU succeeded in positioning issues such as contraception, equal pay, reproduction and sexuality at the centre of feminist debate and activism in Ireland. Many of the women who cut their teeth in feminist activism with IWU would continue to be central to organisations and campaigns for better social conditions for women, reproductive rights, lesbian activism, as well as issues around rape, violence against women and domestic violence, on into the following decades. The strategies of direct action employed by IWU continued to be used by various organisations and women's groups.

Was it a radical organisation? As Cullen has argued, the IWU charter broke new ground 'in sex-related areas, being more explicit with regard to contraception and adding abortion and lesbian rights to its main demands', so for the first time in a country where 'unnatural' birth control and same-sex relationships were regarded as sinful and illegal 'these issues were appearing in feminist manifestos'.[39] However, abortion and lesbianism were not openly included in that first IWU charter, although these issues were discussed in the pages of *Banshee*. As veteran IWU member Marie McMahon said, it was a radical group but 'we couldn't put anything about lesbianism or abortion in the charter … so it was a revolution with limits'.[40]

Despite the limits to its revolution the contribution by the activists of IWU to the campaigns to free Irish women from an ideology of domesticity which had dominated Irish social and political thinking, its challenges to unequal pay for women in the workplace, and to State and Church dictated ideologies on female sexuality and fertility and other issues of gender oppression in Irish society, as well as the introduction of radical ideas and concepts about feminism and feminist activism to a wider national audience, was transformative. Long after its demise many women who had developed their politics and activism with IWU were active and influential in Irish socio-political campaigns which contributed to the fundamental alteration of Irish society in the later 20th century. These future campaigns would, in time, achieve many of the aims laid out in the IWU charter.

NOTES

1   *The Irish Times*, 2 August 1975, p. 9.
2   Mary Cullen, 'Women, emancipation and politics, 1860–1984', in J R Hill (ed), *A New History of Ireland, Vol VII, Ireland. 1921–1984* (Oxford, Oxford University Press, 2010), p. 879.
3   Rosemary Cullen Owens, *A Social History of Women in Ireland, 1870–1970* (Dublin, Gill and Macmillan, 2005), p. 301.

4   Linda Connolly, *The Irish Women's Movement from Revolution to Devolution* (Dublin, The Lilliput Press, 2002) p. 148. For a discussion on women's activism in Ireland between 1940 and 1960 see Hilda Tweedy, *A Link in the Chain: The Story of the Irish Housewives Association 1942–1992* (Dublin, Attic Press, 1992).

5   Connolly, *The Irish Women's Movement* pp 137–138.

6   Connolly, *The Irish Women's Movement* p. 115.

7   Ailbhe Smyth, 'The Women's Movement in the Republic of Ireland, 1970–1990', in Ailbhe Smyth (ed) *Irish Women's Studies Reader* (Dublin, Attic Press, 1993), p. 252.

8   Smyth, 'The Women's Movement', p. 255.

9   Linda Connolly and Tina O'Toole, *Documenting Irish Feminism: the second wave* (Dublin, The Woodfield Press, 2005), pp 28–30.

10   Marie McMahon, member IWU, interviewed by Mary McAuliffe, 11/07/13.

11   http://www.irishleftreview.org/2010/09/30/banshee-journal-irish-women-united-left-dctv/ accessed 07/03/12.

12   Interview with Marie McMahon, member IWU, 11/07/13.

13   Mary Dorcey, member IWU, interviewed by Mary McAuliffe, 09/07/13.

14   http://www.irishleftreview.org/2010/09/30/banshee-journal-irish-women-united-left-dctv/ accessed 07/03/1

15   *Banshee, the journal of the IWU*, Vol 1, No 1, 1975. PDFs of most editions of *Banshee* can be accessed at http://www.irishleftreview.org/2010/09/30/banshee-journal-irish-women-united-left-dctv/

16   *Banshee,* the journal of the IWU, Vol 1, No 1, 1975.

17   *Banshee,* the journal of the IWU, Vol 1, No 1, 1975.

18   http://www.irishleftreview.org/2010/09/30/banshee-journal-irish-women-united-left-dctv/ accessed 07/03/1.

19   Smyth, 'The Women's Movement', pp 259–260.

20   Interview with Marie McMahon, member IWU, 11/07/13.

21   http://www.irishleftreview.org/2010/09/30/banshee-journal-irish-women-united-left-dctv/ accessed 07/03/1.

22   *The Irish Times*, 16 September 1975, p. 11.

23   This Bill was introduced after the Irish Supreme Court had ruled that married couples had a constitutional right to privacy, including contraception (the McGee case, 1973). In the Bill the Minister for Justice, Patrick Cooney, proposed that contraceptives could be sold on prescription from a doctor, and that he was satisfied that only married couples would then

access these contraceptives. Taoiseach Liam Cosgrave voted, with his conscience he said, against this Bill introduced by his own Minister for Justice

24   *The Irish Times*, 16 September 1975, p. 11.
25   Connolly, *The Irish Women's Movement*, p. 143.
26   Interview with Mary Dorcey, member IWU, 09/07/13.
27   Interview with Mary Dorcey, member IWU, 09/07/13.
28   Interview with Marie McMahon, member IWU, 11/07/13.
29   Interview with Marie McMahon, member IWU, 11/07/13.
30   Interview with Marie McMahon, member IWU, 11/07/13.
31   Interview with Mary Dorcey, member IWU, 09/07/13.
32   Patricia Lysaght, *The Banshee: The Irish Death Messenger* (Boulder, Roberts Rinehart, 1986) p. 24.
33   *Banshee*, the journal of the IWU, Vol 1, No 1, 1975.
34   *Banshee*, the journal of the IWU, Vol 1, No 2, 1975.
35   http://www.irishleftreview.org/2010/09/30/banshee-journal-irish-women-united-left-dctv/ accessed 07/03/1
36   Connolly, *The Irish Women's Movement*, p. 132.
37   Connolly, *The Irish Women's Movement*, p. 133.
38   Smyth, 'The Women's Movement', p. 262.
39   Cullen, 'Women, emancipation and politics, 1860–1984', p. 884.
40   Interview with Marie McMahon, member IWU, 11/07/13.

Interview with a Born-Again Feminist: Mamo McDonald

Clara Fischer

In June 2013, I interviewed Mamo McDonald at her house in Clones, County Monaghan. Having invited her to speak at the Irish Feminist Network conference the previous year, I was filled with anticipation for what this veteran campaigner was going to reveal to me about feminism in Ireland. Her presentation at the conference had been a resounding success, and several attendants commented afterwards on what an inspirational, humorous and insightful speaker she was. Given her capacity to make audiences of all stripes sit up in their seats and given her breadth of experience, I felt strongly that her thoughts should be captured in an anthology such as this.

For those unfamiliar with Mamo, the impressive, although never towering, organiser, campaigner and poet, a brief biographical sketch might be in order. Originally from the south of Ireland, Mamo moved to Monaghan, near the border to take up work in a bank. She soon met her husband there, with whom she settled in Clones and had eleven children. Forced to leave her employment owing to the marriage bar, Mamo ran a successful clothing business in the town. She joined the Irish Countrywomen's Association (ICA) on moving north, and eventually took over its stewardship in 1982 during what has sometimes been described as a challenging, if not harrowing, time for women and feminism in Ireland.[1]

Mamo at the National Gallery of Ireland © John Cogill Photography

In what follows, Mamo discusses her presidency of the Irish Countrywomen's Association (1982–1985), her visit to Kenya for the UN End of Decade Women's Conference in Nairobi (1985), her involvement with the Older Women's Network (1993–2012), and her take on political activism, life in the border town of Clones, and her passion for lacemaking.

I have chosen not to incorporate Mamo's insights here into a meta-narrative or academic analysis, but want to present her words, her own words, in as pure and un-interpreted a manner as possible. The idea is that readers will be in a position to draw their own conclusions from Mamo's thoughts and stories, and will experience some of the affective nuances of her words, which necessarily pervade feminist accounts of events and ideas, but which sometimes get skewed or erased in a secondary telling. The emotions spurring and accompanying feminist testimony may span the gamut of our affective repertoire, forcing to light tensions and confrontations that are often left unsaid and unfelt. By presenting Mamo's words in as unadulterated a fashion as possible, I want to allow such tensions to be read directly in the text, and to be felt by readers as they evaluate and interpret Mamo's thoughts for themselves. Mamo's narrative is instructive with regard to the wider historical and political context of feminisms in Ireland, and I anticipate several continuities and ruptures to come to the fore for readers, concerning, for instance: broad-based women's representative organising and the construction of policy agendas; progressiveness and conservatism; women's roles in the home and in the public sphere; women's formal and informal political activism; solidarity, friendship and in-fighting; and the construction of older and younger feminist subjectivities. Ultimately, I hope that Mamo's telling will instil in us an awareness of the potential similarities and dissimilarities across differing contexts, as we continue to work on our respective feminist projects.

BEING A 'BORN-AGAIN FEMINIST'

I didn't start out as a feminist. It was life that made a feminist out of me. I call myself a born-again feminist. But I see the need for feminist action and the need is as great now as it ever was. If you consider the gains in the past century, they really have been minimal. And for every gain there was a loss that negated against the emancipation of women. For instance, women won the right to go out to work, but if they did, it is still accepted by a very large cohort of the other gender that affairs of the house still be their duty.

POLITICS WITH A BIG 'P'

I never got involved with any party. That gave me a freedom to criticise them all, but at the same time, things being as they are, unless you belong to a party, you can't really do much. I had the opportunity. I was nominated by the ICA to go for the Senate one time. This was years ago, and first of all, my organisation were tardy in their decision in who they were going to send, who they were going to put forward, so that other Independents were in ahead of me and were getting support. By the time I got out, and I was expected to do the whole country at my own expense …

Now it was a great bit of craic, I have to tell you! But I wasn't asked by anybody what aspirations I had, or what policies I had. The only thing I was asked was 'what is a nice wee woman like you doing putting yourself to this bother?' Kind of very patronising, tapped me on the head, you know. And I was promised plenty of second or third preferences. I was only promised something like eight first preferences, and that wasn't enough to get you over the hump for the others. It was a very interesting exercise, and I learnt a lot.

I was disillusioned by [the experience of canvassing], partly, but also by the lack of any commitment by the ICA. Now, I got great help from other members. I had places to stay and people that looked after me on the way round, which was good, which was very good – but that was individual members. Had I been a party person … but the

ICA didn't want to nominate somebody who belonged to a political party, because we are a non-party political organisation. The only time that it was ever done, they nominated Patsy Lawlor and told her she was to be strictly non-party.[2] Once she got the nomination she said 'well I've always supported Fine Gael, so I'm going to go and look for their help'. And she got in. She was the only candidate we ever got in, in the normal course of events.[3]

POLITICS WITH A SMALL 'P'

Women like me, who were prevented by law from having paid employment once we married – well if we were active women, we got involved in the voluntary sector. Volunteers have been running an awful lot of this country over the years. Take all the daycare centres, meals on wheels, laundry services. Volunteers have been doing things like that for years and years.

THE OLDER WOMEN'S NETWORK

I set up the Older Women's Network with some others because of the fact that the ICA had an ageist attitude. And I couldn't break through. For several years I hammered at the idea. I said, 'look, don't be talking about getting young women in, forget about that. Young women have other things, and more exciting things they want to be doing. Go for the empty nesters'. And there are thousands of women out there whose children have left, and suddenly realise that there's a huge [gap] – women who have devoted themselves to their family.

But when they are talking about renewal they think in terms of young women. They have a youth officer in federations – I think maybe they've changed it at last to 'sports officer' – but they never had an 'age officer'. I used to say that to them, and for several years at council I would say, 'go for the women in their 50s and 60s'. There were an awful lot of ICA women that joined the Older Women's Network. And there was one president, I remember her saying at a council meeting one day, 'I had an invitation the other day', she said, 'to attend a one day event and we were going to be discussing music and movement and', she said, 'incontinence – imagine, incontinence!'

Incontinence is something that the bulk of older women, especially women that have had big families [have to deal with]. That was her invitation from the Older Women's Network, you see. We would tackle things like that and security in the home for people living alone and stuff like that, things like arthritis.

IN-FIGHTING

The lovely Older Women's Network that was doing so well … then my term was up on the council. It has now broken up. A group of women got in that wanted to get rid, first of all, of the people that had been directing it, and they wanted a particular person as the CEO of it. And they got in and then they started fighting among themselves. It began to get hard to get funding. That's what I say: women can down women. Even in the National [Women's] Council there have been huge battles from time to time. The ICA is great, and it has stuck the course and even though there have been battles at times, they have survived.

YOUNG WOMEN AND THE ICA

We have some young women joining us in our local guild, but we've been very proactive in campaigning and one of the things we've been doing, we've been going back to what we call 'the lapsed' – like 'lapsed Catholics' – the 'lapsed members', women who were in it and sort of dropped out of it. The longer you haven't been a member, the less inclined you are to become a member, and it's harder to be encouraged back into it. But we've got quite a number of members that had been members in the last year now, because it's all to do with leadership, it's all to do with who you have.

FEMINIST LEADERSHIP AND A VISION FOR THE ICA

You have to have loads of energy, first of all. You have to be able to withstand the hard knocks and the people that are trying to do you down. You have to have a wide vision. I think the vision is so important, to see the big picture. You have to have a great sense of humour, and a tough skin, as I say, to disregard the criticisms.

I wanted to legitimise the ICA within the women's movement generally. To a certain extent, I do feel I did. I think that's why I'm remembered when others have been forgotten. If the ICA can be considered as a feminist movement, you can say that feminism has been alive and well and working in Ireland since 1910.

ICA AND THE HISTORY OF FEMINISM

They have stayed steadfast. Oh I'll never forget the day that happened, the day the lecturer in UCD was talking about the organisations that were set up in the late 19th and early 20th century. She listed off the women of the land movement, Cumann na mBan, Inghinidhe na hÉireann, there were quite a number of them. Anyway, I said, 'you didn't mention the women of the cooperative movement'. And she said, 'oh you mean the United Irishwomen, who became the ICA. Oh no', she said, 'we don't include them because they were mostly about the domestic'. I said, 'hold on a minute now', and she said 'stop right there, Mamo, stop right there. You write me an essay', she said, 'justifying the place of the United Irishwomen, justifying their inclusion in feminist endeavour, and make your case there'. This was for my term essay. So I said 'right!', so I did one and I called it 'Homestead Revolutionaries: A Force for Radical Change in the 20th Century'. I talked about … that surely the early aspiration was to be the part of the cooperative movement – it was 'better farming, better business, better living', and we were to supply the better living aspect of it. So it was about making things better in the home.

THE UN END OF DECADE WOMEN'S CONFERENCE, NAIROBI
But the point I was making was, that's exactly what the women out in Kenya, that I met, were doing, exactly 75 years after. That was one of the best experiences of my life. The women I met there, out in Katui! I met nine groups of women on that day. I was taken especially out into the rural because, Nuala Fennell says, I was there representing Irish rural women.[4] So she asked for a chance to get out into the country, and we had this day when we left at four or five o'clock in the morning and went out through these dust roads, out to this place. I said, when she asked the chargé d'affair, 'is there any chance we could go to Katui?' He says 'how do you know about Katui?' I said 'I know about it because the diocese of Clara is twinned with the diocese of Katui', and 'county Waterford is also twinned with Katui. The ICA in Waterford have set up a nutritional centre for children in Katui'. 'Oh', he says, 'you have your homework done'. I knew two of the priests that had gone out, and I made contact, and we went out there.

The diocesan network was a very good network, and they organised for us to meet nine different groups of women on that one day, so it was very busy. The ones that I remember most were the women with the garden. They were learning how to do better gardening by contouring the land, and they had this area of ground that they were renting, and they were learning how to grow better vegetables, all that sort of thing. They were also making crafts collectively and selling them collectively. And when they'd get enough money, they'd buy a goat, and they'd give a goat to each one in turn. That's *exactly* what the United Irishwomen did down in Wexford. They started by buying a goat and setting up a little goat farm. For the women in Ireland, it was to give milk to the members to take home to give their children, because you were less likely to get TB if you were drinking goats' milk. It was seeing them doing the kinds of things that the women down in county Wexford had started doing when they started up the organisation, you know, *exactly* the same!

And then we met the women of the well. There were 42 women, and they had such a distance to go from their village to the well, so they decided there was a place when the rains came, water would come rushing down. So they thought if they could dam that, make a dam, and create a pond. Over eight years they had worked at that, with the most primitive of tools. They had built a dam to conserve the water close to the village so they didn't have the big journey to go. And what were they aiming at? They were trying to make better homes for their families and better opportunities in health and education for their children and themselves. Sure, that's what we started, that's what all women will do, no matter what country I've been to, that's what women have been wanting to do – make a better life for their own children so that their children will have a better life than they had.

When water on tap and electricity came, farmers all over the country started putting it into their byre, but they didn't see any need to put it into the house. 'Wasn't she well fit to go to the well? And what would you want it in the house for?' And when they did agree, they wanted one light in the kitchen and that was it. I know in my grandparents' house there was gas lighting downstairs, now this was further on, but upstairs you took a candle up to bed. And it wasn't a primitive house. My grandfather, now, didn't see the need to put the gas light upstairs.

By the 1960s the ICA were addressing issues like the rights for children with learning difficulties, the autistic children, the Down's children – that they shouldn't be put into the sort of places there were for children, and then when they got to 18, that they wouldn't go into a mental hospital. The Criminal Conversation was a good [campaign issue], the one where a man, if his wife was seduced away from the marriage by another man, had the right to claim financial recompense for it. But a woman didn't have a reciprocal right. If it was the man who was seduced away, she didn't have the right to claim compensation. So we got that Act scuppered.

We were the ones that launched the whole thing for women in the police force. We were the people that actually started the concept of the farm guesthouse, which provided great moneymaking opportunities for women, and we set up a training course at An Grianán for them.[5] You know, practical surely, but for the advancement of women.

I was terrified of her! I remember being taken as observer to a meeting down on the Ormond Hotel, down on the quays, and I remember going into it, and somebody whispered to me 'she's after coming in now', and I was watching her going up. I nearly thought she'd have cloven feet! And sure Nell's a pet! Underneath it all there is a real woman that's vulnerable and that is, you know, they're all women.

CHURCH AUTHORITY

Do you know the way that we grew up in awe of the clergy? Now, the generation before us used to genuflect when a nun would pass them in the street, or a priest – genuflect! But anyway, our generation didn't do that, but still in all, there was this huge respect that gave them the power to do some of the awful things that they did.

CHANGES IN THE 1980s

You see, the difficulty for the President of the ICA was that she had to reflect the membership, and we did surveys. But we were able to show that within the timeframe from one survey to another, thinking had progressed, had evolved. It was a very tough time to be president of the ICA, especially when your own thinking would differ from what you had to annunciate. I wouldn't have been quite pro-choice, now, but I'm not pro-life in the way that the people who call themselves 'pro-life' are. I think they're scary, now. I'd be in favour of abortion under certain circumstances.

I made the point constantly that why were they only asking the president of the ICA? They weren't asking the trade union leaders. They had just as much a right to be asked these questions as I had, but they felt that it was only the ICA had to deal with these issues. Anyway, I got through it.

One thing I tried, but I didn't get away with, was changing the structure of the organisation itself to devolve power down, not to hold so much power at the top by the Executive, and to devolve the running of the organisation to allow the rural areas to do a lot of their own decision-making. There was a strong Dublin lobby, and they hired buses and took to vote down that change in the constitution. They've done it now, because the whole thing was falling apart. It would have saved the association an awful lot of ... [The Dublin lobby] wanted to still have the councils in all the different places to go to, and they liked going. And you see, they had a very easy means of going, because Dublin radiated out to everywhere. You can get transport, so that it was made easy for them. I didn't succeed in that, but you can't win them all.

ASSOCIATED COUNTRY WOMEN OF THE WORLD CONFERENCE
Out in Vancouver, I won the next international conference for Ireland, the tri-annual conference of the Associated Country Women of the World – that's rural organisations like ours all over the world, and they come together every three years. And I won it for Ireland, so that it was in Ireland the year after I stepped down. But I had to do all the organising of it during my term, and it involved a huge amount of work, bringing a thousand women to Ireland for a conference. It was to have been in Dublin, but I could see it was going to be huge cost to Dublin, and I swung it that instead we were going to have it in Killarney. I was talking about 'a *rural* women's organisation meeting in a *rural* [place]' – that's how I sold it to them. And of course, Killarney had a kind of little magical sound to it. Boy, did they step up to the plate in Killarney! They were brilliant, and we had a wonderful conference.

We had a series of talks, and they all focused around the theme of family because focus on family was the theme of the conference. But who did we invite? We had Mary Robinson talking about 'the family and the law'. We had Margaret Mac Curtain, 'the family after women's liberation'. We had Nuala Fennell, who had been the Minister for Women's Affairs. We had 'the family and the first cooperative'. We had a bishop, 'the family in an age of communication' was his topic. And we had Nell McCafferty speaking on 'a family proves you can love anybody' – that was her theme. Ah, she was brilliant! And what family did she take as her example? The Royal family of Britain! It was hilarious, people fell about the place laughing. She started off very nervous – imagine, *she* was afraid of *us*! That was 1986.

EUROPEAN WOMEN'S LOBBY AND FEMINIST COLLABORATION

At one stage during my term of office there was an invitation from Bonn, from the EEC. They were setting up a women's lobby, and they wanted to have the views of Ireland on certain topics. They invited three people: one of them was from Cherish, but she would have been wearing her [National Women's Council] hat;[6] then there was Ann O'Donnell, she'd have been from the real inner core of the feminist movement;[7] and myself, representing rural women. Then we were asked to give a joint report, and it was only to last for five minutes, so the thing was, we had to get together and discuss it. They gave us headings that we were to do this report on. The headings were all the usual things, you know, connected with health, with birth control, with divorce, education for women – there were all sorts of topics. We had exactly the same views on the majority of things ... There were only one or two things that our opinion would have been different from the opinion of the more hard-line feminist movement, so there was very little divergence. I became quite friendly with these women, and so I started to invite them to events of ours. And then gradually, there were others, from the different organisations being invited, so it was taking the edge off the differences between us. It became evident to others within ICA that … we were all women.

Mary Robinson was always a great help to us. Mary Robinson always gave us good, sound advice on matters. You know, the legal spin on it, and how one might get round situations. She was very generous.

'POWER WOMEN' AND EDUCATION

This was a scheme thought up by Ailbhe Smyth and a few others for women's empowerment, but for getting funding [for] that by having a north-south dialogue.[8] That was in the late '80s. I applied for it, and got in. It meant north-south women were doing a women's studies course, a certificate course. We met in six different venues, three in the north and three in the south during the course of a year. We had lectures from the University of Ulster and from UCD.

By doing that course it meant you could go on to university, and do a postgrad sort of course. And, as I said, at the age I was when I was doing it, I was coming up to seventy, and I thought, 'God, I mightn't have a chance again'. I'd always wanted to go to university, and didn't have the opportunity. I was one of a family of six, and they all had to get second level education. I was the second of the family, so it would have been out of the question, but I always thought I would have loved to have gone. Here was a chance to go, so now I had to put my money where my mouth was and go for it.

At that stage I was already a committed feminist, and not afraid to say it. There were two other older women doing it as well, so it was great, the interaction with the young ones and the older. And there was so much that they didn't know about life in our time. The interaction between these young women and the older ones was good for both of us, I think. It was a great experience. I loved it.

FAMILY LIFE

My family didn't suffer as a result of [my involvement]. Some people say, 'you know, with all that carry-on, how did you manage to look after your family?' I think my family benefited from it. I have nine sons who have a very good sense of women's place in society, and have an appreciation for the right of women to have an equal place. And we don't have an equal place yet at all.

UNCOVERING WOMEN LACE MAKERS

Who had made the lace? Who are the forgotten people? I discovered, where it started in Verano (the island of Verano in the gulf of Venice), there is now a centre, kind of a big institute devoted to lace. We organised, in 1993, the European Year of Older People – one of the things we drew down European funding for – a convention of lace makers, and it was held at An Grianán. We had lace makers from a lot of European countries. But the ones that came from Italy ... had the book all about ... this institute, and there was a lot of stuff about the man who was the director of the institute. And then they had this wonderful story about a little lace maker that was immortalised. Her picture was in some museum in Switzerland, because she had been painted ... and she was from Verano. *El piccola merietia*, the little lace maker, was the title of the picture.

You didn't know what her name was, but you were told what the name of the man who painted it [was], who made her famous, but you got nothing about the stories of the women who were making this beautiful lace.

And when it came to women of power and influence [in Ireland], the ladies in the big houses, some of them, for philanthropic reasons, set up lace courses. There was a lady from Thornton House in County Kildare, and she sent down a lace teacher or two to Clones to set up a lace school. She had learnt how to unpick a piece of Venetian point lace, and she'd shown these other girls, who became teachers then. And one of those came to Clones and they could do the Venetian motifs, but do them with a little fine, very fine, crochet hook, which was really the eye of a needle broken to allow just a little, tiny hoop. With a fine linen and thread they were recreating these beautiful Venetian motifs. But after a while, the women here began to get creative. Instead of the flowers of Venice and the fruits of the Mediterranean that they were depicting, they started to do things within their own [surroundings] and they did things like the fern, and the wheel, and the whitewash brush. So they were making motifs that were particular to their own lives and to their surroundings.

And then they devised a particular join, which was the Clones knot, and that was what made the lace from Clones particularly distinctive. From Clones, they started sending out teachers then, and when the Contested Districts Board wanted to set up some means of women earning extra money, over in distressed areas in the West of Ireland, on the Western seaboard, they got teachers from Clones to go to places like Sligo and Galway and Mayo and Donegal, and that's how it spread. And it's known as Irish crochet lace, but we claim a particular lace that is Clones lace with this Clones knot.

We started to find out about the women and to celebrate them. So our little exhibition in Clones is called 'Lace and Lace Makers'. We researched the stories of the women who made the lace, and there were lots of them still alive at the time. Now some of them have died since, but [lace making] would have died out in that generation, only that we got it revived.

LIFE IN A BORDER TOWN

The border towns were just forgotten about by the powers that be at the time. They decided they would sacrifice them, and they didn't give them any help whatsoever. When they closed the border roads, for instance, in Clones, they cut off the livelihoods of [people], because it was a northern town. Our parish is ten miles in Northern Ireland and only three miles in the Republic. Our custom was a northern custom. When they closed the border roads, sixty per cent/seventy-five per cent of our business died. Bringing up a family at that time, and seeing the neglect, the sort of no-care attitude of the government to the plight of towns like Clones, was enough to make raving republicans of them all. I have a couple of raving republicans, but at least I steered them clear of getting involved with any …

When I could see the [clothes] business failing, I started a teashop within the business. That gave me a modest living now for six years, and I loved it. I had two great women working with me, Patsy and Paulie. We were a great team, the three of us. I couldn't have managed it without them. Paulie said it was the six happiest years of her life. Patsy was my great friend. She'd been my housekeeper when I was president of ICA. She kept the show on the road at home. She was like a mother to the boys. It got to, then, that I couldn't afford to keep her, and still I didn't want to lose her, so by starting the teashop, it provided a job for herself and myself. We were good!

ADVICE TO YOUNG WOMEN ACTIVISTS

Women, they need one another to stand for them, you know ... you need other women. There's nobody will listen to you like a woman will listen to you when your back's to the wall. We do need one another very much.

NOTES

1   For in-depth studies on the ICA see Heverin, Aileen, *The Irish Countrywomen's Association: A History 1910–2000* (Dublin, Wolfhound Press, 2002) and Diarmaid Ferriter, *Mothers, Maidens and Myths: A History of the ICA* (Dublin, FÁS, 1995).
2   Patsy Lawlor was the ICA's president from 1976–1979.
3   There were also Taoiseach's nominees from the ICA: Peggy Farrell and Kit Ahearn.
4   Fennell was then Minister of State at the Department of the Taoiseach with responsibilities for Women's Affairs and Family Law.
5   An Grianán is the ICA's adult education centre.
6   Cherish is now called One Family, and is an organisation working on behalf of one parent families.
7   Ann O'Donnell was a founder of the Dublin Rape Crisis Centre.
8   See also Ailbhe Smyth's contribution to this volume.

GIVE UP YER AUL' POWER
THE CHALLENGE TO MEN

Anthea McTeirnan

I just wonder if there are any men that would like to show their
solidarity and leave at this point, out of respect for autonomous
women's space. It's a polite invitation, but I just thought you
might like to consider it, as political allies. Thank you.[1]

It is amazing that a film about women's autonomous,
separatist organisation, lesbianism and community-
building in the 1970s could generate such a *maelstrom* in a
world where Botox, breast enlargement, labiaplasty and
poker-straight glossiness are female orthodoxies, but it
did. When radical lesbian feminist activist Julia Long made
her polite intervention during a panel discussion after the
screening of Myriam Fougère's documentary *Lesbiana – A
Parallel Revolution* at the first London Feminist Film
Festival (LFFF) on 29 November 2012, she was taken aback
by the reaction. Long was even more taken aback at the
metamorphosis of the debate in social and mainstream
media after the event:

I am the kind of nutter that gives feminism a bad name. Barmy. A gender-hating sexist misandrist. Childish. Selfish. Unsisterly. A saboteur and troublemaker who derails feminist debates by indulging in cheap tricks and meaningless grandstanding.[2]

She went on to write, tongue-in-cheek, in *The Guardian's* Comment is Free section:

Such has been the assessment of my character and behaviour from certain quarters, following my participation on a panel after the London Feminist Film Festival screening of the glorious *Lesbiana – A Parallel Revolution*, a film that documents and celebrates lesbian feminism and separatism. According to a previous piece on Comment is Free, I reputedly 'asked all the men in the audience to leave', an intervention which was greeted with hearty applause from much of the audience, but also some consternation.[3]

The 'previous' piece to which Long refers was written by journalist Marta Owczarek, who was at the LFFF panel discussion. She reported that after Long had spoken:

there was an instant uproar: lots of clapping, but also lots of booing. Many men and women got up and left, visibly disgruntled. Long then elaborated on her point, saying how 'politically disastrous' it had been to allow men to attend feminist events and conferences in recent years ... Meanwhile, most questions from the audience, rather than referring to the film, opposed Long's request: 'Some men were here to learn', said one audience member. 'You have to know your allies', said another.[4]

Also on the panel that day, gay rights activist Linda Bellos said that she thought women-only spaces are important. Owczarek said she agreed with Bellos, to some extent:

I agree with her when she says women can't hold men by the hand, that there's work to be done by men to redefine masculinity. I agree that it's not obvious what role feminist men can assume within the movement without derailing it and taking power away from women. However, patriarchy hurts men too – something that does not erase the damage it does to women, but underlines how important it is to reject bankrupt binaries when they are damaging.[5]

This is a central point in the debate about feminism. The conversation about whether there is room for women and men at the same table as we restructure the world into a fair place to be either gender is, for feminists, the challenge that keeps on giving. It's like a game of feminist pinball, with two ball-bearings smashing the hell out of each other to score maximum points. One ball-bearing: the radicalism in evidence in *Lesbiana* (the purity of the vision, the uncompromising decoupling of men's perpetual exploitative treatment of women from the construction of a new lifestyle and social structure); the other ball-bearing, a more liberal, holistic, conciliatory vision of all genders moving forward, together.

FEMINIST FUTURES

I think it was the most embodied revolution to ever take place on the planet. Even if we were not lovers, we were kind of in love with each other, we were in love with ideas and we were in love with what was possible ...[6]

Lise Weil of Montreal uses the L word a lot in *Lesbiana*. The L word being 'love'. But she also makes a hearty contribution to our discussion about the direction we'd like to see this 'new', possibly less radical, probably more challenged, version of feminism go.

Marta Owczarek and I seem to agree that 'women can't hold men by the hand' as we strive for a fair feminist future, but, and I am imagining here, our journeys towards 'Feminism 3.0' may take different routes. Yes, indeed, patriarchy hurts men too. It also benefits them inordinately. Men rule the world. Literally. Men own the world. Literally. It seems churlish, and boringly repetitive to state the obvious, but it is a mantra that needs to be chanted like the oppressive orthodoxy it is. Women do 66% of the world's work and produce 50% of the food, but earn only 10% of the income and own 1% of the property.[7] Up to 70% of women are victims of violence during their lifetime. Women make up nearly two-thirds of the world's 759 million illiterate adults. In the US in 2010, women earned less than men in 99% of all occupations. In Ireland in 2012, only 15% of the Dáil are women: that's 25 female TDs and 141 male ones.[8]

Being a woman can hurt. It can make you angry. It can mess up your chances. It can deny you your actual, physical life. None of these things are our responsibility, but they are something feminists can and will change. Whether, having done a cost-benefit analysis of the financial, social and sexual advantages of being a man, the critical mass of men we need to join us will set off on the path to a feminist, gender-equal future, we have yet to see. Whether the men on the journey can desist from telling us the way to our mutual feminist, gender-equal future before we women co-travellers have had a chance to speak, is open to debate.

Of course, not all men are bastards. Some men genuinely dislike the status quo that gives them their status, just as I as a white woman hate the racist colonialism that has resulted in the injustice of living on a planet where I benefit from the oppression of others on a minute-by-minute basis. I just pretend it's impossible to change the system that mines humanity in the developing world for my cheap mobile phone, my cheap underwear, and supplies my comfortable economic cushion. I seem to keep benefitting from the most inequitable distribution of global resources one can imagine, yet I, like many others, say virtually nothing. Sometimes, rational and just thought can and does triumph, however, and when the advantages of a demonstrable redistribution of power become evident, even in small ways, feminists can convincingly argue that men will benefit directly from a disturbance in the force, and a relocation of power between the genders.

In his book, *The Second Sexism* (2012), David Benatar says that OECD figures show that boys lag a whole year behind girls at reading in every industrialised country. Globally, men are more likely to be victims of violence and more likely to lose custody of their children during divorce.[9] The journalist Julie Bindel says men are 'paying the price that male supremacy gives them'.[10] It is hard to disagree. With the inequality facing women, feminists could be forgiven for holding back on efforts to help men out of the hole they have dug. Yet they are trying. Despite the obvious attractions on offer in *Lesbiana*, I choose to live with three men. Lots of feminists live with men. I don't want them to die young. I want them to be healthy and happy. I want my sons to play a full part in raising their children. However, feminism means men having half the cake. We want half. We want men to have the *other* half. That is fair. That is equal. Whether this message needs to be conveyed to men who are taking up half the space in the meeting room, and more than half the available speaking time, is less clear. Whether we should be apologising and agonising and fighting about when, on rare occasions, women respectfully ask men to give them some space – to talk, to plan, to strategise for a mutually-agreed equal endgame – is open to debate. Like Julia Long did at the London Feminist Film Festival, I am respectfully suggesting that sometimes we have those debates in a darkened room without men present.

BATTLES OVER WOMEN'S BODIES

In Ireland, when it comes to feminism and ultimately to gender equality, sometimes the topics we are debating are so ostensibly about women (they concern only women and are the result of men's need to control women and limit their position in society), that it is hard not to slam the door in the face of the nearest concerned male and ask him to wait outside in the corridor. Men have fought their battles for control on the bodies of women. It is a war that rages globally – the women of the Philippines won part of their battle at the tail end of 2012 when the country's president signed a law to promote both artificial and natural contraceptives as well as sexual education and family planning programmes vigorously opposed by the Roman Catholic Church. Women in the United States and Britain, countries where many assume women's reproductive freedom is taken for granted, are constantly fighting rearguard actions against male-led churches and political groups determined to use women's biology to restrict their choices and curtail women's slow journey towards political and economic equality. In the United States in 2012, 42 states and the District of Columbia enacted 122 provisions related to reproductive health and rights. One-third of these new provisions, 43 in 19 states, sought to restrict access to abortion services. This was a decrease from the *annus horribilis* of 2011, which saw 92 new abortion restrictions enacted.[11]

Here in Ireland, we are used to men fighting their battles over our bodies. The result of the Irish State's colonisation of women's bodies means Ireland continues to abandon its female citizens and residents to the whims of other jurisdictions and offloads the vindication of the rights of half its population to other states – one in particular. It is surely the ultimate irony for a post-colonial state to hand the fate of half its population straight back to its former occupier?

On paper, it looks like change is coming for women in Ireland. But the changes are illusory, free-floating and not anchored by truly equal rights. The Electoral (Amendment) (Political Funding) Bill 2011 says that 30% of election candidates must be women by 2016 – a strangely disproportionate choice given that 50% of the population is female. This measure should mean that women will increase their representation in government, but it will mean nothing for their personal autonomy. The Irish people have elected two fine women Presidents – Heads of State who embodied the sovereignty of the nation, yet who, as women, never enjoyed sovereignty over their own bodies. From 2016, women in Ireland can take up the 30% allocation of places on the ballot paper during elections. But as women they can never be equal in a State that embeds discrimination into its constitution and denies them the right to control their own bodies.

Equality of opportunity will only come from equal rights and equal respect. A mature democracy must take mature decisions. Women must have jurisdiction over their own bodies. And men must also stand up and make sure they do. Men *must* stand up and make sure they do, because silence is acquiescence in gender inequality. Silence means accepting the woman next to you is worth less. Accepting she is worth the same is logical and will produce the optimal outcome for the world – and every man's nation-state. Standing up and making their voices heard without drowning out the voices of the women they wish to (help?) empower is where the challenge lies. Men must stand up, but they must also step back. It will be a tricky manoeuvre.

GENDER QUOTAS AND POWER

In March 2012, the How to Elect More Women Conference took place in Dublin Castle. It was an uplifting and unusual day. Sitting in a seat of male power with hundreds of powerful women felt just like I'd always imagined it would – completely normal. Opening duties fell to the Taoiseach of the day, Enda Kenny. 'What they said about the flaming red hair speaks appropriately for her fight for Cork', he said of conference organiser Minister of State Kathleen Lynch.[12] Mistress of ceremonies journalist Olivia O'Leary was certainly in no mood to cut the Taoiseach any slack. 'There's a lot more to Kathleen than her red hair', she retorted.[13]

The name of the conference was chosen to reflect a very practical approach to getting more women into national politics. The exclusion of women from our democracy challenges the very meaning of the word. Women hold a mere 25 of the 166 seats in the 31st Dáil. That's 15.1%. Of the 4,744 Dáil seats filled since 1918, only 260 have been held by women. Only 91 women have been elected TDs since the foundation of the State, half of them part of a male electoral dynasty. Ireland stands in 79th place in the global gender electoral league table. That means 78 countries are doing better. Globally, the average for elected female representatives is 20%. In Europe it's 22.3%.[14]

The statistics show how unreconstructed Ireland is, and sadly they also underline the fact that gender inequality is a planet-sized problem. One of the biggest obstacles to redistributing power is that no one likes giving away half their sweets. Ask any child. But that's what men are going to have to do. The aforementioned and rather wordy Electoral (Amendment) (Political Funding) Bill 2011, requires that 30% of election candidates must be women by 2016. Women must be selected. *Where* they are selected and *how* their subsequent campaigning is supported by political parties may be a tricky and opaque variable, but women *will* be in the shake-up for a share of the electoral confectionery.

All the political parties have begun to address the dearth of women partaking of this electoral pick'n'mix. Fine Gael general secretary Tom Curran was honest when he told the How to Elect More Women Conference that implementing the quotas would present a 'huge challenge' for all parties. 'The reality is there's going to be blood on the floor', he said. If a party branch fails 'to select enough – or any – women on a local ticket, the party will step in and add female candidates', Curran said.[15] That sounds like positive discrimination. And that is what it will take. Tánaiste Eamon Gilmore went further. Quizzed on whether he would be prepared to stand aside for a woman candidate at the next election, he said: 'To be honest, personally, I'd be very happy to pass it on to someone who's willing to take it on'.[16] Whether he stands aside to let a woman through, we have yet to see, but at least Gilmore told it like it is. Some men will have to step down. Men who are committed to creating a society where everyone has a say will have to take one for the team. The departure of some men will be a new departure for men. And I mean that literally.

Opponents of quotas say men are elected because they are better candidates. We need to ask whether this is true. Meritocracy in the Irish electoral system is a myth. A woman is as capable of representing the electorate as a man. How many of our male politicians have covered themselves in glory? We should be more afraid of the status quo than of change. And so should men. Some men will have to stand aside as electoral lists and quotas will inevitably beget an increase in successful women candidates. And these men will have the opportunity to find a new way to serve their public. It is not a bad place to be. Studies show when given a choice, the Irish electorate does not favour one gender over the other. The people will decide. They are just waiting for their equal opportunity. Former President Mary Robinson once said that 'a society that is without the voice and vision of a woman is not less feminine. It is less human'.[17] It is unacceptable that men collude with what is effectively a form of gender apartheid any longer.

In recent times, Ireland has celebrated its aptitude for power-sharing on this island. Power-sharing as a pathway to peace in Northern Ireland was a challenge met with maturity and dignity, and it is a similar challenge on the pathway to gender equality that must be met again. Some of the men in Ireland's political parties will have to give up their seats for women. And Ireland's women will be ready to take them. Eamon Gilmore sounds like a man open to facilitating a vacancy. It is, therefore, inevitable that men will have to share power as we move towards creating a society that represents all of its citizens, a society that will be stronger and richer as a result.

Men will also have to stop talking so much and will have to listen to women's voices. When they do, the most surprising realisation for some men may be that women don't actually agree on very much at all. Empowered by quotas – in government and, potentially, in business – women will not enter the political, social and economic arenas as a monolith. There is no uniting orthodoxy, no one voice. Given a chance, the resistors and objectors to women's equality might find they actually enjoy this new pugilism amongst the sisters. After all, they did say women's boxing would never take off and now a boxer and Irishwoman, Katie Taylor, is an Olympic champion.

Not listening to women, and thus not fully representing the interests of women as citizens and human beings, can have a disastrous effect. And it can have that effect on any woman. Any woman citizen of the world, who finds herself trapped on an island that equates the life of an adult woman with a foetus is vulnerable to the peccadilloes of a State that has accepted the seepage of scripture into its constitution and into its governance.

SAVITA HALAPPANAVAR, REPRODUCTIVE RIGHTS AND 'EXPERTISE'

On 28 October 2012, Savita Halappanavar, a dentist from India, living in Ireland, died in University Hospital Galway. She had asked for, but been denied, a termination while there was still a detectable heartbeat of the baby she was miscarrying. She went on to die of septicaemia. There were waves of protest throughout Ireland as people, in their shock, grief and revulsion, took to the streets to show solidarity with Savita's husband, Praveen, and her grieving family and friends. Academic Clara Fischer argued in *The Irish Times* in December 2012 that, five weeks after the tragic death of Savita Halappanavar, nothing urgent or meaningful had been done by the Irish Government to protect women's lives.[18] Indeed, the government said it would not 'be rushed' into acting and would take two weeks to read the expert group's report.

The intricacies of the forming of an expert group to consider the implications of the ruling by the European Court of Human Rights (ECHR) in the A,B,C case are considered by Ivana Bacik elsewhere in this volume, suffice to say two years had elapsed since the ECHR ruling and 20 years since the 1992 Irish Supreme Court ruling in the X Case, which saw a 14-year-old girl, pregnant as a result of rape, prevented from travelling to the UK to get an abortion. It was this ruling, giving women a constitutional right to an abortion in Ireland where there is a threat to her life, including from suicide, and requiring the Irish parliament to legislate for said right, that formed the basis of the ECHR judgement.

At the United Nations Human Rights Council meeting in March 2012, the Irish Government stated that the expert group convened to make recommendations on the ECHR judgement, would report in July. Savita Halapannavar died in October. No report had been published. In December a young woman was dead and the masters of several of Ireland's maternity hospitals were highlighting the need for legal clarity on the issue. The Government still would not be 'rushed'. The streets filled with protestors. Meanwhile, as Fischer noted in her article, the nation's airwaves were filled with experts debating the legal framework required and noting the medical problems facing doctors caring for pregnant women in Ireland. And yet,

> women of reproductive age were largely absent as experts in these debates, as were women who have had terminations, or who were denied them. Again, the message was clear: your first-hand knowledge of being pregnant, of having terminations, of being refused terminations, of enduring complications during pregnancy, of your right to health and life, are of little relevance to this debate.[19]

Fischer was right. According to figures collated by the Irish Family Planning Association from UK Department of Health abortion statistics, between 1980 and 2011 at least 152,061 women living in Ireland travelled to England and Wales to access safe abortion services – but their testimonies, the experiential opinions of these real 'experts' were nowhere to be heard.[20] Many male pundits, in our newspapers and on air, wrote powerfully about the nonsensical inequity of denying women their basic human rights. None of the male commentariat, however, handed their space over to the women who might have recounted a personal experience of the issue. 'This sidelining of women as experts can be read as part of the more general exclusion of women from news media', wrote Fischer, who added, 'women are frequently dismissed as experts, even on topics that only they have first-hand experience of'.[21] She quotes the philosopher Miranda Fricker's concept of 'epistemic injustice', and applies it to the Irish abortion debate, arguing that

> the exclusion of women directly affected by the issue of abortion results in distorted public debate on the issue. Moreover, it

limits women's ability to influence political discourse, and
hence our capacity to influence decisions that will – or will not –
be taken about our lives, our health, our bodies...We need to be
able...to influence the debate. Hence, we have to be included
as authoritative knowers in discussions concerning us.[22]

The knowledge and experience of women in Ireland and
across the world – for we are global citizens who must
apply the highest international human rights standards to
the governance of our own land – was too far down the
agenda. Women's voices were too quiet, and too drowned-
out by the voices of male experts and commentators –
some of whom, though admirable, should know better and
learn to throw their considerable weight behind
empowering women by giving them access to the channels
of communication that they themselves enjoy. Men need to
listen to women on this issue that is fundamental to
women's participation as equals in every aspect of public
life. Men need to listen and this will sometimes require
their silence. It will sometimes require the handing over of
their privileged spaces on the airwaves and in the news
media to women. If male commentators are asked to write
a column on abortion or women's reproductive rights, they
could just say no. If male commentators are asked to sit on
a radio or television panel that excludes or under-
represents women, they could just say no. This will
facilitate the emergence of an 'expert group', and this may
change everything. After all, the status quo has changed
nothing and women are still dying.

WOMEN IN MEDIA

It might seem unfair to discriminate against those men
who have actually made positive interventions in women's
fight for reproductive justice, but no one ever said it was
going to be easy, and the silencing of women is an issue

that even the most progressive men should remain mindful of. Of course those more supportive, enlightened media men are not necessarily in the majority in their own profession. In fact they are not. There is a gaping hole when it comes to research on women in the media here, but we may assume that we're not far off global norms, which show that men continue to occupy the vast majority of positions of power in the mass media.[23] Campaigners such as Ireland's Lucy Keaveney and Dolores Gibbons, who spend significant time monitoring the participation of women on Irish airwaves, have made a significant contribution here, but we need more quantitative analysis of women's representation in our national media.[24] Since the 1960s, feminists have argued that 'it matters who makes it'. And in the mass media 'who makes it' continues to be men.

It would appear that women are not worth asking or listening to. There seems to be a fundamental assumption that women don't have a clue what they're talking about even when it comes to their most intimate body parts and most personal decisions – that must be why they are not asked for their opinions. Of course there are some women working in the media, myself included.

Every day at noon the *Irish Times* news conference convenes on the third floor to plan the day's news coverage – online and in the next day's newspaper. This is where the news, business, sport, foreign and features agenda is set and agreed on. As the editor of *The Ticket*, the supplement that appears with the paper on Friday, I attend the Thursday news conference. On Thursday 14 March 2013 there were 19 men and one woman (me) at the daily news conference. On Thursday 21 March 2013, there were 15 men and one woman. On Friday 22 March 2013, there were, again, 15 men and one woman at the conference. On 13 March 2013, the day of the announcement of the new Pope, at the 6pm conference which takes place on the floor of the newsroom, and is the final determiner of the daily Front Page, there were 11 men and one woman. Maybe the Vatican is not so unusual after all. It may be unfair to single out *The Irish Times*, as similar inequities occur in many Irish news organisations, but I would ask: is this what a modern, representative news organisation should look like today?

As we continue to struggle for equal representation, research by Prof Martha Lauzen of San Diego State University shows that significant differences can be made by the women working in the industry. Women in the media have a big impact on the ways women are portrayed, across all types of media. Lauzen notes:

> When women have more powerful roles in the making of a movie or TV show, we know that we also get more powerful female characters on-screen, women who are more real and more multi-dimensional.[25]

It may take a lot of courage to stand your corner in a newsroom where the upper echelons are occupied by opinionated men, but it is where feminists can make those small differences that can lead to a bigger difference.

As the lone woman in the sports department at the time, 12 years ago, I lobbied the Sports Editor to hold awards that specifically and exclusively honoured Irish sportswomen, and the Irish Sportswoman of the Year Awards have just celebrated their 10th year in existence. There are very few women working in sport media in Ireland. Just having a different perspective, someone with a different set of priorities, a different set of values and experiences in a mono-cultural, mono-gendered workplace can make a difference – in this case a difference that has been significant for women in sport specifically, and all women, generally.

In 2000, women editors and journalists took over the newsroom for a single day at a newspaper in Wichita Falls, Texas. In the newsroom, for the day's lead, the journalists had to make a choice between a story about a peeping tom and an item about local women fighting for equal rights. When the women chose the latter story there was a heated debate. Journalist Laurence Pantin reported that 'the women finally won, but only because they held the key positions on that day. All other times, the peeping tom and stories like it would have prevailed'.[26]

The media can be unpalatable, but if we're not in, we can't win. It's not easy. There are night shifts, noise, prejudice and egos to be overcome, but without achieving critical mass women will remain a mass of critics – passive consumers smarting from the sidelines while the men continue to have their say. It is not optimal that women should continue to be viewed through the lens of a media top-heavy with male values. It affects us all. The prism of the male gaze, through which all of human endeavour is judged, has to change as part of the shift towards gender liberation. It has to. Women need to make demands on men both inside and from the outside of media organisations.

In *The Irish Times*, women journalists are doing that as we speak, meeting and organising a strategy to increase the numbers of women in positions across the board. Ireland held its first NUJ Women's Conference in 2013. Its stated aim, according to Nicola Coleman, NUJ National Organiser, was 'to get as many women along as possible, so we can learn from the history of women's struggle and from each other's experience to make sure that we have effective and strong union organisation in our own workplaces and industry'. Having attended, it was a great start. Women do not see themselves and their unique experience reflected back at them in the media. Their voices are under-represented, their views virtually inaudible. In some cases the views of women – all women, but particularly some women – go unheard. The 50:50 Group is doing an admirable job campaigning for equal representation for women in government – the media needs a similar kick.[27] Women are at the bottom of the pile in ever greater numbers, but they need to rise to occupy a critical mass of decision-making positions in the media before they see themselves and their experiences and their vision reflected back.

THE WOMEN'S COALITION

In 1992, after the X Case, I became involved in the campaign for reproductive justice in Ireland. Ironically, such times of abject disempowerment, of devastating tragedy and injustice, proved perversely empowering. The group which I became a member of was called the Women's Coalition. It was the first Women's Coalition on the island, although our sisters in Northern Ireland would also go on to use the name. It was a forum open only to women and we met weekly in a room kindly made available for us on North Great George's Street in Dublin by Cherish (now known as One Family). Many of the members of the Women's Coalition were already politically active, having campaigned against the Eighth Amendment of the Constitution in 1982 and for divorce in 1986. Others had emerged from community action and from student unions. We were a mixed bag. Some of us had children, some of us didn't. We were of all social classes, some of us had jobs, others were unemployed, some of us were lesbians, some of us had disabilities, some of us were involved in political parties, some in trade unions. We came from all parts of Ireland, north and south, but not all of us were born in Ireland.

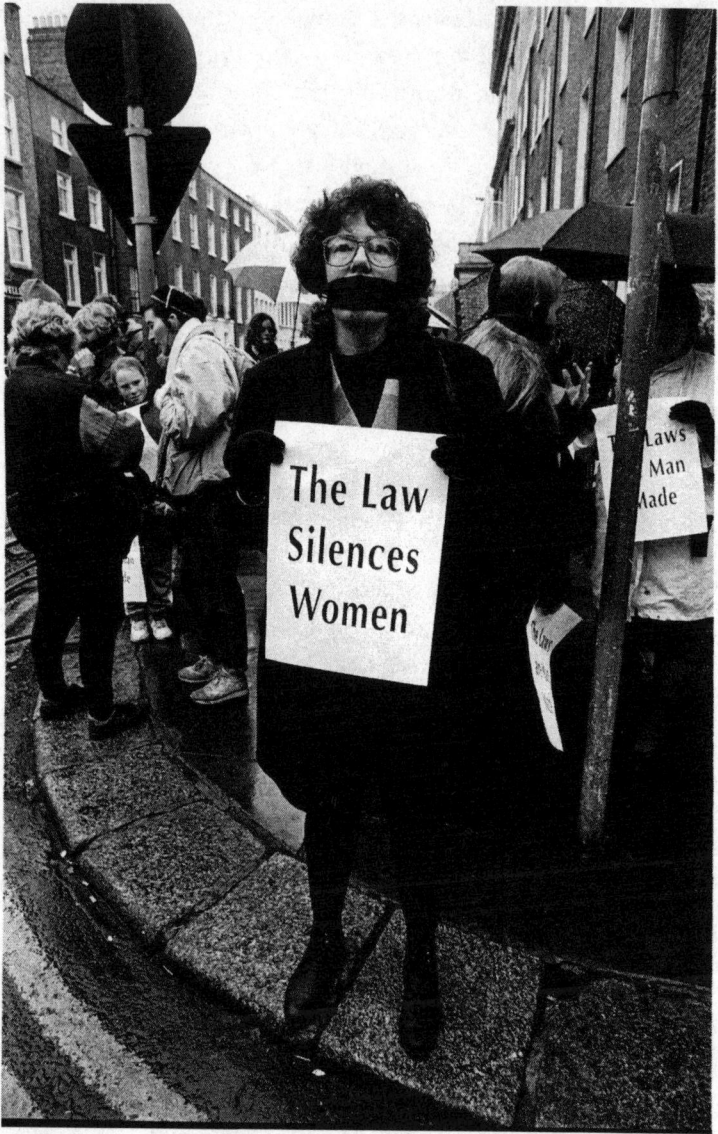

The Irish Times 23/10/1992, p. 7: Ms Melissa Murray, a member of the Women's Coalition, during a demonstration outside Leinster House yesterday. The pro-choice group says that women's voices are not being heard in the current debate on abortion. Photograph: Peter Thursfield/The Irish Times

I didn't attend the first meeting, joining a few weeks in after Grainne Healy, who is now the chairperson of Marriage Equality and writes elsewhere in this volume, suggested I'd fit right in. I was glad I did get involved, meeting remarkable and inspiring women, many of whom I am proud to still call my friends – and many of whom I sadly, but inevitably, found myself marching with again on Saturday 17 November 2012 when we took to the streets to say 'Never Again' after the death of Savita Halappanavar.

16/11/1992: Grainne Healy, of the Women's Coalition, looks on as Joan McDermott and Ann Kinsella (right) sing in St Stephen's Green, Dublin, at the pro-choice rally on Saturday. Photograph: Joe St Leger/The Irish Times

The Women's Coalition's biggest action was to organise a March for Choice to vocalise our demands for reproductive rights. On this march more than 5,000 people took to the streets of Dublin on 14 November 1992 to call for choice in all areas of their lives. The marchers included many members of the lesbian, gay, bisexual and transgender community, some of whom would go on to organise for civil partnership and for marriage equality. Dating from a pre-internet age, and falling foul of women's history repeating itself – as it always does by not being recorded – few records exists of the Women's Coalition. When the broad pro-choice alliance of which I am now a member marched in Dublin on Saturday 28 September 2012, calling for the same things the Women's Coalition did in 1992, there was a salutary moment when one of the speakers congratulated the attendees for turning up to Ireland's 'first March for Choice'. Of course it wasn't. Women's history had slipped through the cracks once more.

A, B, C v Ireland

From the women-only Women's Coalition, I would go on to sit on the board and then become the chairperson of the Irish Family Planning Association (IFPA). Thus, I have been involved in the fight for reproductive justice for more than 20 years. As chairperson of the IFPA, I was part of the team that went to Strasbourg in December 2009, the others were IFPA's CEO Niall Behan, lawyer Julie Kay and Senior Counsel Carmel Stewart, policy officer Meghan Doherty, IFPA head of counselling Rosie Toner, and IFPA staff member Richie Keane. Watching as Julie Kay and Carmel Stewart stood up in the European Court of Human Rights to answer the Grand Chamber's questions on A,B,C v Ireland was an unforgettable moment. Two women, one of them (Julie Kay) eight months pregnant, sat on one side of the room, while the Irish Government's legal team, which included the Attorney General of the time, Paul Gallagher, sat across from them on the other side. The contrast couldn't have been starker. Two men representing the Irish Government spoke. Behind them, there was another man and four women. None of them spoke at the hearing.

The ECHR had spent many months deliberating on the cases involved and had submitted questions in writing to the Irish Government before the hearing. One of the main questions that the court had was how many women have accessed life-saving abortions in Ireland? The Government could not or would not respond. The hearing was more of a procedural formality that gave members of the Grand Chamber the chance to ask brief additional questions that they felt were needed before they retired to consider their judgment. They asked those questions, including the question about where women in Ireland could go for a judicial response in circumstances where their life was threatened by a pregnancy and they needed to access a life-saving abortion in the Irish State. The Government's legal team did not answer this question.

(*from left to right*) Niall Behan, IFPA Chief Executive Officer, Rosie Toner, IFPA Director of Counselling, Anthea McTeirnan, Chairperson of the IFPA, Julie Kay, lead legal counsel for A, B and C, Carmel Stewart, Legal Counsel for A, B and C, Mercedes Cavello, Legal Consultant, descend the steps of The European Court of Human Rights, the Human Rights Building, Strasbourg on 9 December 2009 after responding to questions from the sitting of a Grand Chamber on the case of A, B , C vs Ireland. Photograph: Paul O'Driscoll

Of no legal import, but a graphic microcosmal display of the severing of women's bodies from women's control, Ireland brought men to the European table to argue that its restrictions of women's right to choose to terminate their pregnancies, when that pregnancy might kill them, was pragmatic and the outcomes controlled – even though no-one on the Irish legal team in the chamber of the European Court of Human Rights on that day in December 2009 could say how. Of course the ECHR judgement in the case of A,B,C v Ireland, which was published on 16 December 2010, was a massive step along the road, a step that has brought us to where we are now. It was a step, however, that was, tragically and unforgivably, not acted on in time to save the life of Savita Halappanvar – which is where we come back to men.

MALE POWER AND THE FUTURE OF FEMINISM

Men have, largely, made the laws of this land and many lands. And few men have shown much of an interest in amending these laws that apply so demonstrably only to women. When there has been an interpretation of law that has required the legislature to act to vindicate the rights of women, such as in the 1992 X Case, Dáil Éireann, which has never had more than 15.1% of women in its ranks, has failed to do so. It is surely optimistic and possibly naive to expect an assembly as unrepresentative as Dáil Éireann to act in the optimal way to give full expression to the rights of half the population it represents, but does not reflect?

As feminists, the need to harness male power to advance and win our own struggle can leave us with a dilemma. It also leaves progressive men who support equal rights with a dilemma. Naturally the sexism from which men benefit is the self-same discrimination that gifts men their power – their seats in government, their positions on State and company boards, their newspaper columns. It is the self-same sexism that gives the voices of men the power that makes them such attractive allies for co-option in the fight for gender equality. It is also this engendered power that, in its most unreconstructed form, can drown out the voices of women. As has been pointed out, the voices of women have been lacking from the media's coverage of the debate about abortion rights and women's real experiences of abortion have not been heard. Women's voices are lacking in the Dáil and in the wider Government. It is a dilemma, therefore, for some of us 'more mature' feminists to discover that there is a new resistance to women's autonomous organisation – even around issues that are palpably solely about women.

An issue for feminism has always been – and it has been mentioned here in terms of documenting, understanding and building on our own history – that each new generation of feminists has had to reinvent the wheel. Older feminists move on, bogged down by frustration and the actual caring responsibilities they were optimistic about revolutionising and redistributing. Young feminists unearth the same golden nuggets of revelation that their grandmothers and mothers had dropped. And, their disappointed and frustrated foresisters tire of having the same conversations they had 50 or 20 years previously.

Not all the conversations are had again, though. As a member of a number of new feminist and pro-choice groups and collaborations, I have yet to hear (or, admittedly, to instigate) a discussion about the value – or lack of value – of women organising on their own, or about the role men will have in those campaigning organisations. In a crisis which needs a quick, well-organised, effective response, all hands are on deck. The national 'Never Again' march for Savita Halappanavar on 8 November 2012, was such an event. There was no time for discussion or reflection about the involvement of men – and that was appropriate. The job had to be done and done quickly. We brought our many genders into the room in Buswell's Hotel across the road from the Dáil to organise a response.

Since then we have seen the rebirth of a new pro-choice movement. At the planning meeting in the Gresham Hotel on 8 December 2012 there were a significant number of men in attendance. There were also a number of interventions from the floor (I made one myself), but I counted slightly more speeches from men. So we're back to that old dilemma. We need the support of men, but as feminists we also need to challenge our male comrades about their own sexism and to challenge them about how that might be expressed. Some listening is required.

And that's just our more reconstructed brothers. It is going to be even harder for some of the men in Dáil Éireann to learn to share power with women. In this case sharing power will mean losing power. That is how it will look anyway. Some good therapy and a positive mental attitude might help as the un-seated redefine their positions. Everyone is going to benefit from this creative reconstruction of a more representative society. It just might not feel like it to everyone at first.

It is too pessimistic to see gender inequality as an impregnable fortress, the walls of which we will never scale, but it is too optimistic to expect to get onto the battlements any time soon. Of course, the battle will be won quicker with men on our side. We need them and we want them there – they just don't have to be carrying the flag or giving the battle address every time. In a way it's back to Julia Long and the polite plea she made at London's Feminist Film Festival – the plea that caused the rumpus in the first place:

> I just wonder if there are any men that would like to show their solidarity and leave at this point, out of respect for

autonomous women's space. It's a polite invitation, but I just thought you might like to consider it, as political allies. Thank you.[28]

We're not actually asking all men to leave the political, social and economic space – just half of them ('as political allies'). They can pick who goes.

NOTES

1 Julia Long, 'So I'm a feminist trouble-maker for requesting some women-only space?', *The Guardian*, 7 December 2012, http://www.theguardian.com/commentisfree/2012/dec/07/feminist-troublemaker-film-festival, accessed 27/02/2013.

2 Long, 'So I'm a feminist trouble-maker for requesting some women-only space?'

3 Long, 'So I'm a feminist trouble-maker for requesting some women-only space?'

4 Marta Owczarek, 'How a feminist debate was derailed by asking all men to leave', *The Guardian*, 3 December 2012, http://www.theguardian.com/commentisfree/2012/dec/03/asking-men-to-leave-feminist-film, accessed 27/02/2013.

5 Owczarek, 'How a feminist debate was derailed by asking all men to leave'.

6 Lise Weil in Myriam Fougere (director), *Lesbiana: Une Révolution Parallèle*, 2012.

7 Women for Women International, 'What we do: from victim to survivor … to active citizen', http://www.womenforwomen.org/about-women-for-women/victims-to-survivors.php, accessed 28/02/2013

8 Ami Sedghi, 'International women's day 2012: Women's representation in politics', *The Guardian*, 7 March 2012, http://www.theguardian.com/news/datablog/2012/mar/07/women-representation-in-politics-worldwide, accessed 28/02/2013.

9 Elizabeth Day, 'Lagging at school, the butt of cruel jokes: are males the new second sex?', *The Guardian*, 13 May 2012, http://www.theguardian.com/society/2012/may/13/men-victims-new-oppression, accessed 28/02/2013.

10 Bindel quoted in Day, 'Lagging at school, the butt of cruel jokes'

11 Guttmacher Institute, 'States Enact Record Number of Abortion Restrictions in 2011', http://www.guttmacher.org/media/inthenews/2012/01/05/endofyear.html, accessed 28/02/2013.

12 Christine Allen, 'Olivia's Offside Offence', http://corkfeminista.com/tag/how-to-elect-more-women/, accessed 29/02/2013.

13 Allen, 'Olivia's Offside Offence'.

14 Sedghi, 'International women's day 2012'.

15 Anthea McTeirnan, 'Unacceptable for women to collude with State's gender apartheid any longer', *The Irish Times*, 9 March 2012.

16 McTeirnan, 'Unacceptable for women to collude with State's gender apartheid any longer'.

17 Mary Robinson quoted in Alida Brill (ed), *A Rising Public Voice: Women in Politics Worldwide* (New York, The Feminist Press at CUNY, 1995), p. 156.

18 See Clara Fischer, 'Shameful lack of urgency on abortion persists', *The Irish Times*, 7 December 2012.

19 Fischer, 'Shameful lack of urgency on abortion persists'.

20 Irish Family Planning Association, 'Statistics', http://www.ifpa.ie/Hot-Topics/Abortion/Statistics, accessed 29/02/2013.

21 Fischer, 'Shameful lack of urgency on abortion persists'.

22 Fischer, 'Shameful lack of urgency on abortion persists'.

23 See Women's Media Centre, *The Status of Women in the U.S. Media in 2012*, http://wmc.3cdn.net/a6b2dc282c824e 903a_arm6b 0hk8.pdf, accessed 15/04/2013.

24 See National Women's Council of Ireland, 'Submission to the public consultation on the draft code on fairness, impartiality and accountability in news and current affairs', http://www.nwci.ie/images/uploads/nwci_draft_code_submissi on_bai_final2.pdf, accessed 15/04/2013.

25 Jeannine Yeomans, 'Hey, Hollywood: What's Wrong With This Picture?', Women's eNews, http://womensenews.org/story/arts /000918/hey-hollywood-whats-wrong-picture#.U52_vsb7Wll, accessed 29/02/2012.

26 Laurence Pantin, 'When Women Run Newsrooms, Women are in the News', Women's eNews, http://womensenews .org/story/ media-stories/010406/when-women-run-newsrooms-women-are-the-news#.U53BAMb7Wll, accessed 29/02/2012

27 See http://5050-group.com/blog/.

28 Long, 'So I'm a feminist trouble-maker for requesting some women-only space?'

A FEMINIST REVIEW OF THE LAW ON ABORTION

Ivana Bacik

INTRODUCTION

Ireland has a unique legal and constitutional approach to reproductive health. It was the last country in Europe to legalise contraception, and is the only country in the world with a constitutional provision giving equal rights to life to a pregnant woman and to the foetus she carries.[1] Through the twentieth century, Ireland was a very sexually repressed society.[2] A more liberal culture has emerged in recent decades, but changing attitudes to sex have not been reflected in the Constitution or legal system. There has been huge resistance from conservative and religious forces to any assertions of reproductive rights. Changing sexual attitudes have brought about substantial legal reform on contraception, which is now legalised as a result of extensive litigation and lobbying by feminists and family planning groups. However, conservative Catholic resistance remains much stronger on the abortion issue. From the 1980s onwards, highly divisive debates on abortion have focused on the Constitution, the law and the moral-legal aspects of abortion, rather than the medical-health or indeed women's rights aspects. Abortion is prohibited both in nineteenth-century criminal legislation and in the Constitution. Doctors may terminate pregnancies in Ireland only in the very limited circumstance where the continuance of the pregnancy would pose a 'real and substantial risk' to the life of the pregnant woman, in accordance with a 1992 Supreme Court decision.[3] Yet thousands of Irish women have abortions every year in Britain. Clearly, prohibition does not address the real needs of women with crisis pregnancies.

This chapter will trace the legal, social and political developments in reproductive rights campaigns in Ireland since the passage of Article 40.3.3 in 1983, and will examine options for change in the future. Ultimately, it will be argued that Article 40.3.3 should be deleted from our Constitution, for the important reason that while it remains part of our fundamental law, it devalues the lives of women. By equating the right to life of the unborn with that of the 'mother', it gives unborn life an unrealistically absolute claim on the life of the pregnant woman. This claim is, in practice, untenable. The tragic death of 31-year old Savita Halappanavar in Galway University Hospital in October 2012, following apparent failure by doctors to perform what could have been a life-saving termination of her pregnancy, has highlighted this with a terrible clarity – and has focused international attention on Ireland's highly restrictive abortion law.

The adoption of Article 40.3.3 has not prevented one crisis pregnancy, nor stopped even one woman travelling to England to terminate her pregnancy. Its retention allows maintenance of the hypocrisy that there is no abortion in Ireland, and creates an area of grave uncertainty for doctors in trying to make difficult judgements where the continuance of a woman's pregnancy may pose a risk to her life. This uncertainty may well have contributed to the tragic death of Ms. Halappanavar. Her death has created an apparently unstoppable political impetus for the introduction of legislation to clarify the terms of the Supreme Court test in the X case. Ultimately, however, it is argued that the deletion of Article 40.3.3 is necessary to remove legal uncertainty about reproductive health services generally, and to allow the introduction of sensible legislation to set out a range of conditions under which abortion could lawfully be provided.

17/11/2012. NEWS: Thousands gather to demand legislation on abortion after the death of Savita Halappanavar at Merrion Square, Dublin at the weekend. Photographer: Dara Mac Dónaill/The Irish Times

THE LEGAL CONTEXT FOR ABORTION IN IRELAND

Abortion was made a criminal offence in Ireland in 1861, under sections 58 and 59 of the Offences Against the Person Act. Section 58 makes it an offence for a pregnant woman unlawfully to 'attempt to procure a miscarriage', ie, to undergo an abortion, while section 59 criminalises anyone who assists a woman in having an abortion. The 1861 Act, passed by the UK Parliament, applied to Ireland both before and after independence. These provisions remain part of Irish law. For many years after 1861, prosecutions were taken against persons performing backstreet abortions in both England and Ireland. However, the law was relaxed in England after the 1939 case of *R v. Bourne* (1939).[4] Dr. Bourne was prosecuted under the Act for performing an abortion on a young girl who had been gang-raped by a group of soldiers. The trial judge, Judge Macnaghten, directed the jury that the use of the word 'unlawful' to qualify the procurement of a miscarriage meant that there were circumstances in which it would be lawful to perform an abortion. He said that a doctor would have a defence if he or she carried out an abortion to preserve the life of the pregnant woman, and the doctor would also have a duty to carry out an abortion if the effect of the continuation of the pregnancy would be to make the woman or girl a 'physical or mental wreck'.

This judgment led to an increase in the availability of backstreet abortion in England, as doctors were able to rely upon the *Bourne* defence. As a result, women began to travel from Ireland to England for abortions, and the numbers of Irish prosecutions for abortion and infanticide fell considerably. They rose only during the years of World War II, when restrictions were placed on travel to England from Ireland).[5] The last prosecution for a backstreet abortion in Ireland was the infamous Nurse Cadden case. The nurse, reputed to have performed hundreds of such abortions, was the last woman sentenced to hang in Ireland in 1956 following the death of one of her patients, although this sentence was later commuted, and she died in prison.[6]

In Britain, largely as a result of pressure from the medical profession concerned at the many deaths of women undergoing abortion in poor sanitary conditions, Parliament passed the Abortion Act in 1967 which provides for a range of circumstances in which abortion can legally be carried out. Once abortion became legally available in England under this Act, the numbers of women travelling from Ireland for terminations began to increase significantly, reaching 3,600 in 1981 – the same year that an Irish right to choose campaign was launched. The numbers peaked at over 6,000 per year in 2001 and have fallen since, averaging at about 4,000 per year currently (4,149 women gave Irish addresses at UK clinics in 2011).[7] These figures demonstrate the extent of the need for legal abortion in Ireland. At present, for many Irish women this is addressed through the availability of travel to Britain. But the needs of the most vulnerable women – the young, the poor, or asylum-seekers – for whom travel can be very difficult, are simply not being met. The voices of these women are not heard in the debate on abortion – they have effectively been silenced under the present legal regime. Some years ago, one publication did attempt to present women's experiences of abortion, yet even there women provided their stories anonymously.[8] These are women who face a 'double crisis'. On top of their crisis pregnancy, they also face the added crisis involved in the practical, financial and emotional difficulties in making the journey to England.

The Irish women's movement has been actively seeking to address this double crisis for many years. In late 1979, a group of feminist activists established the first Women's Right to Choose group in Ireland, demanding the legalisation of contraception and abortion. In March 1981 this group held a public meeting at Liberty Hall, Dublin. As sociologist Linda Connolly describes (1997: 561):

> The counter right then made itself visible and increasingly mobilised ... by diverting the abortion debate into the legal/constitutional arena. Tactically, it aimed to block the

women's movement from providing its services by actively campaigning for a constitutional referendum on the 'right to life of the unborn.[9]

THE 1983 EIGHTH AMENDMENT

The counter-right had been galvanised into action by a series of legal events in the US. In 1973 the US Supreme Court held in *Roe v. Wade* building on earlier case law around the right to privacy and contraception, that women had the right to abortion under the American Constitution.[10] This decision acted as a catalyst for conservative forces in Ireland to lobby for a constitutional referendum to 'copperfasten' the legislative prohibition on abortion. The same year that *Roe* was decided, the Irish Supreme Court had held in *McGee v. Attorney General* that a right to marital privacy was implicit in the Constitution, thereby enabling a married couple to import contraceptives for their own use.[11] The *McGee* decision was described by William Binchy, a leading member of the Irish anti-abortion movement, as being a 'time bomb' in the hands of a court. He warned about the 'foreseeable event of some change in attitudes in this country on the question of abortion … the privacy concept espoused by that decision provides the key for opening that door in the future'.[12]

The decision in *Roe*, and the legal reasoning of those who saw *McGee* as offering a backdoor route to the legalisation of abortion had 'a clearly visible effect on the development of Irish law and policy on abortion, in giving an impetus to the Pro-Life Amendment Campaign (PLAC) which resulted in the passing of the Eighth Amendment to the Irish Constitution in September 1983'.[13] The bitter and angry 1983 referendum campaign has been described as a 'second partitioning of Ireland'.[14] The anti-abortion campaign successfully played one political party against another to win promises from the government to hold a referendum, which was passed by a two-to-one majority (67% to 33%, on a 53% turnout of the electorate). Many commentators have analysed this campaign and identified the outcome of the referendum as a pivotal moment in the history of the Irish women's movement.[15] The wording of the Eighth Amendment to the Constitution, which became Article 40.3.3, is:

> The State acknowledges the right to life of the unborn and, with due regard to the equal right to life of the mother, guarantees in its laws to respect, and, as far as practicable, by its laws to defend and vindicate that right.

Article 40.3.3 remains uniquely misogynistic, in that it expressly sets up the right to life of both the pregnant woman and the foetus that she carries in conflict – anticipating that a time would come when somebody would have to decide between them. That time did come, only nine years after the passing of the referendum, after a great deal of litigation had taken place which was to extend the effect of the provision well beyond that publicly envisaged by its advocates. PLAC had promised that it would not use the amendment to pursue individuals through the courts – but that promise was quickly broken.

THE EFFECT OF ARTICLE 40.3.3

Very shortly after the passing of the eighth amendment, the Society for the Protection of Unborn Children (SPUC) began to use the new provision as the basis for a series of cases taken against those audacious enough to provide desperate women with information on abortion facilities in England. SPUC first issued proceedings against two non-directive pregnancy counselling agencies, Open Door Counselling and the Well Woman Centre. Both offered pregnant women information on all the options open to them, including that of termination – in particular, information on the contact details of clinics offering abortion in Britain. SPUC argued that the provision of this information in Ireland amounted to a breach of the constitutional right to life of the unborn – and that the State was failing in its constitutional duty if it did not close down the agencies. This argument clearly required a breathtaking leap of logic in order to succeed – it involved the ridiculous assumption that women would not choose to terminate their pregnancies if they were not provided with information. Yet this argument succeeded – Judge Hamilton ruled against the counselling agencies in the December 1986 *Open Door* case, stating that their right to freedom of expression could not be invoked to interfere with the 'fundamental right' to life of the unborn.[16]

This High Court decision, subsequently upheld by the Supreme Court, established that the provision of information on abortion was unlawful under the Constitution. The agencies however appealed to the European Court of Human Rights, which in the October 1992 *Open Door (No.2)* case ruled that the Irish Government's ban on abortion information was in breach of the freedom of expression guarantee in Article 10 of the European Convention on Human Rights, being 'overbroad and disproportionate'.[17]

The Irish courts' judgments in the *Open Door* case had a dramatic effect on the availability of information, leading to the effective closure of counselling agencies. An underground helpline run by the Women's Information Network (WIN), was established, and linked up with the London-based Irish Women's Abortion Support Group (IWASG), which provided women with information and practical help with travel. Other underground groups in Ireland also provided information through informal networks.[18] However, the only Irish organisations that continued openly to provide information on abortion were students' unions. Shortly after they had initiated the *Open Door* litigation, SPUC began similar legal action against the officers of a number of students' unions, which were providing information on abortion in their handbooks. The student officers, of whom this author was one, were from the national Union of Students in Ireland (USI), University College Dublin, and Trinity College Dublin. Once again, SPUC succeeded in obtaining court orders against the students, prohibiting them from distributing this information. They had at first sought to jail the four officers from Trinity College, who had already distributed student handbooks prior to the High Court case. Mary Robinson, later President of Ireland but then a Senior Counsel, defended the students in the High Court, and succeeded in keeping them out of prison and in referring the issue to the European Court of Justice.

In its 1991 judgment in the *Grogan* case, that Court raised the possibility that a future right to provide information on abortion might be established through EC law.[19] The European Court defined abortion as a 'service' under EC law, and prohibition of the provision of information in one member state on a service lawfully available in another member state would normally be in breach of EC law. However, ultimately the Court concluded that because there was no commercial connection between the students' unions and the British clinics, the information ban could not be regarded as a restriction under EC law. The students' case was thus returned to the High Court, where in August 1992 Judge Morris granted a permanent injunction restraining the students from providing information on abortion. This was finally lifted by the Supreme Court in March 1997, by which time many other more dramatic legal and social developments had occurred. Following the decision of the Court in *Grogan*, in November 1991 the Irish Government negotiated a protocol as part of the Treaty on European

Union (the Maastricht Treaty), stating: 'nothing in the Treaty on European Union ... shall affect the application in Ireland of Article 40.3.3 of the Constitution of Ireland'. The adoption of Protocol No. 17 was to become highly controversial in the aftermath of the X case, which came before the High Court in February 1992.

THE X CASE

Given the wording of Article 40.3.3 of the Irish Constitution, it was inevitable that where the two rights of woman and foetus came into conflict, the courts would have to decide which took priority. This dilemma first occurred in February 1992, with the X case. A 14-year old girl had become pregnant as a result of rape. Her parents took her to England to terminate the pregnancy, and notified the Gardaí that they were going because they wished to use DNA samples from the foetus in subsequent criminal proceedings for rape. The Attorney-General then sought a High Court injunction to stop the girl from travelling out of Ireland for the abortion. This was granted by Judge Costello. The nightmare scenario predicted by those who had campaigned against the 1983 amendment had come to pass: a pregnant child had effectively been imprisoned in her own country. X and her parents, already in England when notified of the injunction, cancelled their appointment at the clinic and returned to Dublin. Political uproar ensued. A protest march unexpectedly drew a crowd of 10,000 people onto Dublin's O'Connell Street. In the face of mounting public pressure, an appeal was heard within a matter of weeks. The Supreme Court reversed Judge Costello's decision, allowing the girl to travel. The Court found that because the girl was suicidal, the continuation of the pregnancy would have threatened her right to life. In such situations, the Court ruled, the right to life of the girl should prevail. Chief Justice Finlay stated that:

> if it can be established as a matter of probability that there is a real and substantial risk to the life, as distinct from the health, of the mother, which can only be avoided by the termination of her pregnancy, such termination is permissible.[20]

In other words, X could legally have an abortion in Ireland. But the corollary of the test was that where a woman was not facing a threat to her life, then it would be illegal for her to have an abortion in Ireland, and she could also be prevented from travelling abroad to avail of legal abortion elsewhere. Further, because of the Maastricht Treaty Protocol, a woman in this invidious position could not rely upon the EC law guarantee of freedom of movement to enable her to travel. When it was realised that the Maastricht Treaty might have this effect, a campaign was launched by the pro-choice movement against its adoption. Faced with the potential defeat of the Maastricht Treaty referendum, the government was again forced to take action. First, in May 1992, the Foreign Ministers of the EC Member States adopted a 'Solemn Declaration' stating that the operation of the Protocol would not affect freedom to travel, or to obtain information. The actual legal effect of this Declaration is uncertain, but its adoption reassured people that girls like X would not be prevented from travelling, and the Maastricht referendum was passed in June 1992.

The government also put three amendments to Article 40.3.3 of the Constitution before the people in November 1992. The aim of the first (officially entitled the Twelfth Amendment) was to rule out suicide as a threat to the life of a pregnant woman, that is, abortion would be allowed where necessary to save a woman's life if she had a physical condition causing a real and substantial risk to her life, but not including the risk of suicide. The second amendment guaranteed the freedom to travel abroad, and the third allowed the provision of information on services lawfully available in other states. The Twelfth Amendment was opposed by pro-choice groups who wished, at a minimum, to maintain the lawfulness of abortion in X case circumstances. It was also opposed by some anti-abortion groups who, while seeking to overturn the decision in X, did not think that the proposed wording went far enough, in that it still allowed for abortion where necessary to save the life of the pregnant woman. It was hardly surprising that the Twelfth Amendment was rejected by the people. However, in a clear victory for the pro-choice movement, the travel and information referendums were passed.

Following these amendments, the Regulation of Information (Services Outside the State for Termination of Pregnancies) Act 1995 came into force, providing for the conditions under which information on abortion may be provided. The first comprehensive study of women and crisis pregnancy in Ireland, conducted subsequently, found that information on both contraception and abortion was still difficult to obtain for many women and girls.[21] In calling the referendum for November 1992, the outgoing government had stated that if the twelfth amendment were not passed, it would introduce legislation to implement the X case. Indeed, the need for legislation had already been explicitly commented upon by the Courts. In the X case, Judge McCarthy, one of the Supreme Court judges, had pointed out that:

> In the context of the eight years that have passed since the [Eighth] Amendment was adopted ... the failure by the legislature to enact the appropriate legislation is no longer just unfortunate, it is inexcusable. What are pregnant women to do? What are the parents of a pregnant girl under age to do? What are the medical profession to do? They have no guidelines save what may be gleaned from the judgments in this case.[22]

The C Case

Yet another case of a tragic teenager came before the High Court in November 1997 – the C case, involving a 13-year-old girl who had been raped and became pregnant. She was in the care of the state and being looked after by the local health board, which was granted permission by the District Court to take her to England for an abortion. However, the girl's parents, having previously supported her decision, changed their minds and appealed the District Court decision to the High Court. There, Judge Geoghegan found on the evidence of psychiatric opinion that the girl was suicidal, and that the continuation of her pregnancy would pose a 'real and substantial risk' to her life. Thus the abortion would have been lawful in Ireland, and so the health board was entitled to take her to England. Once again, however, if there had been no such risk to the girl's life, she would not have been entitled to have the abortion in Ireland, nor to travel abroad for it. Fifteen years later, there is still no legislation in place to protect the rights of young women in C's position; girls who are pregnant but unable to travel abroad without permission because they are in care. Unless they are suicidal or their lives are otherwise at risk if the pregnancy continues, the courts will not grant health authorities such permission. The freedom to travel is only exercisable by those with the means to do so – there is no enforceable right to travel.

The Legislation Vacuum

The lack of legal provision also leaves medical professionals in an uncertain position. Where a woman's pregnancy poses a risk to her life, it may be difficult for doctors to determine what constitutes a 'real and substantial risk' that may justify an abortion. The current edition of the Medical Council Guide to Professional Conduct and Ethics (2009) provides limited guidance, stating:

> Abortion is illegal in Ireland except where there is a real and substantial risk to the life (as distinct from the health) of the mother. Under current legal precedent, this exception includes where there is a clear and substantial risk to the life of the mother arising from a threat of suicide. You should undertake a full assessment of any such risk in light of the clinical research on this issue.[23]

Paragraph 21.4 of the same Guide reads:

> In current obstetrical practice, rare complications can arise where therapeutic intervention (including termination of a pregnancy) is required at a stage when, due to extreme immaturity of the baby, there may be little or no hope of the baby surviving. In these exceptional circumstances, it may be necessary to intervene to terminate the pregnancy to protect the life of the mother, while making every effort to preserve the life of the baby.[24]

This paragraph, which acknowledges that pregnancy may be terminated lawfully in cases of fatal foetal abnormality, for example, is particularly noteworthy in light of recent case law before the European Court of Human Rights.

GOVERNMENT REPORTS ON ABORTION

In the years since the C case, there have been a number of further developments, but no legislation to clarify these issues has yet been forthcoming. The 1996 Constitution Review Group recommended such legislation, concluding that a bill passed within the ambit of the existing constitutional framework was the 'only practical possibility'.[25] Following the C case, a comprehensive Green Paper was published by the Irish government in September 1999, presenting seven options ranging from an absolute constitutional ban on abortion (which was rejected as unsafe) to legislation allowing for abortion on request. This Report was referred to the All-Party Oireachtas Committee on the Constitution (APOCC), which engaged in a further consultation process, reporting to the Cabinet Sub-Committee on Abortion in November 2000. As a result of this report, the Crisis Pregnancy Agency was established in 2002. Now subsumed into the Department of Health, for a time it ran major contraceptive and sex education programmes. The members of APOCC could not however agree on a single recommendation for legal change, so they presented three alternatives. The first was to leave the legal position unchanged, the second to introduce legislation within the existing constitutional framework, and the third to amend the Constitution to rule out suicide as a ground on which threat to life could be established. Of the three options, the anti-abortion movement supported the referendum to rule out suicide risk as a ground for abortion. The government was persuaded by the movement's intensive lobbying to carry out this re-run of the November 1992 referendum, and on 6 March 2002, again put an amendment to the people to reverse the decision in the X case, by ruling out suicide risk.

The campaign around this referendum was dominated by a debate over whether pregnant women or girls ever really became suicidal. This deeply unpalatable debate carried within it a perceptibly misogynistic undercurrent: that pregnant women would pretend to be suicidal in order to obtain abortion. Following extensive campaigning by the ANV (Alliance for a No Vote), the Irish Family Planning Association, the Labour Party, and other progressive groups, the referendum was indeed ultimately defeated, although just as with the 1995 divorce referendum, the majority was tiny.

Following the defeat of the 2002 referendum, abortion slipped off the political agenda altogether for some years, while the needs of women with crisis pregnancy remained unmet. In 2007, the public were reminded of this when a 17-year-old woman with an anencephalic pregnancy sought permission from the Health Service Executive to allow her to travel to obtain an abortion. The High Court ruled that she had a right to travel.[26] In the first decade of the new century, pro-choice activists and lawyers then took on a new strategy: to bring the issue of abortion law back to the European Court of Human Rights. The first such case, taken by an applicant known as D, concerned a pregnancy where fatal foetal abnormality had been diagnosed. The applicant had been forced to go to England to terminate the pregnancy, and argued that this breached her rights under the European Convention. In its decision, however, the Court found the application inadmissible because the applicant 'did not comply with the requirement to exhaust domestic remedies as regards the availability of abortion in Ireland in the case of fatal foetal abnormality'.[27] The Court accepted the rather hypocritical argument made by the Irish government, that:

> there was 'at least a tenable' argument which would seriously be considered by the domestic courts to the effect that a foetus was not an 'unborn' for the purposes of Article 40.3.3 or that, even if it was an 'unborn', its right to life was not actually engaged as it had no prospect of life outside the womb. In the absence of a domestic decision, it was impossible to foresee that Article 40.3.3 clearly excluded an abortion in the applicant's situation in Ireland.[28]

In accepting this argument, the Court made reference to the APOCC Report of November 2000. The Court noted that the Committee during its deliberations had met the Masters of the three major Dublin maternity hospitals. The Court commented that:

All three [Masters] spoke in favour of permitting in Ireland termination of pregnancy in cases of foetal abnormality ... where the foetus would not survive to term or live outside the womb[29]

The Court concluded that there was:

a feasible argument to be made that the constitutionally enshrined balance between the right to life of the mother and of the foetus could have shifted in favour of the mother when the 'unborn' suffered from an abnormality incompatible with life[30]

and found that if she had initiated legal action before the Irish courts, the applicant's case would have been 'an arguable one with sufficient chances of success' to mean that a domestic legal remedy was therefore in principle available to her, and she should have pursued her case through the Irish courts before applying to the ECHR.[31] Accordingly her application was deemed inadmissible. Nonetheless, the judgment of the Court in *D v. Ireland* clearly envisages that terminations of pregnancy in cases of fatal foetal abnormality would be declared lawful by the Irish courts.

Then came the more recent decision of the European Court of Human Rights in *ABC v. Ireland* (2010). Three women, A, B and C, all of whom were living in Ireland when they became pregnant, had been obliged to travel to England to terminate their pregnancies. They argued that this breached their human rights under the Convention. While ruling against the applications of A and B, the Court unanimously ruled that Ireland's failure to implement the existing constitutional right to a lawful abortion in Ireland had violated Applicant C's rights under Article 8 of the European Convention. Applicant C's pregnancy had posed a risk to her life. The Court concluded that the Irish State had violated C's rights because:

> ... the authorities failed to comply with their positive
> obligation to secure to the third applicant effective respect for
> her private life by reason of the absence of any implementing
> legislative or regulatory regime providing an accessible and
> effective procedure by which the third applicant could have
> established whether she qualified for a lawful abortion in
> Ireland in accordance with Article 40.3.3 of the Constitution.[32]

The Irish government was thus required to take positive steps to implement this judgment. A new government was elected in February 2011, just months after the European Court decision, and it committed to establishing an expert group to review the judgment and its implications for the provision of health care services to pregnant women in Ireland.

In advance of the Expert Group's findings, a private members' bill on abortion was introduced in the Dáil in April 2012 by Socialist Party TD Clare Daly. Although supported by pro-choice campaigners, the bill was defeated by the government on the basis that it would pre-empt the report of the Expert Group. The Group finally reported in November 2012, and essentially recommended the introduction of legislation to clarify the criteria under which terminations of pregnancy may be carried out in order to save a woman's life. The same month, however, the nature of the debate was fundamentally altered as details emerged of the tragic death of Savita Halappanavar in Galway University Hospital, following apparent failure by doctors to accede to her desperate requests to terminate her pregnancy once the foetus was deemed non-viable. This tragic and apparently preventable death once again brought out tens of thousands of people onto the streets all over Ireland to protest at the state of Irish abortion laws, and to demand urgent legislation to implement the X case test.[33] Following the outcry over Savita Halappanavar's death, in December 2012 the government announced its intention to legislate for the X case in accordance with the report of the Expert Group. In January 2013, the Oireachtas Health Committee debated the format of the proposed legislation in a series of public hearings with a range of interested groups and individuals. The government published the heads (outline) of the legislation in April 2013, and in May 2013 the Health Committee again held a series of public hearings with invited legal and medical experts debating the substance of the heads. Finally, in June 2013, the text of the Protection of Life During Pregnancy Bill 2013 was published, for introduction in the Dáil and Seanad with a view to securing passage by the end of July 2013.[34] The legislation provides for the procedure to be followed whereby a termination of pregnancy may be carried out by doctors to save a pregnant woman's life, either where the 'real and substantial risk' to her life arises from a physical condition or from a risk of suicide. It does not cover cases of fatal foetal abnormality, despite clear public support for the inclusion of such cases and indeed for the provision of abortion in cases of rape, incest or risk to the health of the pregnant woman.[35]

CONCLUSIONS

Twenty-one years after the X case, the introduction of legislation providing a statutory framework for life-saving abortions is long overdue and very welcome. However, there is now clear public support for legislation allowing abortion on a wider range of grounds than the very restrictive cases provided for under the X case. Legislation is also needed to regulate the provision of other reproductive health services and the carrying-out of embryonic stem-cell research. Until now, the main reason for the failure to legislate for any of this is the presence of Article 40.3.3 in the Constitution (the Eighth Amendment) and the legal status it gives the foetus. The existence of this Article has contributed to the culture of secrecy and silence around the termination of pregnancy.[36] Because of the reluctance of politicians to confront the issue, the judiciary have been left to step into a legal vacuum and have had to create policy. The *Protection of Life During Pregnancy Bill 2013*, along with legislation to provide for terminations in cases of fatal foetal abnormality, would address the needs of women in the most desperate circumstances. *But* in the longer term, more fundamental and far-reaching reform, particularly the deletion of Article 40.3.3, is necessary.

There are positive signs ahead. The prospect of radical reform of the Constitution lies in three particular developments: the clear shift in public opinion which now favours the legalisation of abortion on grounds wider than those permitted under Article 40.3.3; the passing of a referendum in November 2012 which inserted specific protection for the rights of children into the Constitution for the first time; and the establishment of a Constitutional Convention in 2012. We are now facing into a period of genuine constitutional reform, and this could have much to offer those campaigning for women's rights. Ultimately, the courts and the legal system cannot be the only focus of any such campaign. Feminists also need to win the argument for change in the political and legislative arena – on abortion and on women's rights more generally. Following the passage of the X case legislation, the focus of feminist campaigners should now move to winning the argument for deletion of the Eighth Amendment, so that progressive legislation can be introduced to address the real reproductive health needs of Irish women.

NOTES

1   Article 40.3.3 of the Irish Constitution.
2   See Diamuid Ferriter, *Occasions of Sin: Sex and Society in Modern Ireland* (London, Profile Books, 2009).

3   Attorney General v X, [1992] IESC 1; [1992] 1 IR 1, (more commonly known as the 'X Case').

4   *R v. Bourne* [1939] 1 KB 687.

5   Pauline Conroy, 'Outside the Jurisdiction: Irish Women Seeking Abortion', in Ailbhe Smyth (ed), *The Abortion Papers: Ireland* (Dublin, Attic Press, 1992).

6   Ray Kavanagh, *Mamie Cadden: Backstreet Abortionist* (Cork, Mercier Press, 2005).

7   UK Department of Health 2011.

8   Irish Family Planning Association, *The Irish Journey: Women's Stories of Abortion* (Dublin, IFPA, 2000).

9   Linda Connolly, 'From Revolution to Devolution: Mapping the Contemporary Women's Movement in Ireland', in Anne Byrne and Madeleine Leonard (eds), *Women and Irish Society* (Belfast, Beyond the Pale Publications, 1997), p. 561.

10   *Roe v. Wade* (1973) 410 US 113.

11   *McGee v. Attorney General* [1974] IR 284.

12   William Binchy, 'Privacy and Family Law: A Reply to Mr. O'Reilly', *Studies* (1977), p. 330.

13   James Kingston and Anthony Whelan with Ivana Bacik, *Abortion and the Law* (Dublin, Round Hall, 1997), p. 260.

14   Tom Hesketh, *The Second Partitioning of Ireland* (Dublin, Brandsma Books, 1990).

15   Sandra McAvoy, 'From Anti-Amendment Campaigns to Demanding Reproductive Justice: the changing landscape of abortion rights activism in Ireland 1983–2008', in Jennifer Schweppe (ed.), *The Unborn Child, Article 40.3.3 and Abortion in Ireland: Twenty-Five Years of Protection?* (Dublin, Liffey Press, 2008); Ailbhe Smyth (ed), *The Abortion Papers: Ireland* (Dublin, Attic Press, 1992).

16   *Attorney General (SPUC) v. Open Door Counselling Ltd* [1987] ILRM 477.

17   *Open Door No. 2* (1993) 15 EHRR 244.

18   See Conroy, 'Outside the Jurisdiction: Irish Women Seeking Abortion'.

19   *SPUC v. Grogan (No. 2) Case* 159/90 [1991] 3 CMLR 84.

20   The Attorney General Plaintiff v. X. and Others Defendants [1992 No. 846P].

21   Evelyn Mahon, Catherine Conlon and Lucy Dillon, *Women and Crisis Pregnancy* (Dublin, Government Publications, 1998).

22   *Attorney General v. X* [1992] IR 1.

23 Medical Council Guide to Professional Conduct and Ethics (2009) paragraph 21.1.

24 *Ibid.*, Paragraph 21.4.

25 *Constitution Review Group* 1996: 277, 279.

26 *D v. HSE*, 2007.

27 *D v. Ireland*, 2005, at para 103.

28 *D v. Ireland*, 2005, at para 69.

29 *D v. Ireland*, 2005, at para 40.

30 *D v. Ireland*, 2005, at para 90.

31 *D v. Ireland*, 2005, at para 92.

32 *ABC v. Ireland* (2010). Para 267.

33 See for example Ivana Bacik, 'Time for Government to Stop Talking and Legislate', *The Irish Times*, 16 November 2012.

34 After much contentious debate this Bill was signed into law by President Michael D Higgins on 30 July 2013.

35 See *The Irish Times*, 13 June 2013.

36 For further commentary, see for example Jennifer Fletcher 'Silences: Irish women and abortion', *Feminist Review* 50 (1995), p. 44; Ann Rossiter, *Ireland's Hidden Diaspora: the 'abortion trail' and the making of a London-Irish underground, 1980–2000* (London, IASC Publishing, 2009), and Jennifer Schweppe (ed), *The Unborn Child, Article 40.3.3 and Abortion in Ireland: Twenty-five Years of Protection?* (Dublin, Liffey Press, 2008).

'RESIST, FALL, FAIL, RESIST'
DIARY OF A FEMINIST ACADEMIC

Ailbhe Smyth

FOREWORD

I am not going to write it how I thought I would. The reasons are personal and political, certainly real, but that is no guarantee of satisfaction.[1] They come crowding in, arbitrary and entirely contingent, until I know only what I cannot or should not write, and why not. Post-modern *anomie* or *angst:* a condition I started to half-believe in just lately, when it may be already post. Or simply fatigue. That would not be unreasonable. But it won't do. The heaves and turmoils of change are supposed to produce quite other effects.

In fact, feminism and the academy is something I spend a lot of time thinking about, shuttling between mainstream and margins of one kind and another, although more often than not wandering somewhere in the spaces between, liminal or lost.[2] Romantic self-dramatisation, *hero fails to overcome obstacles*, or plain truth of the matter. I had grown used to being at home on the edge. Now, the relation of periphery to centre has been shifted by central control in ways that are difficult to identify, often volatile and unpredictable. *Strange attractors.*[3] Peripheral challengers are being systemically and systematically incorporated, *no loose uncanonical bodies need apply.* Expressing outrage, exposing and condemning the persistence and particularity of oppressions, even more taking action to end them, are anachronistic solecisms. Ordinary common or garden opposition, never mind revolution, is being stifled by discursive stealth.

You think I exaggerate for rhetorical effect? Just the other day, I heard someone say: 'We on the Left don't use the word "opposition" any more: we prefer "alternative"'.

Left-wing lite. No, I don't prefer 'alternative'. Oppositional politics – feminist, anti-racist, lesbian, gay, queer, anti-corporatist – are not pick-and-mix, customised, consumerist options, co-existing harmoniously in the mainstream. I oppose (that is I confront, contest, resist, seek to change) specific socio-economic, political and cultural systems based on arbitrary hierarchical divisions which intersect with one another in remarkably consistent and persistent ways, to produce and maintain unequal relations of power, with acute and deleterious material consequences for people in their everyday lives and life possibilities. *A politics without adversaries is not a politics at all.*

When the Left is merely an 'alternative', when 'revolutionary' and 'radical' are unacceptable self-descriptors for intellectuals and activists alike, when 'feminist' is a term used sparingly if at all, even by feminists, when 'gender mainstreaming' is about as political as it gets in this (allegedly) 'post-feminist' era, you have to wonder (and whatever the explanations) if you're in danger of becoming one of the adversaries you once opposed (and how would I know if I were?).

Feminism is being stripped of its feminist voice.

Therefore, non-consequentially, I'm writing a diary.

DAY 1

It never is 'day 1' of course. Always *in medias res*, in the thick of it. Yet another convention I don't know how to subvert. The onward march. Where will it lead us (*pace* Virginia)? Must come back to that. *Make time to think.*

Get up the minute alarm goes off, make strong coffee. Surprisingly cheerful. Back to work today, so think this diary thing not altogether arbitrary. Academics must never be arbitrary, we must always have reasons, a rationale. Am pleased with this. *Chaos under control.* That's the key. *Irish Times* piece on UN Human Development Index says Irish poverty rates second highest in developed world. Government says UN report based on out-of-date figures and that it's all changed now. *Plus ca change ... etc* is hardly a suitable motivator for a feminist academic so locate briefcase and head for the car.

Office untidy as ever but yellow walls great (practically had to pay Buildings Office to paint the Centre yellow – significant subversion in context of regulation 'broken white'. What is it with universities and interior aesthetics? Why is 'dreary' corollary of non-arbitrary? It's true though about the payment business. Have worked out (you don't have to be gifted) that an office in UCD costs roughly 100,000 euro in research grants. Our university is now dedicated to research which will determine the 'future of the nation' no less, and which pays hard cash on the nail. No grants, no offices. A Chair costs a bit more I reckon. No more un-market un-driven un-funded research. Or only standing up, outside.

Check up on general state of affairs with J. No emergencies. Centre running smoothly. Could have stayed away. Postpone budgets until next week. Sort out desk, make phone calls, skim huge e-mail (no exciting invitations, one article to revise, two draft PhD chapters, three draft MA dissertations, various interview and reference requests, one million bureaucratic edicts, two million messages of no interest whatsoever), check up on course book orders, organise meetings, plan work schedule for next couple of weeks. Want to go away again immediately. When are we supposed to get any work done? Thinking? Reading? Writing? Research? Course preparation? Writing papers? (Ha!) Connecting? Dialoguing? Co-operating? Confronting? Resisting? Strategising? Inventing? Creating? When can feminist academics transform the academy, never mind the world? What do I mean by 'work' anyway? Realise am starting internal whine so exit to café with draft dissertations, two urgent refs, article for revision. August is a quiet month.

Buy more ciggies (will not think about consequences right now), and order doppio cino (*how IS a girl to survive?*). K arrives and I tell her about Australian conference. Incredibly invigorating, on 'Poverty, Violence and Women's Rights'. An up-front radical agenda:

> We believe that, now more than ever, there is an urgent need for women to get together to discuss male violence and its effects (including terrorism, war, racism, fundamentalism and corporate globalisation), and to plan more effective feminist responses. Indeed, we believe it is time for women to set the agenda.[4]

The crucial questions: Who? Where? How? For what purposes? Raised, debated, argued (in detail, in several languages) by 400 feminist activists, researchers, writers, artists and (even) academics plus the odd politician, mainly from South East Asia and the South Pacific. Well, the ones who could get visas. Pakistani, Indian and Indonesian feminists were refused entry. Not me, or other

Europeans or North Americans. There were protests of course (press release, petition, strong letters) but it didn't magic them over to Oz. A dissonant undertow to our discussions. Insistence on the vitally necessary integration of practice, politics and theory: this is no time for disconnection; *this is no time to turn our backs*. Commitment to a radical analysis of power relations as a central, non-negotiable, grounding element in the feminist project, and to a clear politics of structural change, however diversely construed, however much radicalism is derided and denigrated. Refusal of individualist analyses, as of parochial responses and 'solutions' which assume global relevance: the hegemony of unreflective, introverted White North American and European feminist perspectives must be named and resisted. Finding ways to understand and respect differences between women, while resisting the inequalities in which they are rooted. Recognising the effectiveness of collective action, local and global, in the struggle to change the social, political and economic systems which structure inequality.

Oh the sheer relief of being able to speak directly. Why should we apologise for being – still – radical and political, when the oppressions feminists identified have got worse, not better, for the majority of women in the world? Why are we so afraid to say it straight? K agrees. Decide to do next conference in Dublin. Oh well. We can fantasise.[5]

Later – a sad irony – I read in *Sojourner* of the death of June Jordan, one of my heroes for the past 30 years. Poet, activist, essayist and teacher, she died this summer, aged 66, of breast cancer. A true revolutionary who never stopped believing. On the wall over my desk I have pinned up a quote from an essay she wrote in 1989:

Let's not sit inside our sorrows, let's not describe things to death. My orientation is activism. Other than that it's like a kind of vanity or a decadence.[6]

Hard time getting to sleep. Worrying about undone budgets, X's dissertation (argument all over the place and dreadful referencing, but a great whoosh of intellectual energy and passion – will it be enough?), UN Human Development Index, deradicalisation of politics, being (or not) a 'feminist academic', and the arbitrariness of our living and dying. Reach no conclusions.

DAY 2

Not keen on getting up. Weather terrible. Energy low. One of my sisters is seriously ill in hospital. Call her to chat. She's amazingly upbeat and says tests are ok. Am relieved, but wish I could help more. I feel very anxious and sad.

Have to start working, and think will get more done at home, no meetings till afternoon. Phone rings when half-way through dissertation number two and I hear that the Higher Education Authority has decided, after more than a decade, to close down forthwith its Equality Unit – the only watchdog for the entire third-level sector in the country.[7] I note, *en passant*, as one does, that the closure coincides with the conference the unit has scheduled on 'Gender Matters in Higher Education in Ireland'. Coincidences bother me, but of course I don't subscribe to conspiracy theories – I'm an academic. The decision just dropped down out of the blue summer sky. Someone arrived in Cork early one morning in July and told the staff: you'll be gone, *finis,* unwritten history before you can formulate a thought, never mind organise a protest, or words to the same effect. As far as I know, they told nobody else, and by the time Academe gets going again after the summer break, it will all be a *fait accompli*.

I'm boiling mad. This is so arbitrary. With a non-coincidentally miniscule budget and very few mostly part-time staff, the unit has been tracking equality policy and practice in the system through conferences and publications, and across a whole range of areas: gender, race and ethnicity, sexuality, disability, poverty, social class divisions. Now is the time for the unit to be expanded and supported, not disappeared, when Ireland is on the brink of having to acknowledge that equality is more than a buzz word, because 'the mainstreaming of an idea is not equivalent to creating its reality'.[8] But it's an idea we are clearly not nearly as committed to as we like to think we are. Academic institutions have been among the most resistant of all. A lot of lip service in the form of policy statements and superficial compliance with legislation, but not much concrete, material, tangible changes on the ground (or not the ground I walk on). The closure of the Unit is inexplicable, the timing and method cynical, to put it mildly. And the difficult truth is, those who are passionately committed to fighting inequality (i.e., those who bear its brunt) do not have the power to stop this happening.

This is not being a good day. Have meeting with high-up in UCD about one of our grants. Funders have said they're withholding second tranche payment because the university has failed to deliver on one of the key performance indicators (I marvel at how such phrases trip off the tip of my feminist tongue in this new entrepreneurial environment). It had agreed to increase core funding to the Centre and to improve our staffing levels. They've done neither, although we've exceeded our project targets by 150%. High-up most affable and utterly, maddeningly non-committal, until I say (equally affable), I don't see why the Centre should be discreet about the university's failure to honour commitments it has entered into. I mention Academic Council, Governing Authority, and (in a perfectly modulated rising crescendo), the media. We end up agreeing the matter 'will be looked into'.

Race back over to Centre (on the edge of the campus, surprise surprise – more coincidence), where the sun is at least metaphorically shining (this is Ireland after all) and I cheer up something considerable. Applications are high this year for our PhD and MA programmes. Yes! We're doing ok despite all the usual obstacles. Am extremely relieved as have nightmares of WERRC being disappeared – it's happening in the UK where some programmes have been shut down over the past couple of years, and problems elsewhere in Europe too. A climate not exactly conducive to the flourishing of feminism with governments falling over themselves in their rush to the neo-liberal centre, where the consequences of the inequalities and injustices people experience in their lives are being drowned in a mainstreaming morass of vacuous equality-speak. We now have equality policies which evade the use of the term 'women' entirely – or indeed of any specific group of workers. Women are redundant, obsolete, over! Long Live Equality! Problem solved. Except that a policy with no one and nothing at its heart cannot deliver on anything for anyone.

I think for the nth time that 'gender' is killing women's studies and feminist politics, oh so politely, softly, definitively and ironically. 'Genderisation' disconnects feminist theorising and research from political action, and effectively removes women – conceptually and materially – from intellectual and political discourse. 'Gender', sans feminism, sans women (it's absurd!), will never transform the academy, much less the world. I argue all the time with post-structuralist, deconstructionist et tutti frutti friends about the evacuation of politics from theoretical projects (who will be left when there's no one left?), but it is, at the very least, a constructive debate which makes me think. 'Gender' isn't even a debate anymore – it's a hollow cold thing, and I don't want to be in it.

Take ten deep breaths, re-focus, face into e-mail then go back home, desperate to do some real work. Diverted by call from girlfriend who almost certainly thinks academics are weird (not exotic, just weird). I do too, of course, but hold on to the notion (arrogant of course) that feminists do it differently. She suggests swimming, which is even weirder given the weather, but I go along anyway and feel much better. As doing diary later, thought crosses my mind that I'm probably considered to be well beyond 'girlfriend' age. But as Iris Murdoch said, in another context entirely, *sic disintegrat bisquit.*

DAY 3

I'm with a judge, who has a long composite name, a handsome woman, very warm and supportive. She's telling me things, giving me important information. I'm to appear in Court on 'non-specific charges'. Strangely, I'm not at all alarmed about this. Then I notice my skirt keeps falling down because I've no belt and it's too loose. I excuse to go and hike it up. When I come back, I'm relieved but eventually see I've exchanged skirts with the judge. I know mine isn't suitable for a judge and I'm anxious now. Still, I tell myself that it goes with her wild and glamorous high-heeled boots. Vive Madame le Juge! We enter the courtroom and now I see she's put on a disguise, or maybe dragged up. I'm in the dock, skirt around my feet, shivering and swearing what must be an oath to tell the truth, the whole truth in a language I don't understand and cannot speak. It's a cacophony. A catastrophe.

I wake up, but want to go on dreaming. I want to understand what's being said, I want to be able to speak. Fail, so get up, read newspaper and drink too much coffee. I feel hazy, spacey. Put off having to revise article on men's violence against women but eventually get down to it. Try hard to keep tone neutral (why? what's happening is horrible), although it doesn't really work. At least the footnotes are ok. If they don't like the politics, they don't have to publish it, and they probably won't. Even women's studies journals tend to prefer 'real' academic articles. Am not a sociologist or a psychologist or a philosopher or a historian. Was trained (oh was there ever such a misnomer) as a *litteraire*, and think of myself (we all have our pride) as a 'properly' interdisciplinary Women's Studies person. But it can be dodgy. I still haven't sorted out the question of feminist methodology, even though I teach it. I dread the earnest conference question, 'So, what are you actually working on now?' It doesn't have a name I think. Academic boundaries are tough to break and we transgress them at our peril. Careers are at stake. But I like the crossing, however unfitting, and it's far too late for me to be having career qualms. I'm certainly not on a fast-track to anywhere, but they can't get rid of me either. I have nothing to lose in this place, at this time. Free to go for broke all the way. I never expected roses – did I? Foolish to dream of roses if your goal is to challenge and change the dominant order. Sometimes, though, I feel bewildered.

Spend afternoon in yellow office, and check up with C on progress of one of our research projects: on refugees and asylum-seekers in the labour market. It's policy-oriented, and you have to watch that kind of research now like a hawk to make sure you don't end up working for the government agenda. A growing problem, and a dilemma. We want to participate in policy-shaping, but on our own terms. I think it's going really well.

Then A comes in to discuss our big outreach certificate programme. We started doing a non-graduate certificate in women's studies 10 years ago, and it's boomed and bloomed beyond our dreams. We did it because one of our aims is to work to increase women's access to the academy (transformed or not), and specifically for those euphemistically known as 'non-traditional students', i.e. women who because of their age, socio-economic or geographical location, or for whatever reason, wouldn't otherwise have a hope in heaven of getting to university. We work in partnership with community-based women's groups to develop what I think of as 'site-specific women's studies'. We have up to 10 programmes, all around the country, at any one time, upwards of 200 students, and hundreds of graduates. Over the years we've introduced specialist women's studies certificates in areas such as rural development, community leadership, north-south issues, and most recently the first ever accredited Lesbian Studies course in Ireland. More boundary crossings. I love it, I love teaching these courses, we all do. You feel somehow you truly understand what developing feminist critical awareness and education is all about.

End afternoon in state of apoplexy when I read in university *Newsletter* that President has made speech about the growing importance of responding to the needs of mature students without once acknowledging the work we're doing. You'd think he'd be proud, but he's not a feminist (ha! just teasing), plus community-university partnerships are not exactly a major money spinner, or (it would appear) about building the future of the nation. Oh no. Mind you, the programme doesn't cost the university a single penny. All the funding comes from outside. When will the university put equal money where its mouth is?

Go home exhausted via gym and local deli. *Must shop!* Call my mother who wants to know where I am, as in 'are you ringing me from Ireland or are you at a conference?' Feel bad. Have I been that busy? Yes. Wonder how we hold everything together in our heads, and what happens to our hearts and souls when the head is so busy. Remind myself *primo* to watch out for my soul because knowledge-making is a betrayal of the spirit without it. Remind myself *secundo* that although I rail against the academy, I have the immense privilege of being paid to think, teach, research, write, organise *de facto* from the place of passion and imagination, as much as from intellect and reason.

Have two glasses of very dry white wine and read Elizabeth Bishop in bed. Soul-watching. Set radio alarm for 8am. This is still August after all.

DAY 4

You think they can't stop you. But suppose you're wrong? You may get hurt, for all your bravado.

Surfacing slowly, I hear my name and sink back down into my dream state. Suddenly, I realize this is not a dream. I really do hear my name on the morning news. 'Feminist academic Ailbhe Smyth has lost her gender discrimination case against University College Dublin'. The report goes on, but I can't concentrate, my mind has gone blank. The phone rings. A friend, hoping I haven't been listening, to break the news gently. She gives me the details I missed and much love. Phone goes again immediately. A journalist. I say 'no comment at present', hang up and it goes again. After four 'no comment' calls, I get through to my Union rep's mobile. Yes, I should have been told in advance. Yes, it's appalling. No, they didn't release it to the media. Yes, they're as stunned as I am. They're issuing a 'no comment until we've read the judgement' statement immediately. We'll talk about the situation later in the day. Ring current girlfriend, still asleep, who says 'Oh my god, hold on, I'm on my way'. Take phone off hook. Item on again at 8.30. Stop listening after that.

I feel as if I've been stripped. Lonely, humiliated, hung out to dry. It's so public.

The case, ongoing since 1997, was straightforward: I made a routine application (not for the first time) for a long overdue internal promotion to Associate Professor, a post for which I was more than adequately qualified. I was turned down. Of 20 people promoted to the grade that year, 19 were men, only one was a woman. Several of us senior women academics protested to university Governing Authority, and informed the Equality Authority, pointing out that UCD was failing to deliver on its mandatory equality policy, that indeed the institution appeared intent, *au contraire,* on flouting the law and reproducing deeply embedded historical patterns of discrimination against women. Two other colleagues and I decided to take gender discrimination cases against the university. The decision generated heated debate (by no means all women academics were supportive) and caught the attention of the media. The Registrar of the university (a woman) claimed that the statistics (93% of full professors were male) were not indicative of any gender bias in the academy. Oh my! What does it take? However, the university was thus forced to set about cleaning up its gender equality act, reviewing and revising promotions criteria and procedures, record-keeping and accountability, gender balance on appointment panels and so forth. The following year, both of the colleagues who had taken cases at the same time as me were promoted, an effective 'divide and rule' tactic. After all, the university could put its hand on its heart (heart?) in court, and say: 'Oh no, we're not guilty, we're purer than pure (and whiter than white – literally true). We even promote women who challenge our authority'. The Equality Authority then softened its threat of a full-scale gender audit of the university on foot of these procedural revisions (are we to be haunted forever by revisionism?) and promotions. Meanwhile, I continued to teeter out on a chilly ledge, as head of a discipline that wasn't even a discipline and that probably didn't 'really' exist for heaven's sake. *In the freshly gendered knowledge economy, there is no logical need for women's studies.*

But I decided to stick with my case, although I reckoned I had at best a 50:50 chance. Gender equality cases are extremely difficult to win (track-covering has now become an institutional fine art), and especially so in Academe. I didn't know anyone who had already won such a case. I persisted because I was angry on my own account at having 33 years of hard and effective academic work discounted, angry because it was a denial of worth and status not only to me personally but to the area of research, scholarship and teaching I am in – women's studies – angry because it is still so difficult for women academics to achieve equal representation and respect, (parity of esteem, if you like), and angry because all women who work in the system are liable to exploitation, treated as a permanently expendable underclass. I was angry because I knew, although this I could indeed not prove, that I was being targeted because I was, am, and intend to remain a feminist, lesbian, radical. And I don't keep quiet about it. I owe no allegiance or loyalty to hetero-patriarchal, post-capitalist, racist, elitist, market-driven systems. It is my job to theorise, research, teach and oppose existing power relations in such systems. I am not naïve or stupid. I know that persistent challenges to the dominant order will not be tolerated. I know they will be punished, one way or another. I also know that this is part of the way of change, however paradoxical it seems to me just now.

I call my daughter in California, my mother in Dublin. Such immense distances between our three generations. Such amazing connections in spite of them.

My friends are wonderful, comforting, supportive. They come with consolation, love, brandy, sushi, cream cake. I think they're brilliant, and know how lucky I am. There is real community, solidarity. They tell me not to take it personally. I say 'No, of course I won't'.

But of course I do. That's me out there, my body, heart and soul, flapping in the wind. I feel so tired.

Later, I turn to other things. I must not 'sit inside my sorrows'. There's a lot to think about – definitely political and certainly personal. But that's for the future. Now, always a practical girl, I buy very cool bright red shoes for the first time in my life. Now is indubitably the time. Lesbian, feminist radical etceteras need great footwear to kick ass. Yes! Ever onwards!

DAY 5

Today in town, I saw a young girl – 14 or 15 at most – lying in a doorway in broad daylight. Very thin, smooth-skinned, with brown eyes. Totally out of it. Drugs? Glue? I don't know. In her left hand, she was holding on tightly to a small teddy, or maybe a bunny, with pink ears. I walked past her. Everyone walked past her. A not unusual urban phenomenon after all. I didn't know what to do, didn't think I could do anything, did nothing. I went about my business as a feminist academic, activist, radical *et cetera*.

Home again – so cool, calm, clean, orderly – I stand waiting for the kettle to boil. I want the comfort of hot tea and toast with butter and jam. Conscience is such a weak thing in the face of destitution. Idealism useless if it leads nowhere beyond itself. Knowledge pointless if it turns its back on the will to act.

Fragments of my week swim back to me in arbitrary disorder: delights, dreamings, dilemmas, disappointments. June Jordan's warning about vanity and decadence especially.

I think about the reasons why we resist, and why we fail. I think about reason. *'Be reasonable, Ailbhe'*. I hear it all the time. Yes, I am capable of reason when reason is appropriate. No, I will not be reasonable when what I encounter in the world is beyond human reason and understanding. Oppression, exploitation, poverty, violence, greed, war, injustice, indifference. I have no reason to be reasonable about such things.

Decide not to resign from my job, emigrate, hide my head or mince my words. I will not desist from future resistance. Decide it's a waste of my allotted time to worry any more about being a 'proper' academic. Determine to focus on being a feminist in the academy and out – 'up for women', as my daughter used to say when she was little. Realise we have to be rigorous, steadfast and brave in what we do: our scholarship, writing, teaching, organising. Recognise we have to be clear-sighted about the toll this takes on our lives. Think about the solidarity that comes from working together with others. Think how we have to be careful of ourselves and of each other because hearts and souls are always fragile. This does not mean that we cannot or ought not to be critical: why should debate and disagreement be destructive?

I will not say we must be uncompromising, for in truth it is impossible to live your life without compromise. But I believe that all those who resist – feminists and so many others – need to choose lucidly what we will and what we will not compromise on. It will be different for each of us. This is not about homogeneity. For my part, I will try not to compromise on my right to express my ideas, my analysis and my experiences in explicitly political and personal terms. That is what I can do.

Yesterday, losing that case, I felt somehow I had failed all the women who get a raw deal (and it is indeed very raw), all the many women who are silenced, sidelined, worked to the bone, not just where I am, but everywhere.

Today, walking on past that young girl in such a terrible state, I knew I had failed myself at some profound level I can't even name yet.

I drink my tea, and try to appreciate the love, kindness and courage that surround me in my life, the security and the freedoms that my privileged location brings me. I remind myself of Muriel Rukeyser's powerful, compassionate exhortation: 'RESIST, FALL, FAIL, RESIST'[9]

AFTERWORD

A ritual is a symbolic performance, typically collective, solemnly signalling (and sometimes celebrating) our recognition of the meaning and importance of certain material realities, experiences, and beliefs. It is a sequence of pre-ordained acts or gestures, performed at particular – marked – moments and in particular – 'sacred' – spaces, contained in time with a clear beginning and end. Its ceremonial incantations are so familiar to us we can repeat them by rote, without pausing to consider the precise meaning of the words. While there is space for internal additions, variations and modulations, the basic structure and form of a ritual are always maintained. Their very repetition, and the familiarity which derives from the sameness of their re-iterated performance, comforts and consoles the participants, reinforces community, and consolidates the status quo. Rituals are thus fundamentally conservative, designed to maintain and sustain systems, meanings, values and beliefs. Transformation is taboo.

Standing before you at a conference entitled *Gender Matters in Higher Education*, giving what must be my fiftieth talk on women in the Academy, it is difficult for me to avoid the sense of this being a re-iterative performance, which has much of the quality of ritual about it.[10]

What, I ask myself, is the purpose of yet another

conference on the issue? When the same terrain has been exposed and explored over and over again and again for so many years? As I ask myself when I see still more statistics, yet another institutional report, even more high-sounding statements? And (of course) what is the purpose of my intervention here? Is it, can it be anything other than a ritual reminder? *That the problem is not solved.* That there is no evidence of serious, sustained 'top-down' leadership and investment in seeking and implementing a solution to the problem of persistent gender inequality? That the typical institutional response to the 'question' of Gender in Higher Education (formerly known as Equality for Women) is that time is doing its work, over time the situation will change, in the fullness of generational time women will be equal?

Which shows firstly, a remarkably dismissive disregard for current generations of women caught in a seemingly ineluctable warp of inertia, plurally waiting (the classic stance of femininity) for time to move them forward; and secondly, a convenient (and entirely non-credible) ignorance of processes of historical change, since the equalising of complex hierarchical relations of power (from which gender is never absent), in Higher Education as throughout our social systems, cannot be realised without a whole series of strategic redistributive moves. Is there any purpose, I wonder, in performing this ritual statement of the bleak reality of women's locations in the Academy with and to those who already know and have no need to be convinced, persuaded, encouraged or incited?

These questions to myself are interruptions, disruptive of rituals which will brook no such thing. *More or lesss unanswerable anyway.*

When I wrote a straight-up proposal for this paper some months ago, I was in a more optimistic, or perhaps just more preoccupied frame of mind. Since then, my belief in the momentum of positive change (much change is laterally retrogressive) for women working in the Higher Education sector has been undermined by various sobering encounters and events, both public and personal. And I don't know how to talk about it anymore. The language has left me. Yet it matters.

For of course gender matters in Higher Education. Truly, I am appalled at being here, two decades after the first report on the status of women academics in Ireland was made, making the very same points again. Gender matters 'in here', because it matters 'out there', in the real world. Gender matters because it's not generally optional, never equal, and oh man, is it ever hard to shift.

Whose gender? Your gender matters, if you're a man (more chances, more money, higher stakes, higher status); my gender, your gender matters, if you' re a woman (fewer chances, less money, more leg-work, lower stakes, lower status). Men behave as if there's only one that matters, because that's in their best material and political interests. Women wish gender would disappear, and sometimes try to behave as if it has and it doesn't matter, because it does us no good in here. Gender is a bonus for men, and a great big persistent problem for women. Which is not the same as saying, mark you, that women are the problem.

No, the question we have to answer unequivocally, is why men continue to thrive on gender, and women do not, and what is going to be done to change this?

So I am not going to go through the impersonal body-counting ritual (although I do have a paper which does that, yet again). I want, instead, to get really personal and political about this matter of gender inside the academy, and read you a non-consequential diary.

1   This paper was delivered as a keynote speech to the Gender Matters in Higher Education Conference, organised by the Higher Education Equality Unit of the Higher Education Authority, at National University of Ireland Galway (NUIG), 8 November 2002.

2   When I wrote the diary – and of course when the events took place – I was Director of the Women's Education, Research and Resource Centre (WERRC) at University College Dublin (UCD), and Senior Lecturer in Women's Studies.

3   Horrocks glosses Jean Baudrillard's borrowing from astrophysics of the term 'strange attractors' as 'the irresistible gravitational pull of the universe towards forces lying at its periphery'. See Chris Horrocks, *Baudrillard and the Millennium* (Duxford, Icon Books, 1999), p. 74.

4   'Poverty, Violence and Women's Rights: Setting a Global Agenda'. James Cook University, Townsville, Australia. 2–7 July 2002.

5   Fantasy became reality (it happens) in July 2004 when WERRC at UCD hosted the 17th Annual Women's Studies Association (UK and Ireland) conference.

6   June Jordan interviewed by Pratibha Parmar, *Feminist Review*, 31, 1989, p. 62.

7   The Higher Education Authority is the major regulatory body for Higher Education in Ireland. The Education Equality Unit (HEEU) was indeed closed down in 2002 and has not since been re-established.

8   Zillah Eisenstein (1996): 'Stop Stomping on the Rest of Us: Retrieving Publicness from the Privatization of the Globe', in *Indiana Journal of Global Legal Studies*, Volume 4, Issue 1, p. 75.

9   Allusion to lines from Muriel Rukeyser's powerful poem *Letter to the Front* (Part V11): 'Full agonies:/ Your evening deep in labyrinthine blood / Of those who resist, fail, and resist'. Muriel Rukeyser, *Selected Poems*, edited by Adrienne Rich (Bloodaxe Books, 2013, new edition).

10 I first wrote about women academics way back in 1984, in a commissioned research study, *Breaking the Circle: The Position of Women Academics in Third-Level Education in Ireland* (Dublin, Dept of Education, 1984).

WOMEN'S ROLES IN IRISH POLITICAL PARTIES: CONTINUITY AND CHANGE[1]

Claire McGing

INTRODUCTION

In the western world, gender politics and party politics have had an uneasy relationship. Periods of accommodation and understanding have been interspersed with longer periods in which party attitudes towards gender roles privileged the patriarchal status quo. While first wave feminists in Ireland regarded women's enfranchisement as key to equality, their second wave 'daughters' were, at first, more cynical about electoral institutions. They saw male-dominated structures as the problem, not the solution, and sought to effect change from outside the walls of Leinster House. Meanwhile, tea-making and minute-writing became the groundwork of women who were members of parties, many of whom had joined following their father or husband. By the mid-1970s, however, a section of the women's movement had come to realise the potential of party politics for their claims. They began to join parties in larger proportions and an increased number ran for office. Furthermore, broader shifts in gender roles created space for more traditional and non-feminist women, mainly in Fianna Fáil, to mobilise for increased representation.

Between the 1980s and 2000s, the issue of gender waxed and waned in every party, though some took women's inclusion more seriously than others. As part of a broader appetite for political reform, women's representation became a popular issue during the 2011 general election campaign and the Irish government has since legislated for gender quotas. This chapter examines the changing roles of women in party politics in Ireland. It focuses on the four main parties with current representation in Dáil Éireann, Fianna Fáil, Fine Gael, the Labour Party, and Sinn Féin, but this is not to discount the important contribution of female activism in other parties in Ireland's weave of electoral history, as detailed elsewhere.[2]

At a global level, proportional representation (PR) tends to facilitate the election of more women than single-seat electoral systems like First Past the Post (FPTP). As constituencies elect multiple representatives, the argument goes that PR gives parties more 'room' to select women candidates without displacing a man. Feminist scholars of late, however, have come to accept that PR offers no fixed guarantees for women and increasingly concentrate on the importance of 'informal' factors like party traditions in grounding gender representation.[3] As Krook notes, 'a closer look reveals that PR systems promote women to the extent that their structural features combine with concerns to actually select more women – that is, practices and norms that support and even compel the recruitment of female candidates'.[4] On the island of Ireland, the Single Transferable Vote (STV) variant of PR has been found to be relatively friendly to women, suggesting female underrepresentation is attributable to internal party cultures.[5]

Though female party membership has risen slowly but steadily across the western world since the reawakening of feminism in the 1970s, parties largely remain places of male privilege. A mere increase in women's bodies does not necessarily equate to full integration and studies show continued patterns of inequity. By some, women are seen to be less active than their male party counterparts.[6] This is largely related to life cycle processes: once married and in motherhood, women's leisure-time declines at a much great rate than men's. Others take a more critical stance, arguing that women are not necessarily less active but participate in parties differently. In California, Costantini's older survey of Republican and Democratic activists shows how women 'tend to specialise in functions associated with their party's internal affairs and with roles variously characterised as supportive, nurturing, helpmate, and cheerleader'.[7] Though increased numbers of women are seeking out positions of party power in place of making tea and buns and supporting male candidates, parliamentary elites worldwide continue to be mostly men. Research suggests that as the hierarchy of power ascends, female presence in associated structures will decrease.[8]

Thus, we need a broad framework from which to understand women's roles in political parties, such as that provided by Childs and Webb.[9] They argue that research on the 'feminisation', or not, of parties must investigate broad gendered patterns. This would include female participation in party structures (not just limited to the parliamentary party), and whether measures are used to guarantee, or at least encourage, women's representation. Importantly, feminists should consider whether women participate equally across all party spaces, or whether they are limited to certain 'symbolic' roles. Party mechanisms to enhance female representation, if used, vary widely in scope and broadly fit under the headings of equality rhetoric, equality promotion, and equality guarantees, each of which will be considered in turn.[10] Firstly, equality rhetoric is the public acceptance of women's claims for inclusion. Examples can be found in party manifestos and in the speeches of political leaders. This discourse may increase the common ground for action and make strategies for change seem possible. Equality promotion, on the other hand, is the introduction of 'soft' measures such as future targets for female candidates and training or mentoring programmes. Finally, in recognising that political parties are the main 'gatekeepers' to women's representation, equality guarantees focus on the 'demand' for women candidates. Electoral gender quotas are an example of such a measure and ensure a certain percentage of women are selected or even elected to party bodies and elective office. Quotas are regarded as a 'fast track' strategy for change and can be quite controversial, particularly in more conservative party environments.

Parties might have very different reasons for pursuing the feminisation of power structures – gender will cut across party ideology. While feminists argue for parity to ensure principles of justice are upheld, and also advocate for the representation of women's interests, political organisations may chiefly consider the electoral benefits of more female candidates. Pursuits for women's equality within social democratic, socialist and green parties are more likely to converge with feminist aspirations than their centre- and right-wing counterparts. Nonetheless, pragmatism, too, may play a part in facilitating change on the left. In western democracies, left-wing parties are usually the first to introduce mechanisms to better enhance women's representation and often prove the starting point for reform across the party system. The literature on party change speaks of 'contagion' effects, whereby more traditional parties feel electorally pressurised to field increased numbers of female candidates if one of their rivals, usually on the left and in a minor party role, selects more women.[11]

Periods of party modernisation may give party leaders a 'mandate' to consider gender representation. In times of political crisis or electoral decline, new female faces might give parties a 'fresh' look and court an increased women's vote. Moreover, the 'mood' among the wider party membership will be more positive to change if it is linked to wider electoral strategies. However, parties are not monolithic organisations, and internal power arrangements determine the extent to which party elites are able to oversee rapid improvements for women. Research illustrates the benefits of centralised selection procedures for female recruitment.[12] Where party elites hold power over local constituencies, they can 'sponsor' or even 'impose' women candidates on tickets. On the other hand, decentralised structures, in which local members are given primary autonomy over selections, tend to favour anointed 'local sons'. Female inequality only becomes readily apparent when constituency decisions are totalled together prior to the election. At this point, it is too late for change.

Crucially, women's internal party activism proves the most significant variable to achieving change.[13] The success, or even starting point, of women's mobilisation, though, will ultimately depend on their 'place' within party hierarchies – individually and in group terms – as well as on political ideologies and vote strategies. When party institutions reach a point of 'critical juncture' like an electoral meltdown, the wishes of party women and party elites may converge, though perhaps out of different motivations. In the UK, for example, younger feminist activists in the Labour Party of the 1980s were able to take advantage of modernisation processes and vote-expansion plans to 'push' internally for greater female representation. Furthermore, party women across the western world have converged with non-party grassroots feminists, state feminist actors, and transnational institutions to further pursue their claims.[14] Thus, PR electoral systems and centralised selections do not always guarantee equality. Numerous informal intra-party and external factors are just as, if not more, important in enhancing or hindering women's political roles.

GENDER ROLES AND PARTY ROLES IN IRELAND:
HISTORICAL BACKGROUND

In 1972, the Commission on the Status of Women undertook a review of women's participation in Irish politics. While women accounted for one-quarter of the combined membership of Fianna Fáil, Fine Gael and the Labour Party, very few held any positions of influence. Society saw women as wives, mothers and homemakers, creating immense barriers to their participation in the public sphere. Tellingly, only six women dominated female Dáil representation from 1948 until the 1970s, and all came from established political families. The situation slowly began to change after the emergence of second wave feminism in the 1970s. The newly founded Women's Political Association (WPA) lobbied party leaders for more women candidates, and encouraged females to join parties and to seek office. Wishing to capture women's newfound consciousness, parties enhanced their numbers of women contenders relative to earlier contests, though party men continued to disproportionality progress to ballot papers. At the 1989 general election, women accounted for 14 per cent of candidates and won just eight per cent of Dáil seats.

The 1992 general election marked a watershed in the representation of women. The number of female candidates reached a record high of 19 per cent, while 20 women (14 per cent) were elected. The enthusiasm for gender politics was, in part, sparked by the 1990 presidential election, when Mary Robinson was elected as the first woman president of Ireland. Alas, the fervour for political women was not to last long. Little numerical progress was made between 1992 and 2011. At 18 per cent, the percentage of female candidates in 2007 was marginally lower than it had been in 1992. Just 22 women TDs (13 per cent) were elected in the 2002 and 2007 general elections. Winning 25 seats (15 per cent), the 2011 general election marked a record high in women's Dáil representation. This has risen to 26 seats, following Helen McEntee's by-election success for Fine Gael in Meath East.

Women of the Oireachtas, past & present © Mick Quinn Photography

Given this history, the legislation of gender quotas by the new Fine Gael-Labour Party government in 2012 is hugely significant. The Electoral (Amendment) (Political Funding) Act 2012 requires parties to run at least 30 per cent women candidates and 30 per cent men candidates in future general elections or else lose half of their state funding. The threshold will rise to 40 per cent after seven years. Ireland became the seventh country in the EU to introduce quotas through the law.

CANDIDACY AND ELECTORAL OFFICE
Labour Party

Party women and feminists on the political left were the first in Ireland to initiate the struggle for increased numbers of women in politics. The social democratic Labour Party, founded in 1912 to represent working class interests, has been the most willing in considering interventionist policies for female candidature. Still, the battle has not always been easy. Change slowly emerged from the late 1960s as the party began to express a more radical, civil liberties-based agenda.[15] Party modernisation created a space for feminism and women members grew concerned with Labour's highly paternalistic culture. Only two women Labour Party TDs had ever been elected fifty years after the establishment of the Free State and one (Eileen Desmond) had succeeded her deceased husband. A National Women's Committee was founded in 1971 by women members, but was not formally recognised by the party hierarchy until 1979.[16] The committee researched women's representation globally, attended seminars in Europe, and networked with other women's organisations abroad to exchange information. In 1981, the leadership agreed to reserve two seats for the committee on the party's national executive, a huge success.

In the mid-1980s, party feminists, aware of strategies used by other social democratic parties in Europe, initiated the long struggle for gender quotas. The party leadership agreed to adopt a 25 per cent quota of female candidates for the 1985 local elections. While the measure did not lead to the selection of more women, it opened up a broader debate within the party on the need for change. Women activists again came to the fore and a Gender Quota

Committee was established in 1989 to consider options. The party elite may have partly agreed to this for pragmatic reasons, as Labour elected no women TDs in the general election that year. A minimum 20 per cent 'quota' was proposed for party officerships and selections for the 1991 local elections. The Gender Quota Committee wanted at least 40 per cent, but the party leader feared resentment from party men in his constituency and refused to implement a figure this high. In the end, local selectorates continued to rally around men, as women accounted for just 14 per cent of the party's candidates in the 1991 elections. By 1995, the aspirant figure had risen to 25 per cent, with a commitment to further increases. In reality, these strategies were more targets than quotas and usually fell short of full implementation. Nevertheless, they did act to improve the broader participation of women in the party throughout the 1990s, relative to other parties. Party ideology appears to have been crucial here, as Labour's traditional concern for class equality allowed feminists to challenge inequities along other axes of difference.

The benefits of women candidates were further illustrated to the party leadership in 1990 when Mary Robinson, who had been nominated by Labour, was elected president. The party had a hugely successful general election in 1992, winning 33 Dáil seats, of which five (15 per cent) were women. This was a significant achievement, given an all-male slate had been elected in 1989. By the 1997 general election, 27 per cent of the party's candidates were women. While far from parity, this was significantly higher than the percentage put forward by Fianna Fáil (12 per cent) and Fine Gael (17 per cent). Thus, over the years, the Labour leadership has accepted feminist demands for more women candidates, largely out of electoral calculation. However, local structures have been much less open to this.

Feminists knew 'hard' reform measures would be required to effect significant change and, by the early 2000s, began to push the party to adopt a policy in favour of legal gender quotas. At its 2003 National Conference, the Labour party aimed to ensure at least one-third of its candidates for the 2004 local elections were women. It again failed to meet its self-imposed target, and 80 per cent of nominees were male. In response to this, the leadership commissioned a report in 2005 on women's participation in the party. As well as a recruitment drive for women members and further targets for female candidates, the report advised Labour to 'lead the way' on the gender issue by introducing a private members' bill while in opposition to legislate for quotas. This would tackle party state funding, along the lines of the French quota system. The proposal was adopted as party policy, largely due to the mobilisation efforts of Labour Women (the modern name for the National Women's Committee), and found its way into the party's 2007 general election manifesto. The party continued to set internal targets, aiming to run at least about one-third women candidates in the 2009 local elections and 2011 general election, though in the end it selected 23 per cent and 27 per cent, respectively. Again, however, these figures were considerably higher than the proportions recruited by Fianna Fáil and Fine Gael in these contests.

Party feminists, supported by the elite, continued to lead the way on the quota issue in the late-2000s. Ciarán Lynch, a Labour TD, introduced quota legislation as a private members' bill in 2010. Although the bill failed, it paved the way for further action. The party's 2011 general election manifesto promised to tie state public funding to 'the level of participation by women as public representatives' and that the party would set out targets in legislation. That year women won just over a fifth of Labour's 37 Dáil seats, outranking the other main parties. After the election, the agreed Fine Gael-Labour Party Programme for

Government stated that public funding for parties would be linked to the selection of women candidates. The section was taken almost directly from the Labour Party manifesto and ultimately became part of the Electoral (Amendment) (Political Funding) Act 2012. Without the long struggle of women within the Labour Party, it is highly doubtful such a law would form part of the statute book today.

Fine Gael

Historically, Fine Gael's approach to women's representation has been marked by a more *laissez-faire* approach.[17] Liberal economic ideology made it difficult for female activists to advocate for equality guarantees. The issue of women first came to light in the late 1970s. Under Garret Fitzgerald, the party sought to modernise its image. To this end, the leadership sponsored the nomination of increased numbers of women candidates and young candidates (though they did not always come through the selection process easily). Personally, Fitzgerald was also sympathetic to the feminist movement and wished to see more women elected. New female candidates constituted a mix of well-known feminists, mainly in middle-class urban constituencies, and more traditional party women in rural Ireland. Interestingly, of the nine women Fine Gael TDs elected in the general election of November 1982 (women now accounted for 13 per of the party's TDs, up from 4 per cent in 1973), three had established profiles through the women's movement.[18] Additionally, a women's group was founded in 1985 and funded by the party. While the group aimed to support, train and encourage women to seek office, its policy fell short of advocating for quotas. As the economy weakened towards the end of the decade, Fine Gael's support levels fell. Women's issues went into decline and unemployment and public finances became the main topics of the day. Men continued to disproportionally progress as candidates and the party's percentage of female TDs declined to just 10 per cent after the 1992 general election.

The party elite also resisted quotas. In 1993, Fine Gael commissioned a report on mechanisms for party renewal. In line with party ethos around equality of opportunity, the report stopped short of recommending rigid gender quotas 'because of the danger of compromising democratic principles'.[19] In 1997, after a further wave of party modernisation, the leadership commissioned an audit on Fine Gael women. This proposed the appointment of a full-time women's officer (which was carried out) and the adoption of affirmative action.[20] By the early 2000s, perhaps influenced by these conversations, Fine Gael had slowly come to accept the structural impediments to women's representation, though feelings on quotas remained mixed. When surveyed, card-carrying members revealed recognition of the lack of equal opportunities for women in the party. Just 41 per cent of members, however, found the idea of quotas acceptable.[21]

Following Fine Gael's electoral meltdown in the 2002 general election (losing 23 seats) and the election of a new leader (Enda Kenny), gender again became a modest part of a much wider party rebuilding process. Plans to elect between eight and ten women TDs in the 2007 general election (up from just two in 2002) did not lead to large-scale change. Just five Fine Gael women won seats, despite the party regaining 20 seats. Interestingly, it appears to have been easier for Fine Gael to enhance women's participation at a highly local and therefore relatively weak level of office. Party headquarters decided to implement gender directives on selection meetings for the 2004 town and borough council elections, a practice that was continued for the 2009 elections. They did not, however, extend this policy for the relatively more powerful city and county councils. The lesser importance placed on town councils perhaps made it easier to 'make room' for women here. Selection conventions in 2004 and 2009 were instructed by party headquarters to select at least one woman candidate, unless they had a sufficient reason not to do so. There is little evidence to suggest local selectorates found it difficult to recruit more women and the policy was highly successful. After the 2009 elections, women constituted 31 per cent of Fine Gael's total town councillors, considerably outranking other major parties.

Nevertheless, internal controversy surrounding quotas for higher levels of office would continue, even at an elite level. In March 2010, the party leadership was forced to back down on an attempt to introduce internal quotas after it was vocally opposed by parliamentary party members, including some women TDs and senators. In advance of the 2011 general election, amid growing public concerns about Ireland's 'broken' political system, Fine Gael published its *New Politics* document. Only five lines were devoted to 'Women in Politics' – one of the shortest sections in the whole document – and its proposed solutions were vague. The party wished to establish a Citizens' Assembly to *consider* a range of political reform options, among them how the representation of women would best be increased, 'including some form of quota system for women candidates'. Influenced by parliamentary party events a year earlier the leadership was, at this point, reluctant to tie itself to quota legislation. The party was more affirmative on the need to tackle the Dáil's 'long hours' culture. The party's 2011 election manifesto recognised the need to enhance women's representation in politics, but put no firm solutions forward as to how this could be achieved. Again, it proposed that a Citizens' Assembly deliberate and make recommendations. After the election, 11 Fine Gael women won seats in the Dáil, constituting 15 per cent of the party's total number.

When Fine Gael entered into negotiations for government with the Labour Party, a commitment to quota legislation was one of the compromises the leadership was prepared to make. Indeed, the legislation was introduced to parliament by a Fine Gael Minister, Phil Hogan, just two months later. Ultimately, this proved a radical shift in direction for the party and, in the legislative process, the bill was criticised by a number of its representatives. The considerable emphasis placed by the coalition on 'new' politics may have helped its introduction. The legislation provided a way of quickly responding to societal demands for political reform, yet did not require immediate attention.[22] It was also, of course, the reality of coalition government – compromises had to be found. As noted elsewhere: 'conceding to Labour's social and equality agenda was a trade-off for Labour support for the implementation of tough austerity economic measures'.[23]

Fianna Fáil

Fianna Fáil's record on women's representation has been very poor. Historically, a number of its few women TDs have relied on familial connections to enter politics, showing a reluctance to promote women outside of the 'party fold'. Illustratively, the youth wing (founded in 1975) was originally termed 'Macra Fáil' and translates from Gaelic as the 'young men' of Fianna Fáil. Representatives of the future were envisaged as men, so women took on mostly subordinate roles for the first half century of the party's existence. The situation began to change in the late 1970s when then taoiseach and party leader, Jack Lynch, sponsored the nomination of six women candidates in the 1977 general election, bringing the total number of Fianna Fáil women contesting the election up to ten. This was part of an attempt to 'woo' women voters and it worked, as the party saw its share of the vote rise 4 per cent, largely from the female electorate. Under Charlie Haughey, however, the party failed to further build on these female candidate numbers, and women members began to mobilise for change. Unlike Fine Gael, Fianna Fáil did not recruit feminist candidates, but broader societal shifts in gender roles created space for more traditional women members to push the issue.

A Women's Consultative Committee comprising female parliamentarians and executive members was established in 1981 and was re-organised as the Fianna Fáil National Women's Forum in 1985. Party women, however, were reluctant to advocate for quotas and, like the Fine Gael women's group, instead relied on rhetorical and promotional measures. This was further reflected by party policy, which undertook a positive action programme in the mid-1990s to foster a friendlier environment for female participation.[24] While modest progress was made during this period in women's internal representation, elective office largely remained the preserve of men.

Over the next few years, the party's Women's Forum went into decline, further dispatching gender democracy to the sidelines. The matter of women's representation in Fianna Fáil again came to light in the mid-2000s, when then party leader, Bertie Ahern, commissioned an action plan. The aspiration was to have women comprise 25 per cent of the party's local election candidates in the period 2008 to 2010, and 30 per cent of general election candidates in the period 2010 to 2012. Like other parties, however, decentralised nomination processes made it difficult to achieve change at a national level. Just 19 per cent of the party's candidates in the 2009 local elections were women and 15 per cent in the 2011 general election. The party's 2011 manifesto called for the replacement of STV with a mixed-member proportional system, which would include the introduction of measures for sex balance on the national list, but was unclear as to what this would entail.

The election was a disaster for the party and it entered the opposition benches with 58 less seats and all-male representation. When the new Fine Gael-Labour coalition announced its plans to legislate for quotas in 2011, Fianna Fáil's parliamentary party welcomed the proposal and even (unsuccessfully) proposed an amendment to extend the law to local elections. In a common theme, Fianna Fáil's failure to elect any women, and the swing of female voters to Labour, may have spurred a pragmatic incentive for the elite to support quotas. Nevertheless, events to follow revealed a persistent gap between the party elite and party membership on this issue, as a motion against the quota legislation was supported by delegates at the 2012 Ard Fheis. However, party headquarters is determined to run higher numbers of women in the 2014 local elections and, under the auspices of Senator Averil Power, established a taskforce on increasing female participation. Time will tell the success of these measures.

Sinn Féin

Sinn Féin's percentage of women candidates in recent elections, ranging from 19 per cent to 25 per cent, reflects its low percentage of female members. Although the party speaks of equality in rhetorical terms, it has yet to sanction affirmative action for female candidates in its constitution. As a cross-border republican party seeking a unified Ireland, issues of ethnicity have trumped gender politics, while its armed history ensured masculinity was deeply embedded in the organisation. Since the 1990s, however, women members have spoken of their struggle to find an equal voice. The situation slowly began to change in the period leading up to the Good Friday Agreement. Nationalist parties, largely in response to the relative success of the cross-community Northern Ireland Women's Coalition (NIWC), began to better prioritise women's representation. Across the island, Sinn Féin encouraged its female members to aspire to office and also heightened its stance of women's policy issues. In advance of the 2007 general election, in an attempt to court more women voters, Sinn Féin published a 'women's manifesto'. While it proposed quotas for semi-state and public bodies, its approach to elections was based mostly on promotional efforts. This was further reflected by internal policy. Sinn Féin's Equality Department ran seminars for party members on gender issues and the Ard Chomhairle adopted a comprehensive strategic plan for change.

A 'soft' 30 per cent target was applied to selections for the 2009 local elections, though women ended up accounting for 23 per cent of the party's candidates. As Sinn Féin saw its support ratings rise in the polls, the elite seems to have reconsidered quotas. Their political reform document in advance of the 2011 election argued for one-third quota legislation under a new partial list PR system. Two of the party's 14 successful candidates in the election were women. When the Fine Gael-Labour coalition announced its plans to legislate for quotas in 2011, a number of Sinn Féin politicians spoke of it favourably. Interestingly, at the party Ard Fheis in 2012, a motion against the government's proposal was passed by delegates. It regarded quotas as 'insufficient' in addressing women's underrepresentation in politics and said 'greater steps must be taken to address the gender imbalance within our political system', though no alternative measures were put to delegates. The elite remains determined to advance more women candidates at the 2014 local elections.

Positively, female presence on the national executives of political parties in Ireland has grown over time, though parties differ in their propensity to guarantee gender balance. In 1991, women accounted for 7.9 per cent of Fianna Fáil's national executive, 27 per cent of Fine Gael's, and 17 per cent of the Labour Party's. By 2008, these figures had risen to 30.5 per cent, 32.1 per cent, and 26 per cent, respectively.[25] Women's integration here is crucial given party power in Ireland has become increasingly centralised in recent years. While the supreme decision-making bodies of Fianna Fáil, Fine Gael, Labour and Sinn Féin are the national conferences (officially called the *Ard Fheis* in all parties but Labour), which comprise delegates from various levels of the party, the day-to-day organisation of parties rests with the national executive (or its equivalent). Members include elected representatives and local delegates elected by party members, while ex-officio officers hold seats in some parties.

In 2004, Bertie Ahern, then leader of Fianna Fáil, disbanded the party's women's section and instead adapted STV rules to ensure females comprise half the Committee of 20 (this was increased from 15 members to facilitate balance), which is the more powerful section of the Ard Comhairle (national executive). Though controversial, this measure has been highly successful in creating acceptance of females in Fianna Fáil. This is all the more important given women, at least in 2011, constituted just over one-third of party members.[26] At the 2012 Ard Fheis, the rule made no difference to the final outcome as, based on the count, equal numbers of men and women would have been elected anyway. In 2013, it was men who stood to benefit from parity. Had the count run strictly on vote lines, twelve women and eight men would have joined the new committee. Furthermore, the gender rule may have contributed to a sea change at other prestigious party levels.

Without any equality measures, four of Fianna Fáil's five elected vice-presidents in 2012 were female and one of its two honorary secretaries. These figures are all the more extraordinary given the party returned no women TDs in the 2011 general election and has just two female senators. At more locally-focused ranks, however, structures remain male-dominated. Only nine of the Ard Comhairle's 48 constituency delegates in 2012 were women, suggesting constituency organisations prefer to be represented by males or, more likely, that well-connected men are better positioned to seek this role in the first place. Meanwhile, largely reflecting the Leinster House situation, an all-male slate of frontbench and parliamentary representatives joined the executive.

Fine Gael, on the other hand, applies no strict rules for female representation on the party's Executive Council. Two seats, however, are reserved for the relatively weak Women's Group, chosen by its members.[27] Interestingly, despite the party's low percentage of elected female representatives, the Executive Council has shown incremental signs of gender balancing in recent years, with parliamentary, regional (apart from the three Dublin representatives), and local councillor panels including at least one woman in each case in 2012. Overall, 31 per cent of the body is female at present though this falls well below their proportion of card-carrying members, which equalled 42 per cent in 2011.

The Labour Party has had a long tradition of ensuring women's seat holding at various levels of the party. In 1981, as discussed, the leadership agreed to reserve two seats for the National Women's Committee on the national executive. Since 2009, Labour has reserved three places for women and three places for men, which are elected by delegates at party conference, on its modern 12-member Executive Board. Unlike elections to Fianna Fáil's Committee of 20, where delegates can vote across sex lines, the Labour Party constitution specifies that members vote separately for women and men. In 2012, there was no contest for women's representation, as just three went forward, while five male candidates appeared on the ballot paper. Additionally, the two parliamentary party representatives on the body must comprise a man and a woman, while a 30 per cent gender quota is required for any committee it establishes. In 2011, women accounted for 43 per cent of the Executive Board, outstripping their 36 per cent rank-and-file figure.

Internally, efforts to enhance women's stature in Sinn Féin have been much more rigid than their selection strategies. In 2003, the Ard Fheis marginally passed a motion requiring 50–50 sex balance on the Ard Chomhairle, influenced by the overrepresentation of men in previous contests. Reflecting Sinn Féin's historical disposition towards male power, this motion was not passed without conflict. Since its enactment the rule has enhanced women's role in the organisation, even beyond the proportion of card-carrying female members, which stood at just 25 per cent in 2011.

LOCAL PARTY STRUCTURES

At a party constituency and branch level, women party activists continue to hold supportive roles, largely as secretaries, in much larger numbers than they do leadership positions. In all parties, the constituency chair is most likely to be a man. The chair is the most influential local officer and presides over meetings, exercises chief supervision over constituency affairs and, more informally, is a key recruiter of potential candidates. Male dominance in this role may impact on women's representation as studies in Canada suggest female party chairs might be more inclined to find and encourage other women to run.[28]

Combining chairs and secretaries, just under a third (31 per cent) of Fianna Fáil constituency officerships were held by women in 2011.[29] This marks a considerable improvement on the situation of 1991, where only 2 per cent of chairs and 15 per cent of secretaries were female.[30] In 2008 one-fifth of constituency chairpersons were women.[31] In the past, Fianna Fáil has set plans for women's local participation and such measures appear to have modestly benefited female members. In 2008, women held only 7 per cent of constituency chair positions in Fine Gael, yet accounted for nearly half of all constituency secretaries.[32] Worryingly, inequality in Fine Gael's local spheres has actually enhanced over time. Women comprised 12 per cent of constituency chairs and 63 per cent of secretaries in 1991.[33] Proposals in the mid-2000s to annually alternate chairpersons by sex met with little approval in the party.

In Labour, despite a wider history of women's activism, the role of secretary, too, forms the point at which female constituency seat-holding peaks. Women held 13 per cent of chair positions in 2011, yet comprised 35 per cent of secretaries.[34] Moreover, progress appears to have reached a plateau. 20 years previous, following the introduction of 'soft' targets, women accounted for 12 per cent of Labour's constituency chairs and 32 per cent of secretaries.[35] At lower party levels, information is more difficult to piece together. Of Fine Gael's 42 per cent women members in 2011, 49 per cent held some type of branch officer role,[36] though position-by-position figures are unavailable. Interestingly, an older mass survey of Fine Gael members shows that the proportion of female branch secretaries actually exceeds their rank-and-file numbers. Even though they accounted for 30 per cent of members at the time, 42 per cent of branch secretaries were women.[37] In 2011, women constituted a fifth of Labour Party branch chairs and, mirroring their membership, 35 per cent of secretaries.[38]

YOUTH ORGANISATIONS

Given that traditional gendered barriers to political participation (like motherhood) form less of a hindrance among younger party members,[39] one might expect young women and young men to come up through youth ranks in similar numbers. On closer examination, however, gender biases are as evident within party youth structures, though change is slowly emerging. As young members constitute potential future candidates, it is crucial equality for women is achieved at this stage of the electoral 'pipeline'. In February 2013, Ógra Fianna Fáil elected its first ever female president, Kate Feeney. Below her, however, male-dominance continues. Currently, women comprise just 30 per cent of Ógra's Central Officer Board which is elected by the National Youth Conference and responsible for the organisation's management.[40]

Young Fine Gael has a current female membership of 46 per cent, yet has elected only three women presidents of 26 since 1978 (the first in 1984 and not another for fifteen years). Its last three presidents have all been men. At present, three of Young Fine Gael's eleven-member Executive Council are women, including the vice-president, meaning female power-holding falls well below women's membership proportion. In the Labour Party, conversely, young women in top positions appear to outrank their registered numbers. In 2011, females accounted for 30 per cent of Labour Youth members, though women currently hold four of seven positions on the National Youth Executive, including that of National

Chairperson. Nevertheless, historical patterns also reveal male advantage. Of Labour Youth's 23 former National Chairs, just two have been women, the last elected in 2002. Finally, looking at Sinn Féin Republican Youth, women attained just five seats on its 21-member Executive Council in 2012. The relatively more powerful positions of National Chair, Secretary, Public Relations Officer and Finance are all held by men, though both youth delegates to the senior party's Ard Comhairle are presently female.

Conclusion

In mapping the gendered histories of Fianna Fáil, Fine Gael, Labour and Sinn Féin, this research has shown that women's representation is not fixed across the party spectrum. As institutions, parties possess their own distinct ideologies and norms, and respond to demands for change in different ways. Though all parties bar Fine Gael have introduced creative measures to place women on the national executive, candidate quotas remain a relatively new phenomenon to party members aside from those in Labour. Despite suggestions in the literature, there is little evidence of a 'contagion effect' whereby one party out of electoral calculation follows another in selecting more women. The Labour Party had gendered conversations and strategies almost two decades before their competitors decided to act. While actions did not fully live up to the rhetoric, the fact Labour possesses the best record of all with regard to women's representation is testament to this long history. Indeed, the quota legislation enacted by the Irish government in 2012 first emerged within the Labour Party. The key ingredient seemingly lies with party women's insistence on equality guarantees, something that was missing in the stories of Fianna Fáil, Fine Gael and, despite its left ideology, even in Sinn Féin.

Overall, the picture is one of male dominance, but is very slowly changing for the better, particularly within parties. Quotas should 'shake up' the status quo of selections, as parties who fail to comply will be hit financially. Although the legislation does not apply to local government, it is crucial parties seek out talented women to take council seats in the 2014 local elections, who can then go on to contest Dáil elections. Locally, all parties have work to do in ensuring female members are better represented at a branch and constituency level. Meanwhile, though women are increasingly attaining positions in party youth structures, men continue to be overrepresented here, whether as members or elected officers. Better emphasis must be placed on ensuring young women and young men in parties are equal, as they constitute potential candidates of the future.

Finally, though not the focus of this chapter, it is also important to note the role of civil society groups like the WPA in pressurising parties to run more women candidates in the 1970s and 1980s. In fact, many joined political parties themselves to try and change the situation from 'the inside'. In recent years, a new generation of feminists established the *50:50 Group*,[41] which in many ways started where the WPA had left off. The *50:50 Group* played a key role in lobbying the government for quota legislation and, through public meetings and social media outlets, has contributed to public education on quotas. Future research should detail the role of civil society in the campaign for enhanced gender democracy in the Irish Republic.

NOTES

1   This research was funded by the Irish Research Council. See http://www.irchss.ie.
2   Dáil Éireann is the lower house of the Irish parliament. See Yvonne Galligan and Rick Wilford, 'Gender and Party Politics

in the Republic of Ireland', in *Contesting Politics: Women in Ireland, North and South*, Yvonne Galligan, Eilis Ward and Rick Wilford (eds) (Oxford, Westview Press, 1999), pp. 147–167.

3   Claire McGing, 'Women's Representation and the Single Transferable Vote (STV) in Ireland', *Irish Political Studies* 3 (2013, forthcoming), pp 322–340.

4   Mona Lena Krook, 'Beyond Supply and Demand: A Feminist-Institutional Theory of Candidate Selection', *Political Research Quarterly* 63, 2009, p. 712.

5   Clare McGing, 'Women's Representation and the Single Transferable Vote (STV) in Ireland', pp 322–340.

6   Ronald Inglehart and Pippa Norris (eds), *Rising Tide: Gender Equality and Cultural Change Around the World* (Cambridge, Cambridge University Press, 2003).

7   Edmund Constantini, 'Political Women and Political Ambition: Closing the Gender Gap', in *American Journal of Political Science* 34, 1990, p. 763.

8   Joni Lovenduski, *Feminizing Politics* (Cambridge, Polity Press, 2005).

9   Sarah Childs and Paul Webb, *Sex, Gender and the Conservative Party: From Iron Lady to Kitten Heels* (Hampshire, Palgrave Macmillan, 2012).

10 Lovenduski, *Feminizing Politics*, pp. 83–104.

11 Richard E. Matland and Donley T. Studlar, 'The Contagion of Women Candidates in Single-Member District and Proportional Representation Electoral Systems', in *The Journal of Politics*, 58, 1996, pp 707–733.

12 Joni Lovenduski and Pippa Norris (eds), *Gender and Party Politics* (London, Sage Publications, 1993).

13 Miki Caul, 'Women's Representation in Parliament: The Role of Political Parties', in *Party Politics*, 5, 1999, pp. 79–98.

14 Pamela Paxton, Melanie M. Hughes and Jennifer L. Green, 'The International Women's Movement and Women's Political Representation', in *American Sociological Review*, 71, 2003, pp 898–920.

15 Galligan and Wilford, 'Gender and Party Politics in the Republic of Ireland', pp 147–167.

16 Galligan and Wilford, 'Gender and Party Politics in the Republic of Ireland', pp 147–167.

17 In economics, *laissez-faire* means minimal government interference in the economic affairs of individuals or society.

18   These were Nuala Fennell, Gemma Hussey and Monica Barnes.

19   Fine Gael, *Report of the Commission of Renewal of Fine Gael* (Dublin, Fine Gael, 1993) p. 44.

20   Galligan and Wilford, 'Gender and Party Politics in the Republic of Ireland', pp 147–167.

21   Michael Gallagher and Michael Marsh, *Days of Blue Loyalty: The Politics of Membership of Fine Gael* (Dublin, PSAI Press, 2002), pp 63–68.

22   Fiona Buckley, Yvonne Galligan and Claire McGing, 'Some Day Girls, Some Day: Legislating for Candidate Gender Quotas in Ireland' (20 March 2013). Available at SSRN: http://ssrn.com/abstract=2236481 or http://dx.doi.org/10.2139/ ssrn.2236481.

23   Buckley, Galligan and McGing, 'Some Day Girls, Some Day', p. 11.

24   Galligan and Wilford, 'Gender and Party Politics in the Republic of Ireland' p. 34.

25   Yvonne Galligan, 'Women in Politics', in John Coakley and Michael Gallagher (eds), *Politics in the Republic of Ireland* (London, Routledge, 2010, fifth edition), p. 271.

26   In all cases, 2011 party membership figures were provided to the author by the various parties.

27   When interviewed by the author, members of the Fine Gael women's group spoke of its weak nature, lack of recognition from the party elite and the fact it was underfunded.

28   Christine Cheng and Margit Tavits, 'Informal Influences in Selecting Female Political Candidates', in *Political Research Quarterly*, 64, 2011, pp 460–471.

29   Personal communication between the party and the author.

30   Yvonne Galligan, 'Party Politics and Gender in the Republic of Ireland', in *Gender and Party Politics*, edited by Joni Lovenduski and Pippa Norris (London, Sage Publications, 1993).

31   Galligan, 'Women in Politics', p. 272.

32   Galligan, 'Women in Politics' p. 271.

33   Galligan, 'Party Politics and Gender in the Republic of Ireland' p. 161.

34   Personal communication between the party and the author.

35   Galligan, 'Party Politics and Gender in the Republic of Ireland' p. 161.

36   Personal communication between the party and the author.

37   Gallagher and Marsh, *Days of Blue Loyalty: The Politics of Membership of Fine Gael*) pp 63–68.

38   Personal communication between the party and the author.

39   Membership of Ógra Fianna Fáil is open to anyone between the ages of 16 and 30 inclusive. Young Fine Gael members must be at least 15 and no older than 30. Labour Youth is open to anyone under the age of 27. Republican Youth Sinn Féin members are between 15 and 29 years old.

40   The eleventh position of National Youth Officer is, at the time of writing, vacant.

41   See http://5050-group.com.

Feminism and Migrant Women in Early 21st Century Ireland

Salome Mbugua

Introduction

Since I was 16 years old I have been challenging the patriarchal system that undermines and oppresses women in Kenya, Uganda, Ireland and recently D.R. Congo. My activism has led me to speak in many meetings and conferences, and over the years I have sat on several committees that either look into equality between men and women, or that address issues of violence against women. At the age of 25 I converted my small flat in Nairobi to serve as a women's refuge and many times I risked my life by hosting women who had escaped domestic violence. Two of the women that I supported joined me in 2010 to establish Okuda, an organisation in Kenya that works with women affected by violence and conflict.

I view and introduce myself as a 'black African feminist', as an African and woman of colour. Feminism actually comes with many labels attached to it in accordance with behaviour, norms and cultural expectations from my society. I recall here sexism that I experienced in 2007, when I was approached by an African man who owns and publishes a magazine in Ireland. He wanted to gauge if I am a true feminist. This is what he quoted in his interview with me: 'you must read an explosive interview with Salome Mbugua. She has been happily married for good ten years. *Yet she is an unrepentant feminist.* So is the National Director of AkiDwA having her cake and eating it?'[1] As a woman of colour you are tied to many other labels that include black, African, third world. Identifying myself as a Black African Feminist encourages me to express solidarity with other women and helps me to engage in national and global struggles for liberation.

Feminism is a question of human rights. Feminist movements have done so much to improve our world. There have been very great changes in women's lives in the past few decades. In Kenya and many other parts of Africa, for example, girls are getting educated up to high levels, meaning that not many of them are now married off at an early age. In Ireland, the lift of the marriage bar and access to contraceptives is a great achievement. It is now acceptable to have women as heads of households. Cultural practices, such as wife inheritance (where women are inherited when their husbands die), have been abandoned. Women now own property, and can travel to every corner of the world without being accompanied by a male. There is more openness about sexuality. Millions of mothers are going out to work, and women are breaking into new industries and professions. They are elected or appointed to parliament, and even elected presidents, as in the case of Joyce Banda in Malawi and Ellen Johnson Sirleaf, the 24th President of Liberia. It is now acceptable that women can work outside the home, have children outside marriage, and have the right to control their own sexuality.

I admire the courage and strength of the women who have pushed for these changes. I also see how much still needs to be done. For example, in the 21st Century, 42 million women every year have an abortion. 21.6 million of these are unsafe, and 47,000 women die unnecessarily from complications of unsafe abortion every year.[2] In Europe, abortion is still severely restricted in three countries (Ireland, Malta and Poland). Every minute, 29 women are raped, and every 3 seconds an underage girl is forced to marry against her will. The World Health Organisation estimates that between 100 and 140 million women worldwide have undergone female genital mutilation (FGM) and 3 million girls are at risk in Africa annually. This equates to 6000 women and girls undergoing FGM daily.[3]

The growth of the global sex trade is also a threat to the dignity and survival of women and girls. Sex trafficking is a modern form of slavery for many girls, especially for those who are poor and uneducated. Can we imagine telling our daughters that they can grow up to be 'sex workers', that prostitution is now a job like any other? Millions of victims of trafficking are enslaved in the sex trade and are dying of AIDS. Women suffer exploitation and still shoulder the double burden of family and childcare. Women's traditional role as wives and mothers has not disappeared, but has been reinvented to fit in with new forms of exploitation. They are now expected to juggle all aspects of their lives and are blamed as individuals for any failings in family or work life. Women are still underrepresented in the political arena, still earn less and are the most poor.

It is this understanding of gender issues, and my belief in equality and justice that led me to mobilise African women in Ireland and thus establish AkiDwA (Swahili for sisterhood) in 2001.

The evolution of the Celtic Tiger in Ireland attracted men and women as immigrants, changing a once homogenous society into an emerging multicultural society. Demographics and diversity in Ireland could easily be noted in late 1990s as a reflection of different cultures, different languages and entertainment taking place in the streets of Dublin. According to Kelleher and Kelleher, 'over the last decade, as immigration has increased, the changing nature of Irish national identity has been accompanied by increasing ethnic and religious diversity'.[4]

The demand for services and resources saw the Irish government signing contracts with foreign governments mainly in IT, humanitarian and health service sectors. Human resource was sought from different countries, including South Africa and the Philippines. In 2002, Ireland was the third largest importer of Filipino nurses after Saudi Arabia and the UK.[5] In the same period, the number of people seeking protection from other countries increased, which led the government to implement, in 2000, a policy of dispersal. Government introduced a system of accommodation for asylum applicants, which provided them with full board and a weekly allowance of €19.10 per adult and €9.60 per child. This approach was adopted as means of controlling recent immigration trends.

Due to critical changes in the flow of immigrants, many support groups emerged to provide support and to welcome the 'stranger'. There was a mixture of reactions from the indigenous Irish, the majority of whom felt threatened by the newcomers. The fear of the unknown was very apparent. This led to incidences where immigrants became vulnerable to individual and institutional racism and discrimination.

In August 2001, a group of African women gathered at the Catherine McCauley Centre of the Sisters of Mercy in Baggot Street. For the first time, the women shared their appalling experiences of racism and how they had continued to fight verbal racial abuse and some physical abuse. Two in the group were experiencing domestic violence within their own home. The experiences of these women formed the work and objective of the group. While still at its developmental stage, the women felt the urge to reach out to other women living outside Dublin and to find out how other migrant women were coping.

CREATING SPACE AND A PLATFORM

AkiDwA women's group, at the time, was a small and reasonably young group, set up for survival and the combating of problems experienced by women. The group decided to familiarise itself with its new environment, to highlight issues and to look for support from existing women's organisations. Links and visits were made with Banúlacht, National Women's Council of Ireland, Longford Women's Link, Waterford Women's Centre and Clare Women's Network. This route of seeking solidarity with Irish indigenous women was thought to be the most effective strategy. All the women's organisations approached were very supportive and provided opportunities for migrant women to share their experiences with other women. In its early stage, AkiDwA got the opportunity to make two submissions to the Department of Justice, Equality and Law reform: one on the National Plan for Women, the other on the National Action Plan Against Racism.[6] After several meetings, the group developed a common vision – a vision of a just society, where there are equal opportunities and equal access to resources in all aspects of the society, be these social, cultural, economic or political.

The group members faced a lot of obstacles at the beginning, mainly at an individual level. Women were denied permission to attend meetings by their partners. There was a lot of violence, as women's roles changed in contrast with many African cultures where men are decision-makers in their families, and manage and control resources. Child benefit in Ireland is mainly given to the mother. Because of this, women faced huge problems vis-à-vis their husbands. Disputing the management of child benefit, some were even physically abused. AkiDwA has been working with such women over the years as victims of domestic violence. In recent times, as part of the organisation's objectives, AkiDwA has engaged men in addressing violence against women. The majority of men that attended most of its workshops alleged that the Irish laws are very protective of women, that their migrant wives had been given power, and that thus they had lost control over them.

AkiDwA has been working towards building an inclusive society, one in which all people are valued and treated with dignity. The organisation advocates for inclusive policies that recognise diversity among women and the need to be culturally sensitive while rendering services. As an organisation, we also continue to challenge institutional and individual racism, sexism, sexual harassment and exploitation, and have published research documents, such as, *No Place to Call Home: Safety and Security Issues of Women Seeking Asylum in Ireland.*[7]

AkiDwA has already done significant work to counter these issues, and continues to strengthen the voices of migrant women in Ireland by developing migrant women's capacity to participate in Irish society, and to represent themselves and their concerns with decision-makers. We achieve this through capacity-building, training, consultative meetings, conferences, research roundtables and information provision.

As an organisation, we continue to seek equality of opportunity, access and treatment for the women that we represent. However, many of us are often ignored, undermined, laughed at, and sometimes we feel like we are not listened to. But we are still hopeful and keep on moving with a positive attitude for change.

GENDER AND RACISM

Migrant women have, over the past decade, experienced racism and discrimination in Ireland in many ways, including through exploitation in the domains of reproduction, caregiving and sexuality. Black women tend to be especially subject to discrimination. In the early 2000s, many women were treated with suspicion: they were followed around shops, and some were recipients of verbal abuse. Personally, I was spat on while pregnant in 2000 outside the General Post Office and told not to bring 'another n ... r' in this country.

The failure to recognise the specific needs of migrant women and women from ethnic minorities in Ireland is itself a form of racist and gender discrimination that needs to be challenged. Migrant women often carry with them the effects of violence, rape, sexual harassment and other forms of physical and psychological trauma (including being separated from their husbands or from other members of their families). This vulnerability often causes them to hide their experiences, and may feed into their exploitation. This needs to be acknowledged in service provision, particularly, but not exclusively, in relation to culturally appropriate counselling and support. Like all non-indigenous Irish nationals, migrant women are victims of negative media representations.[8] Migrant women have been largely excluded from national planning processes and decision-making in all levels in Ireland. Therefore, migrant women's specific perspectives and views are not included in policies. AkiDwA have, over the years, been advocating for inclusive policy and the need to engage and consult with migrant women while developing laws and policy. The organisation has helped both government and non-governmental organisations to organise for consultation meetings with migrant women around the country.

Many migrant women, especially African women, have struggled and continue to struggle with managing racism directed toward them and their children. In the early days, migrant women were not comfortable letting their children go to school alone. They always escorted their children and went to meet them after school to ensure their safety. This was a protection measure, as most of the migrant children were vulnerable to racist bullying in school or on their way home. Women also highlighted their experiences of discrimination and racism while trying to access public services. Racism, in this area, came in many different forms, including in the manner and tone used by officials, in prejudiced behaviour, and sometimes in the denial of services. Others have reported sexual harassment while walking on the street or trying to access services.[9] Many migrant women members of AkiDwA have expressed reluctance to report racist incidents to Gardaí, as they experience feelings of intimidation at Garda stations, where they are asked of their immigration status and are treated with suspicion.

Acts of racism and unlawful racial discrimination, including incitement of racial hatred and racist attacks, are serious violations of human rights and should be combated by all lawful means. Ireland lacks a legal framework for this. Education is key to changing racist, xenophobic and intolerant attitudes, and to building a society based on tolerance, respect for cultural diversity and non-discrimination. This should be promoted in all sectors and should be reflected in the school curriculum, institutions of higher education, statutory and non-statutory sectors. Women's human rights, and necessary protections with regard to racism and discrimination, must be ensured through gender-mainstreaming of existing legislation and polices, and through consideration of gender within new legislation. Equality of participation and outcomes must be measured quantifiably within government services and must include gender breakdowns. The government should commit itself to responding to the specific needs of migrant women by providing culturally appropriate services and supports in relation to, for example, female genital mutilation, sexual abuse, domestic violence and forced marriages.

CAMPAIGN AGAINST DEPORTATION OF PARENTS OF IRISH CITIZENS

Since the establishment of the Republic of Ireland until the 2004 Irish Citizenship Referendum, all persons born on the island of Ireland were entitled to automatic Irish citizenship. Many migrant parents had gotten the right to reside in Ireland because of the birth right of their children. However, this was overturned in 2003, when the Supreme Court decided that non-national parents have no strong case to have the right to remain in Ireland to bring up their citizen children.[10] A cry for help came from five migrant women and members of AkiDwA, who had received deportation orders. I was working that day in Edenderry, county Meath, when the call came from one of the women crying on the phone after being served with a deportation order. She had to present herself to the authorities within fifteen days. I later learned that over one hundred women, who were members of AkiDwA, had received such a letter. I quickly contacted all migrants and other Irish friends to notify them of the panic and stress that AkiDwA members were going through. Together with Dr. Ronit Lentin (of Trinity College Dublin), we organised for an emergency meeting, and within a week over 26 people, including legal specialists, activists and academics, attended the meeting. The Coalition Against the Deportation of Irish Citizens was formed with the leadership of Dr. Lentin.

During the meeting clear strategies were developed. We were to organise for a meeting with the affected women to give information and support. AkiDwA booked Liberty Hall for the first public meeting and over three hundred people turned up. Also, parents with buggies occupied the streets, including outside City Hall. In the following months the campaign continued. The National Women's Council of Ireland held a press conference a few days before the referendum on Irish citizenship, where they cautioned the government on using women as scapegoats of its own failure in providing services to women. But the most significant and influential element of the campaign against the deportation of parents of Irish citizens was the vigil and street demonstration, both of which were held with women and children due to be deported, and were supported by the coalition.

I got the opportunity to present the views of AkiDwA to the Joint Committee on Justice, Equality, Defence and Women's Rights, and was accompanied in the Dáil by Judith Magaji, one of the women with a pending deportation. In my presentation, I emphasised the need for an immediate and fair system of hearing cases and, where necessary, the reopening of cases of non-national parents of Irish-born children. I also suggested that the government give a general amnesty, granting leave to remain to all non-national parents of children born in Ireland before the Supreme Court judgement, and argued that it would be the fairest way of dealing with all the complexities of each individual case. The requirement was that adjudications be made, and consideration be given to applications based on social justice and humanitarian considerations, rather than on the basis of negative racist stereotypes. On this point, I contended that negative racist and sexist stereotypes of Africans and African women developed around the issue of childbirth. There was a perception that the primary concern of African women, when giving birth, was to obtain leave to remain and to live on the welfare system.

Migrant parents of Irish children would have entered Ireland in a vulnerable position, and now faced the prospect of being returned home more vulnerable and in greater poverty and insecurity compared to when they arrived. Their children could expect to contend with cultures to which they hadn't been socialised and would have reduced life options. In the event of parental separation or divorce a further question arose over the custody of the child. In most African traditions priority would be given to men to take their children if they so chose, thus the mothers would again be the losers. The fears, concerns and needs of women needed to be catered for. In this respect, I pointed out that the needs of a child are best served with its mother in a safe and secure environment. Within my work in AkiDwA, I had encountered women with psychological trauma, as they envisaged the prospect of deportation and the dangerous and difficult situations to which they would return. I also highlighted specific forms of violence against which women are not protected in many African societies (for example, female genital mutilation, death sentences for alleged adultery, and domestic violence as an accepted norm in many African societies), and that these are not covered by the terms of the Geneva Convention as grounds for asylum. Nonetheless, they do warrant consideration on humanitarian grounds. Most African societies do not give priority to the mother in the case of a dispute on child custody – all the more reason for the Irish State to protect both Irish-born children and their mothers by granting leave to stay. Overall, I stressed that the best interests of the child would be served by creating an enabling environment for African women. Migrants spell opportunity and progress, and investing in a multicultural society would result in positive returns for all.

In September 2004, parents facing deportation were given the opportunity to apply for residency in Ireland. The application had only to be made by parents whose children were born not later than 31 December 2004. The 'Irish-born' unit was established within the Department of Justice to deal with applications, and the scheme ran until March 2005. Almost 18000 applications were received by the department, and over 16500 applicants were granted leave to remain for a period of two years initially. The applicants were given conditions, however, including that they should not apply for family reunification and that they had to become economically viable if their application was to be considered for renewal after two years. This was a difficult measure, since the country was entering into economic crisis. Many parents of Irish citizens ended up taking up training.

WOMEN SEEKING ASYLUM
Ireland has seen many people arriving during the last decade seeking protection. Many women, mostly lone parents, have made long journeys to Ireland in the hope of safety, security and a better life. Women may not benefit equally with men when looking for asylum. Their experiences in their countries of origin often differ from those of men. For example, women's involvement in political protest and action is not as widely publicised as

men's, and their inability to produce evidence, both oral and documentary may alter their asylum claim. The 1951 UN definition of a refugee does not incorporate gender as a ground for seeking protection, and yet many women victims of gender-specific harm, such as rape during war, honour killing, FGM and forced marriage, continue to be denied protection.[11] Ireland's rate of granting refugee status has been low compared to other countries in Europe.[12] There is a belief in Ireland that most asylum seekers are bogus, and that people are coming to Ireland to scrounge off the social welfare system. Migrant women in Ireland, in particular, were used as scapegoats for government's failure to address other problems, such as congestion in maternity hospitals and failures in provision of social housing. Myth and stereotypes surrounding women seeking asylum have reinforced racism and discrimination.

AkiDwA has challenged the treatment of women in direct provision centres, where living conditions and indefinite time periods are not conducive to bringing up children.[13] Direct provision has impacted on the psychological and physical wellbeing of women seeking asylum as mothers and women. Many immigrant women living in Ireland today are victims of gender-specific harm including female genital mutilation, marriage-related harm, violence within the family, forced sterilisation, forced prostitution and abortion, trafficking, and societal and legal discrimination. While some women asylum seekers may not qualify for refugee status under the strictest interpretation of the Geneva Convention, gender-specific harm has to be taken into account. Governments have been urged to adopt asylum gender guidelines to facilitate the needs of women seeking asylum. Countries such as Canada, Australia, and the USA have introduced such guidelines. AkiDwA has, over the years, advocated for similar gender guidelines to be adopted and implemented in Ireland.

Ireland needs to be more sympathetic in how it deals with asylum cases, especially in the cases of women and children. It is quite worrying that in recent times refugee status or protection is being denied to women from war-torn countries such as Somalia, DR Congo and Liberia, and southern and less developed countries that have very poor human rights records.[14]

FEAR, THREAT AND DEPORTATIONS

In early 2000, many people faced the threat of deportation, and actual deportations happened largely to Nigeria and Romania. Recently, women and children in the asylum system have been made to feel like criminals, and constantly feel under threat and insecure. As well as carrying the effects of specific cultural and physical abuse with them, their psychological wellbeing and that of their children has been under attack. The majority have spent five, and others eight, years in accommodation centres for asylum, only to be returned back to their countries of origin by force.

In 2005, I worked as a development coordinator with a voluntary organisation in Athlone. As part of my work, I had to support asylum seekers in Lissywoolen Accommodation Centre for asylum seekers, which is located in Athlone and is the second largest accommodation centre in Ireland. It is mainly occupied by families housed in mobile homes. The deportation of two women in particular, Elizabeth and Lyabo, which occurred on 15th March 2005, brought the community from Athlone close together. A group called Athlone Families Together was formed to campaign for Elizabeth and Lyabo to be brought back to Athlone, where they had lived for 4 years.

Three of their children were left behind. They were not given time to prepare, or to look for their children. The normal routine of reporting to the Athlone Garda Station saw them being put in a van and being informed that they were going to be returned back to Nigeria. These two women were traumatised before coming to Ireland, but they left Ireland more vulnerable and traumatised than before they had come.

Lyabo and Elizabeth spoke of the inhuman treatment and humiliation of those who were being deported at Dublin airport. 'One woman was very upset, she was very disturbed, tore her clothes off. A number of Gardaí lifted her into a wheelchair and then called a female doctor who stuck a needle into her arm'. The women said they felt they were treated like criminals, yet they had not committed any crime. While the campaign of Athlone Families Together did not succeed in bringing Lyabo and Elizabeth back to Ireland to reunite them with their children, it still managed to expose the way deportations are carried out, and the treatment of those being deported.

DEALING WITH GENDER-BASED VIOLENCE

Migrant women's experience of gender-based violence is not unique, as indigenous Irish women may also share this. However, migrant women exposed, for the first time, other forms of violence against women that were not familiar in Ireland, including female genital mutilation, forced marriages, and rape experienced during conflict in one's country of origin or during the immigration journey. AkiDwA's work on FGM goes back to its founding times. In 2000, AkiDwA joined Comhlámh, an organisation for Irish returnees from overseas, and aimed, together with other groups, to raise awareness on FGM and its impact.[15] The coalition started campaigning on the establishment of law prohibiting the practice in Ireland. AkiDwA later took the lead on FGM work, and the organisation is known for its expertise and work in this area.

Over the years, AkiDwA has carried out research, campaigned tirelessly, delivered training, and raised awareness at all levels. According to AkiDwA 2013 statistics, there were 3780 women in Ireland who had undergone FGM. The Criminal Justice (Female Genital Mutilation) Bill was passed in the two houses of the Oireachtas in March 2012, signed into law on 2 April, and commenced on 20 September. It is now a criminal offence for someone resident in Ireland to perform FGM. The maximum penalty under all sections of this new law is a fine or imprisonment for up to 14 years or both. It is also a criminal offence for someone resident in Ireland to take a girl to another country to undergo FGM. AkiDwA continues to work with the Health Service Executive and other organisations in developing a referral pathway and support for women that have undergone FGM.

Migrant women also continue to challenge issues of domestic violence among the various migrant communities in Ireland. In recent years, other organisations, such as the Immigrant Council of Ireland and Doras Luimní, have joined AkiDwA in advocating for laws and policies that protect migrant women. Often women's residency depends on the residency permit of the spouse, meaning that migrant women are more vulnerable in violent situations. Many migrant women feel they have to remain in violent relationships to avoid losing their residency by leaving a violent partner. Women seeking asylum are always at a disadvantage, as they have to expose their experience of violence to managers at their resident centres in order to receive help. Additionally, they can't leave the accommodation centre as doing so may put them at risk of losing their accommodation, which might also affect their claim for asylum.

Trafficking of women in Ireland has become a significant problem in recent years. Many women have been trafficked to Ireland for sexual exploitation or labour. Ireland has also been used as a transit country by traffickers, with most trafficked women ending up in brothels or held captive by traffickers. Organisations such as AkiDwA and the Immigrant Council of Ireland (ICI) have, in recent years, joined efforts to challenge the trafficking of women in Ireland, and ICI is leading a campaign on the issue, the Turn off the Red Light campaign. AkiDwA has also worked with the Global Alliance Against Traffic in Women, based in Thailand, and the Black Association of Women Step Out (BAWSO), based in the UK.

Rape continues to be used as a weapon of war in many developing countries, and many women now living in Ireland carry with them the trauma of experiencing rape during conflict in their country of origin. AkiDwA has been involved in the development of Ireland's National Action Plan for Implementation of UNSCR 1325 on women in armed conflict.[16] The Irish government cannot continue to ignore the fact that there are women living in Ireland, who have suffered and still suffer with trauma owing to their experience of armed conflict. AkiDwA continues to advocate for involvement and engagement of such women. The organisation is involved in the monitoring of the implementation of the National Action Plan.

PARTICIPATION AND REPRESENTATION

'Opportunities, not empathy' is a verse that I use quite a lot while advocating for the representation of migrants in Ireland. According to Ireland's 2011 census, 12% of residents in Ireland classify themselves as 'non-Irish nationals', and represent 199 different nations.[17] However, the level of democratic participation by immigrants in Ireland is very low. Despite the emergence of a relatively large number of organisations focusing on integration, representation of migrants is not reflective of the migrant population. AkiDwA has been a member of the National Women's Council of Ireland (NWCI) since its foundation. But while the organisation supports the campaign to increase women in decision-making, AkiDwA also has to advocate and challenge the lack of encouragement and support to have migrant women involved in all levels of decision-making. Organisations such as the NWCI have taken up this step by reviewing their policy on board membership, and by ensuring they are maximally inclusive. Migrants, particularly women, find it difficult to get involved at any level due to their experience of discrimination, racism and marginalisation. Ireland has changed significantly in the last twenty years. Its diversity should be reflected in all public spheres. Better policies and laws need to be put into place to ensure people from different backgrounds are involved in all levels of decision-making.

In 2003, AkiDwA received funding from the Department of Foreign Affairs to develop and deliver training to migrant women, mainly to equip them with skills so that they can represent themselves and participate fully in meetings. The organisation has, over the years, delivered training on capacity-building to more than two thousand migrant women. AkiDwA has previously been contacted by organisations and government departments to recommend women to be involved in decision-making at regional level. One of the greatest challenges in keeping women in representation and participation spaces has been barriers such as childcare and travelling expenses. Many migrant women have more than one child, and as they lack a family support network, they find it challenging to leave their children with strangers. There has been a tendency to treat migrant women's representation and participation at events as a token of inclusion. Having one or two migrant women in a meeting does not mean that they represent the whole migrant community. While challenging patriarchal society, it is very important that we acknowledge, as feminists, the diversity among women and the need to have diverse representation at all times.

CONCLUSION

Migrant women's activism in Ireland has been fraught with challenges. However, many migrant women now feel that this activism is so much part and parcel of their new home in Ireland. While women worldwide share similar experiences of marginalisation and discrimination, we must acknowledge the diversity among women and make ourselves aware of different experiences and issues affecting women around the world. In Ireland today, we do not need to travel to Afghanistan, Iraq, Congo, Somalia, Sudan, or Algeria to learn about the circumstances of women, as they largely live among us. We therefore need to engage and reach out further to increase our self-awareness. As feminists, we have a responsibility to be aware of the women in the world around us. We must fight to give those women the same freedoms we demand for ourselves.

NOTES

1   Peter Anny-Nzekwue, *Xclusive Magazine*, Issue 06, 2006.
2   World Health Organisation, *Unsafe Abortion: Global and Regional Estimates of the Incidence of Unsafe Abortion and Associated Mortality in 2008*, 6th edition, 2011, p. 1.
3   AkiDwA and Royal College of Surgeons, *Female Genital Mutilation: Information for Healthcare Professionals Working in Ireland*, 2008, p. 7.

4   Patricia Kelleher and Carmel Kelleher, *Voices of Immigrants: The Challenges of Inclusion* (Dublin, Immigrant Council of Ireland, 2004), p. 3.

5   Nicola Yeates, 'Changing Places: Ireland in the International Division of Reproductive Labour', *Translocations: The Irish Migration, Race, and Social Transformation Review*, Vol 1, No. 1, 2006.

6   AkiDwA and Islamic Cultural Centre of Ireland Women's Project, 'Submission on the National Action Plan Against Racism in Ireland', August 2002, accessed 04/05/2013 online at http://www.akidwa.ie/publications/general-publications/file/4-the-national-action-plan-against-racism-in-ireland-napar.html

7   AkiDwA, *No Place to Call Home: Safety and Security Issues of Women Seeking Asylum in Ireland*, AkiDwA stakeholders survey report, 2012.

8   Eithne Luibhéid, 'Globalization and Sexuality: Redrawing Racial and National Boundaries through Discourses of Childbearing' in Ronit Lentin and Eithne Luibhéid (eds), *Women's Movement: Migrant Women Transforming Ireland* (Dublin, Trinity College, 2003), p. 82.

9   AkiDwA, *Am Only Saying it Now: Experiences of Women Seeking Asylum in Ireland, 2010*, accessed online 07/05/2013 at http://www.akidwa.ie/publications/women-and-asylum/file/1-am-only-saying-it-now-experiences-of-women-seeking-asylum-in-ireland.html, p. 20.

10   Ronit Lentin, '"There is no Movement": A Brief History of Migrant-Led Activism in Ireland' in Ronit Lentin and Elena Moreo (eds), *Migrant Activism and Integration from Below in Ireland* (London, Palgrave, 2012), p. 22.

11   AkiDwA, *Briefing Paper: Gender Guidelines in Asylum Processes in Ireland*, 2008, p. 5

12   Aideen Sheehan, 'Only 25 Granted Asylum Last Year, Lowest Rate in EU', *Irish Independent*, 30 November 2012.

13   Direct provision is a means of meeting the basic needs of food and shelter for asylum seekers directly, rather than by cash payment, while their claims for refugee status are being processed. Direct provision commenced on 10 April 2000, and from then on, asylum seekers have received full board accommodation and personal allowances of €19.10 per adult and €9.60 per child per week.

14 Anti-Deportation Ireland, *Preliminary Report on Deportation in Ireland: The Human and Economic Costs of Deportation*, 2012.

15 The organisations involved were AkiDwA, Amnesty International, Barnados, Cairde, Children's Rights Alliance, Christian Aid, Integrating Centre, Integration of Children in Ireland, Irish Family Planning Association, National Women's Council Ireland, Somali Community Ireland, Somali Community Youth Group, UNICEF.

16 Department of Foreign Affairs, *Ireland's National Action Plan for Implementation of UNSCR 1325, 2011–2014*, accessed on 05/05/2013 at http://www.peacewomen.org/assets/file/National ActionPlans/ire_nap_nov2011.pdf

17 Central Statistics Office, *Census 2011: Profile 6 (Migration and Diversity)*, 2012, pp 7–8.

RESPECT AND RESPECTABILITY

Susan McKay

1

Opening the Irish Feminist Network's 2012 conference, the poet Phil McCarthy talked about a 'deeply subversive vision', and this is what feminism must always be.[1] If it ceases to be that, and becomes instead a cosy circle to which only those who affirm its established values are admitted, then it is no longer working in the interests of the women outside that circle. It will not compel their respect or support; it has no right to claim to represent them; and it won't change a thing.

It was moving to enter that room full of young feminists at the Sean O'Casey Centre, ready for action and willing to engage with women from other generations of feminism. This suggests a generosity of spirit, because it must be frustrating to hear the constant refrain from older feminists: 'young women nowadays don't know how lucky they are, how hard we had to fight for things they take for granted, etcetera'. Feminism has to be inter-generational, but it will always be the prerogative of the young to break the mould, to challenge, defy and even overthrow those who've gone before them.

2

I'm not sure what wave of feminism I belong to, or belonged to. All I know is that it has always been very damn stormy on this particular sea. My first active engagement was as a volunteer in the Dublin Rape Crisis Centre in 1979, one of the first intake of volunteers to join the original group. I moved to Belfast in 1981 and became one of the founders of the Belfast Rape Crisis Centre. We quickly found that the violence of the conflict was masking horrific levels of violence against women and children, some of it carried out by men who saw themselves as heroes within their communities and felt that they had a right to do as they pleased to women and children. The legacy of that silencing of women is still emerging.

After Belfast, I moved to Sligo to run a centre for young unemployed people. The needs of the young women who used it included information about contraception and counselling about abortion. Providing this was regarded as subversive by some of those dominant in youth services in the town at the time, particularly by the Catholic Church. It still is.

Histories of the 1980s tend to emphasise the gloom as church and state rallied and combined to knock back gains made by activists in the 1970s, and economic recession ensured that funds for existing feminist activities were slashed while new projects struggled on social welfare-type schemes or on the work of volunteers.

The election of Mary Robinson as President in 1990 was a welcome and wonderful break in the clouds.

In the 1990s, as a journalist, I became my newspaper's first female Northern Ireland correspondent. I included women in my stories, and wrote about issues relevant to women, including explicitly feminist ones. My first book, *Sophia's Story*, is the biography of a young woman who overcame her brutal father, and then took on the state which had allowed him to dominate and violate his family.[2] I wrote the book in close co-operation with Sophia and we got many messages from women for whom it had proved a catalyst to escape from intolerable situations.

The only bad review we got was from a Northern Irish feminist magazine. The reviewer argued that we should have put more blame on Sophia's mother. This despite the fact that in the book, Sophia is quoted saying of her mother: 'she could not save us – she was one of us'.[3]

3

In 2012 I heard Nell McCafferty and Margaret Mac Curtain – both brilliant women who have made a huge contribution to feminism in this country – talking on the radio about how the second wave of feminism had ended after the 1980s, and that while feminism might return some day, it was, for the time being, over. As I was the Director of the National Women's Council of Ireland at the time, this was demoralising.

Nell, in her time, was the cheeky young upstart who came down to Dublin fresh from the North with its street drama of riots and revolutionary demands, to urge a bit of radical action in the South. It was a mark of the wisdom of the late Hilda Tweedy, founder of the Irish Housewives Association, that she welcomed and understood the scorn the ungrateful young poured on all that was being done for the cause of women's rights. She was however, frustrated by the fact that, as she put it, 'so many people think that the women's movement was born on some mystical date in 1970', when in reality it had been 'a long continuous battle ... each generation adding something to the achievements of the past'.[4]

In her book *Sisters*, the late June Levine described the yielding of the Irish Women's Liberation Movement to Irishwomen United, and noted that the energy and brilliance of the new young feminists was such that 'change was inevitable'.[5]

Those women too got older, more set in their ways. They got nostalgic for their own youth and they did not hand over the mantle graciously. This is, I think, partly a wider problem with the sixties generation. The second wave of Irish feminists, with honourable exceptions, seemed not to notice and certainly not to acknowledge those who built on the ground they broke, the generation that set up services and began to fight for policy change at local, national and international levels. The contraceptive train was a wonderful and iconoclastic gesture, but it was to take hard and unglamourous toil by many other people to bring widespread access to contraception to Ireland.

4

Feminists who set up or run institutions need to open them to the young, to share the limited resources available, and to resist the urge to hold onto control and to 'mammy'. When I was at the NWCI, we got funding from Atlantic Philanthropies for a project designed by young women. We designed a suite of offices in our new premises so that the project could have its own space.

While I was researching my book on the history of the Dublin Rape Crisis Centre (DRCC), *Without Fear*, Olive Braiden spoke about starting out with a list of 'notables' when becoming a director and setting up the Centre's first board in 1990.[6] The DRCC was in trouble – it was seen as being too radical, it had not managed well the paltry funding that had been allocated to it, and now it was being starved of state funds. One of the notables, the distinguished journalist Cathal MacCoille, said he realised that Braiden's tactic was to give the beleagured organisation an establishment image. This worked and the Centre survived.

However, this model of activism has its tensions. Certainly, the conflict between feminist radicalism and the imperative of holding on to state funding is one that has continued to dog Irish feminist organisations. Protecting the institution may come into conflict with the need to be radical in making demands on the state on behalf of women. It may be deemed safer to remain silent, or at least to tone down a critique that is met with disapproval.

Time and again the state has used the crude tactic of divide and conquer when it comes to funding. It has done so in recent years in its dealings with feminist organisations that struggle valiantly to change attitudes and policies, and that provide services for women who are victims of domestic and sexual violence. The excellent work those organisations do continues – but activists have been hurt and have hurt others to no good end.

5

Feminists have played their part in every attempt at revolution in this country but the cause of women has always had to wait. Anna Parnell was so wounded by how the Ladies' Land League was dismissed that she left Ireland and said she would never trust an Irish man again. The 1937 constitution was a travesty of the 1916 ideals. The Women's Coalition played a significant role in bringing about the Good Friday Agreement, not least in the way it supported other small parties that had little political experience. However, it got shouldered aside once the new regime took hold, and Northern Irish politics remains intensely male.

When the recession hit, Fianna Fáil dismissed arguments it had nominally accepted – arguements that were part of the National Women's Strategy, that included the active promotion of women's equality, not only as a matter of justice, but as an essential driver of economic recovery. The Fine Gael-Labour coalition continued the damage.

6

Gemma Hussey recalled bringing a bill to tackle rape to the Senate in 1979: 'you were regarded with terrible suspicion. What you were up against was a strange hostility that gave you a shock each time you encountered it'.[7] Hatred, distrust and disrespect of women have surfaced again and again, notably in the debate about a woman's right to control her own fertility.

Women have internalised some of this absence of respect. A woman who has been raped is likely to feel as much shame as she feels rage, and often the shame will silence her, turn her rage loose on herself. Women in a male dominated society may choose the tactic of silence if to speak means denigration. Until a few years ago, women rarely spoke about having chosen to terminate a pregnancy. This, thankfully, is changing, particularly in the aftermath of the Savita Halappanavar tragedy.

Feminism is not, generally, respected. During one interview I did on Irish radio the presenter talked over all of my answers to his sneery questions. Feminist blogs and articles often provoke outbursts of misogyny in the comments section. To counter this, feminism must open up its imagination. It must constantly seek to renew itself, to explore ideas and identify new voices in all kinds of disciplines. Sexism isn't funny but tackling it can be, and sometimes humour is a powerful weapon against those who believe feminists incapable of it. These are often people who are themselves anything but amusing.

Unfortunately, some feminists are only comfortable with women as victims in need of assistance. They don't know how to tackle the phenomenon of anti-feminist women, and they are often deeply ambivalent about their own leaders. This makes for a sullen and defensive politics. Meanwhile, the conservative men who still dominate Irish society blithely continue to assist other men in their own image up the ladder. It is good to see young women and men setting up new and upbeat campaigns to take on the issue of the under-representation of feminists in Irish public life, and doing so with flair and obvious enjoyment.

7

I have met brilliant women who are strongly feminist in their practice – in business, politics and community development – but who shudder at the thought of working in 'the women's sector'. They point to examples of the classic pattern of female bullying, the retreat to the clique, jobs for the girls, and the hoarding of resources that should be shared. They deplore the exclusion of critical voices, the closing of ranks against dissenters, the sheer bitchiness.

It is certainly true that the history of Irish feminism is littered with women who have been driven to feminism by the injustices of a male dominated society and driven out of feminism by the injustices of feminists. Too many women have been 'disappeared' from our collective memory because it is inconvenient or embarrassing to talk about them. Too many women become activists in a spirit of idealism only to be traumatised by their experience of it. Sisterhood is powerful, we used to say, and often it wonderfully is, but sisterhood turned sour can be powerfully destructive. June Levine describes the 'tyrannical superego' of the women's movement in the 1970s, the voice which interrogated women constantly as to their loyalty to the cause. It created, she noted, a dense and frightening claustrophobia.[8]

There is something terribly complacent about those within the women's movement who deplore the unwillingness of many women, including young women, to identify themselves as feminists, without admitting that maybe that is because these women just don't like and can't identify with what they see. You have to be inspired if you are to engage in feminist activism. You have to inspire if you wish to be trusted to lead the way.

There are many excellent women's groups and organisations in this country, and some of the best of them have a feminist ethos that encourages and welcomes the participation of women of all ages and backgrounds. There are groups that reflect the diversity of women from all around the world who are now in Ireland with their own gendered issues. They remind us that there is an urgent need today for a global perspective in feminism.

8

The new, young feminist groupings have huge potential – and they must be supported, as must the voices of individual young women and men who speak out against sexism. As young feminists you have new ideas on how to tackle old oppressions, and you have new experiences of sexism and misogyny. You also have new media with which to communicate in ways many older feminists just don't, for the most part, understand.

The times they are a changing. Always. Those who fear what they can't understand when faced with the feminism of the young should heed the great Irish designer, Joan Bergin, who, speaking after she won an Irish Tatler Woman of the Year Award in 2009, urged women to help younger women in every possible way. 'They are nipping at your heels', she said. 'They need our support, and we need them to take over from us'.[9]

And for those of you who are young and nipping, by all means, respect the magnificent work that has gone before, but demand respect as well and a share of the scarce resources that are made available for feminist work. Remember what the poet said, 'feminism is a deeply subversive vision'. The women's movement in Ireland will fade into insignificance unless it is revived by a new generation riding a new wave. Make solidarity with others who share your feminist vision, your guiding principle, constantly review the way you put your vision into practice, be honest, and let no one stand in your way.

NOTES

1   This essay is based on my speech at the IFN conference held on 19 May 2012.

2   Susan McKay, *Sophia's Story* (Dublin, Gill and Macmillan, 1998).

3   McKay, *Sophia's Story*, p. 174.

4   Hilda Tweedy quoted in *Hilda Tweedy and the Irish Housewives Association: Links in the Chain* edited by Alan Hayes (Dublin, Arlen House, 2012), p. 143.

5   June Levine, *Sisters* (Dublin, Ward River Press, 1982), p. 282.

6   Susan McKay, *Without Fear: 25 Years of the Dublin Rape Crisis Centre* (Dublin, New Island, 2005), p. 144.

7   McKay, *Without Fear*, p. 29. Gemma Hussey is a former Fine Gael politician, who acted as the party's spokesperson on Women's Affairs from 1981–1982, and was a founder member of the Women's Political Association. See also Claire McGing's contribution to this volume.

8   Levine, *Sisters*, p. 268.

9   Bergin quoted in Hayes (ed.), *Hilda Tweedy and the Irish Housewives Association*, p. 144.

'YOU MEMORY THAT?'
THEORISING FEMINISM IN IRELAND THROUGH FEMINIST STORYTELLING AND REMEMORY

Clara Fischer

... I turned to Professor Trevelyan again to see what history meant to him. I found by looking at his chapter headings that it means – 'The Manor Court and the Methods of Open-field Agriculture ... The Cistercians and Sheep-farming ... The Crusades ... The University ... The House of Commons ... The Hundred Years' War ... The Wars of the Roses ... The Renaissance Scholars ... The Dissolution of the Monasteries ... Agrarian and Religious Strife ... The Origin of English Sea-power ... The Armada ...' and so on. Occasionally an individual woman is mentioned, an Elizabeth, or a Mary; a queen or a great lady. But by no possible means could middle-class women with nothing but brains and character at their command have taken part in any one of the great movements which, brought together, constitute the historian's view of the past.[1]

With this quote, Virginia Woolf relates the pervasiveness of male endeavour and pursuit passed down to us through the ages in tomes of recorded material collectively termed 'history', while illustrating the exclusion of women from such stories of import told about the past. Writing almost a hundred years ago, Woolf could not have anticipated the increased interest women's lives and thought would garner throughout the twentieth and twenty-first centuries. And yet, her basic exhortation to record and learn more of women is as relevant now as it was then. Indeed, despite efforts by feminist academics to unearth women's preoccupations – as Woolf says, 'what they did from eight in the morning to eight at night'[2] – such work has only recently intensified. Forty years of herstory seems like a drop in the ocean when it comes to our knowledge of womankind.

While this work is of course invaluable, and increasingly accepted, even by the mainstream, as valid and worthwhile scholarly pursuit, the existing relative lack of documentation on women's lives, beliefs, desires, and activities, should alert us to the continued need for recording our experiences and thinking. For, the danger in women's omission lies not just in our metaphorical erasure, but also in the very real-life denigration of women that comes with elisions and one-sided historical accounts of events and ideas. If women are absent as agents, or merely starring in bit part roles in the stories we tell each other about the past, then the likelihood of women being seen as complete human beings is diminished. The sad consequences of this are evinced by the many inequalities women continue to be subjected to, as highlighted by the contributions in this book.

Although we may know little about women, certainly compared to men, during the Crusades or the Hundred Years War, the Nine Years' War in Ulster or the Battle of Clontarf, we do know one 'great movement' women were and are a part of – the feminist movement. Of course, there is recovery work to be done in this regard also, as more and more unknown women are gradually rescued from obscurity, and their resistance to patriarchy, since time immemorial, comes to be revealed by historians. In Ireland, as elsewhere, such feminist documenting has proven invaluable to successive generations of women, who are enabled to learn from what has come before.

This chapter will form an instance of feminist recording by documenting and exploring aspects of contemporary Irish feminism. In particular, it will capture the activities and aspirations of recently formed feminist group, the Irish Feminist Network (IFN). Since the impetus for such recording lies in the need for present and future knowing and remembering, my account will be contextualised through a theoretical exploration of feminist memory and the affective, reflexive understanding feminists hold of feminism itself. Under discussion, then, will be the stories we tell each other about feminism, positioned relative to my original story of the Irish Feminist Network.[3] It should be emphasised that the latter is of course *my* story – that is, a partial account, reflective of my interpretation of and engagement with the IFN. I make no claim to an objective retelling of singular Truth, nor do I purport to describe feminist activism in Ireland exhaustively or as a whole. What follows represents merely a 'slice' of feminist action and thought as seen through my eyes – a story told to record and make sense of the current renaissance of feminism in Ireland; a story told to add to the many stories we tell each other under the aegis of 'history'.

STORIES OF FEMINISM

At the outset, it should be noted that the very assertion that feminism is indeed undergoing a period of renewed invigoration could be construed as controversial. Feminist historiography has perpetuated the story of intensification and slackening of feminism by drawing upon the wave metaphor. This metaphor has been critiqued, as it masks pre-suffrage feminism and feminism of assumed 'trough' periods, while at the same time elevating crest periods as pinnacles of feminist endeavour. On the other hand, 'first', 'second', 'third' and even 'fourth wave feminism' are terms routinely used as a shorthand with which to refer to certain periods in feminist history. They immediately denote a certain time, and bring to mind specific political achievements and well-known feminist personalities. In Ireland, the first wave is synonymous with Hanna Sheehy Skeffington and the franchise, while the second wave evokes images of the famous contraceptive train, and high-profile activists such as Mary Robinson and Nell McCafferty. It is by now generally acknowledged, though, that a reduction of feminist history to peaks and lows significantly diminishes the role played by less prominent feminists, by marginalised women, and by groups often unjustly deemed too conservative and conformist to carry the label 'feminist'. Organisations such as the Irish Countrywomen's Association, for instance, have only recently been credited with undertaking feminist work during assumed trough *and* crest periods of the twentieth century.[4]

And yet, the wave metaphor is appealing in its ability to capture moments of heightened feminist energy. Indeed, it seems instinctively accurate to acknowledge increased levels of feminist action during certain periods. While the precise causes giving rise to this might be debated,[5] certain eras appear to have witnessed a more or less intense feminist activism. Much of this can be gleaned from the prevalence of activist groups at a certain time, from the level of campaigning, from the impact feminism has on public discourse, from the support for feminism in formal organisations and institutions, from the incidence of mass mobilisation, media engagement and other opportunities for feminist consciousness-raising. With that said, I think it is fair to characterise the present time as another period of enhanced feminist engagement, although perhaps not in the sense of entailing the achievement of a feminist pinnacle, the crest of the contemporary, fourth wave. Indeed, given that the extreme characterisation of feminism in terms of peaks and lows (action and non-action) risks erasing certain feminist experiences, it might be best to understand the wave metaphor in terms of undulating 'ebbs and flows',[6] of continuous, ever-present movement that sometimes eddies and intensifies, and sometimes constitutes stiller waters.[7]

The story of the Irish Feminist Network needs to be understood within this context, then – within the meta-story of feminist ebbs and flows in Ireland, and the sub-stories that are told by feminists about feminist movements as such. The latter tales have, perhaps, not always painted a rosy picture of feminist accord, and a generational divide has sometimes emerged from these stories which often ardently champion allegiance to a certain feminist wave. The announcement of a third feminist wave in the 1990s, for instance, was framed in terms of a clear differentiation from perceived second wave ideology and practice. It professed its own, new values of pluralism, spontaneity, and fluidity, and juxtaposed these to the rigidity of a seemingly monolithic, overbearing second wave feminism.[8]

While it is hardly surprising that successive generations of feminists wish to lay claim to their unique experiences, the generationally reactive reading of feminist waves has proven to be somewhat problematic. Debates concerning the relationship, or non-relationship as the case may be, of second and third wave feminists, have sometimes resembled spats between a petulant child and her stern, defensive mother. At the very heart of this lies the telling of feminist stories, with some self-identified third wave feminists telling one story about the second wave (homogenous, disapproving, overshadowing, essentialist) and second wave feminists telling another (encompassing the very pluralism and diversity the third wave espouses as quintessentially 'third wave').[9] Conversely, the third wave has been characterised as uncritical, consumerist, unduly influenced by popular culture, and expressive of an internalised anti-feminism.

It has been pointed out that the sometimes adversarial and contradictory narrative of successive feminist waves can feed into patriarchal backlash movements, and may be unnecessarily divisive.[10] On the other hand, conflict among feminists may, in itself, create a certain energy that propels movements forward, and invites reflexivity and reassessment of feminist storytelling. Central to such analyses of feminist stories should be what has been termed the 'affective economy of feminism'.[11] In her 'Telling Feminist Stories', Clare Hemmings argues that feminist work is heavily imbued with emotion, hence the need to conceptualise feminist stories not just in theoretical terms, but also in affective terms. Thus, 'feminist emotion … is central to the feminist stories we tell, and the way that we tell them. Challenges to these stories, from within as well as outside feminism, are frequently experienced and responded to at an emotional level, and as a result an account of ways of telling feminist stories needs to be attentive to the affective as well as technical ways in which our stories about the recent feminist past work'.[12]

It is precisely because we care, because we are emotionally invested in feminism, that feminist storytelling is affectively important, and can be a source of great pleasure or hurt. The content of feminist stories matters, as feminism matters to us. Hemmings critiques the common story of steadfast feminist progression from essentialist, monolithic second wave to post-structuralist, diverse third wave feminism, and shows how the creation and reproduction of this story is carefully implemented through misleading or exclusionary citation practices in feminist texts.

At this juncture, it might be said that much of the above does not apply in an Irish context. Indeed, I agree that on the face of it, there seems to be less of a polarisation between feminist generations in Ireland, with some prominent, established feminists working alongside their younger counterparts. Much of this might be attributable to Ireland being a small country, with an attendant smaller cadre of active feminists, and a history of intense political hostility toward feminism.[13] One could speculate on the need, in such a setting, for increased solidarity and cohesiveness for sustaining campaigns and feminist organising. Jo Reger's model of 'political generation' supports such a reading, as she understands feminist waves to be structured by the specific socio-political, historical context that spurs people from different generations, backgrounds and ideologies to become activists at a particular moment. On this account, more hostile political contexts result in diminished disidentification and increased cross-generational alliance-building, while contexts more open or conducive to feminism allow for greater dissension among feminists.[14] Recent research also suggests that the partial consolidation of feminism in Ireland into state feminism has had an arguably greater impact on the nature of feminist accord and discord than the 'progress' narrative from second to third wave feminism.[15]

Hemmings' work on feminist storytelling does resonate somewhat, though, with the Irish experience in the context of the second dominant narrative identified by her – the narrative of loss. This story establishes second wave feminism as a politically committed force for change that is undermined and eventually surpassed through academic corruption and ideological splintering. Post-structuralism is upheld as the final death knell of an already career-driven feminist enterprise, as the golden age of 1970s feminism is forever lost to apolitical fragmentation. Dean takes this reading of feminist storytelling further, and assesses the effective erasure this narrative entails for younger feminist activists. In 'On the March or on the Margins?' he examines why the feminist story of loss continues to hold traction in the UK, despite empirical evidence refuting any lack of interest by younger women in feminism and political activism. It seems that although a younger generation of feminists has been increasingly visible in media, activist and academic fora, 'attachments to loss remain remarkably intransigent'.[16]

This is also the case in Ireland. Despite the proliferation of younger feminists' work, it is not uncommon to hear the mantra that young people are apolitical, and that younger women, in particular, only come to see the value of feminism – if at all – when they encounter discrimination later on in life, such as when they are overlooked for promotion or experience parenthood for the first time.[17] Hence, prominent feminists, such as Nell McCafferty, have announced the present-day decline of feminism in Ireland.[18] While it is true that Celtic Tiger Ireland disparaged all dissenting voices – including feminist ones – and its reduction of social and political life to a rampant economism discouraged questioning, critical analysis and thought, feminism did not disappear during the boom years. Moreoever, Ireland today is a very different place than it was even five years ago.

In the wake of the banking crisis, economic recession and troika bail-out programme – not to mention the huge human cost incurred through the political mismanagement of our affairs – public discourse in Ireland has sought to make sense of the values and mind-set that gave rise to our speedy economic success and spectacular subsequent bust.[19] Terms such as 'groupthink' are now part of the common vocabulary, and yet, the connection to gender and marginalisation of women in spheres of influence is less often made in mainstream debates on such issues.[20] Many younger women, though, who are particularly disadvantaged by mass youth unemployment, forced emigration, rises in student fees, and cuts to services and welfare provisions, have been making that connection, and have questioned established political and moral authority on a range of gender equality issues. It is no coincidence that Ireland has seen a particularly intense reengagement with feminism since the onset of the economic crisis.

Given the erasure of younger women's feminism by the perpetuation of the affective story of feminist loss, it is perhaps time now to counter the contemporary 'death of feminism' narrative by setting out, in detail, the recent activities of some younger feminist activists in Ireland.[21] I shall do so by drawing upon my experiences with the Irish Feminist Network.

STORY OF THE IRISH FEMINIST NETWORK

The Irish Feminist Network was set up in 2010 by a group of Masters students from the Centre for Gender and Women's Studies, Trinity College Dublin, in response to the perceived need for a space specifically dedicated to younger feminists. When I joined as a co-ordinator in 2011, it had already undergone several transformations, reflecting the transitory nature of people's lives in mid-economic crisis Ireland – a circumstance that is to date unchanged. The then sole co-ordinator of the network, Madeline Hawke, had published an ad encouraging new people to take over the reins of coordination with a view to building upon the already considerable achievements of the IFN. The latter included a discussion group called 'Feminism in the Pub', which travelled across the country; an International Women's Day event, 'Suffragette City'; a Reclaim the Night march; and a series of videos showcasing young women leaders entitled 'Y-Lead?'[22] Several women replied to Madeline's ad, and in July 2011 five of us – Emma Regan, Jessica Connor, Alison Spillane, Erin Gell and I – assumed our voluntary posts as IFN co-ordinators. Since then, the IFN has undergone further changes, with Amanda, Colette Fahy, Emer Delaney, Jennifer Wilson, and Claire Marshall coming on board, and previous coordinators moving on.[23] During my two years with the IFN, I've felt privileged to know these women, and to further develop the work of the network.

The Irish Feminist Network marches in the Pride Parade, Dublin, 2012 © Karina Bracken

Back in 2011, it was decided that we needed a statement of priorities and values, hence a Strategic Plan was written, which outlined five key strategic areas for us to focus on: economic gender justice, reproductive freedom, prostitution and sex trafficking, political representation, and engaging people in feminism.[24] Since then, we have been active in each of these in advocacy and campaigning, outreach and events, and policy and research. On the theme of economic gender justice, we initiated a campaign on Equality Budgeting, which seeks equality-proofing of economic policy measures, the publication of draft budgets, and increased transparency and engagement of stakeholders in political decision-making.[25] Having been established for just eleven months, the Equality Budgeting Campaign, a broad coalition of civil society organisations and concerned individuals,[26] saw legislation giving effect to its goals tabled in our national parliament on 2 July 2013 by Sinn Féin. The bill was rejected by the Fine Gael-Labour government, however, all members of the opposition voted in its favour. It will be reintroduced in the Senate at a later stage, as we continue to work with elected representatives on making government accountable for detrimental political decisions taken largely in secret, by four men, and with disproportionate impact on women and many marginalised sections of our society.[27]

Other campaigns we are involved with include the Turn Off the Red Light Campaign, which has forced a review of current prostitution legislation in Ireland; and the Abortion Rights Campaign,[28] which comprises several pro-choice, feminist and women's organisations, and was set up in the wake of the tragic death of Savita Halappanavar.[29] We've contributed to national and local debates on these, as well as other justice and equality issues, by giving interviews, participating in and organising press conferences, writing articles and blog posts, distributing press releases, utilising social media, and speaking at seminars, debates and activist meetings. Our events have also provided a great opportunity for collective reflection on gender-related topics. In May 2012, we organised a conference on the theme 'Feminist Activism in Ireland: Past, Present and Future', with the aim of creating a dialogue between different generations of feminists in Ireland, allowing for a pooling of intellectual resources and knowledge for future activism.[30] As part of the Equality Budgeting Campaign, we also organised a seminar on 'Equality in Policymaking',[31] held a letter-writing group on reproductive rights,[32] screened and toured feminist movies,[33] and facilitated monthly discussion groups and a feminist book club.

We've collated research and policy, and have made several submissions to Oireachtas committees and government departments (including on proposed abortion legislation and improving the lives of children and young people).[34] We successfully applied for a grant from the Community Foundation of Ireland's Women's Fund to run a training programme for young women activists, and also obtained funding for the collation of an information booklet on Equality Budgeting from the Equality Authority of Ireland. Good fun was had at photo stunts we organised or took part in,[35] as were protests and marches we joined with our purple and white banner.[36] At the 2013 National Women's Council AGM, we proposed a motion that will see a woman under the age of 27 sit on the NWCI board from here on in.[37] Basic logistics and organisational infrastructure, such as the setting up of websites, social media accounts, bank accounts, and incorporation for charity status, were also undertaken.

All of these activities took place with a view to providing an explicitly feminist voice in contemporary political debates, to open up intellectual fora and cultural spaces for feminists in Ireland, and to be part of a general enthusiasm for feminist movement building, which women as young as fourteen were expressing to us. My involvement with the IFN has been wonderful and exciting, but also sometimes draining. In a climate where government and philanthropic funding are simply missing, it is difficult to sustain work. As the network continues, so will debates concerning issues we haven't quite yet managed to resolve around sustainability, the building of a responsive members-based organisation, and structure. With that said, I've learnt so many new skills, and feel grateful for the friendships I've made.

Given the above, it should be clear that the Irish Feminist Network has been rather busy. Unless one does not engage with any kind of media at all, it is likely that one will have heard of us, especially in activist circles.[38] Furthermore, we are just one of many groups, campaigns, university societies and feminist blogs that have sprung up in recent years (see for example, Feminist Open Forum, Action on X, Cork Feminista, 50:50 Group, Rag, Sibéal, UCC Feminist Society, NUI Galway Feminist Society, the Anti Room, and Consider the Tea Cosy). It remains to be seen why, then, in the face of ample evidence to the contrary, the story of feminist loss persists.

FEMINIST LOSS NARRATIVES IN IRELAND

The tale of a feminism lost by an apolitical, even anti-feminist, younger generation is nothing new.[39] Sadly, though, its persistence results not only in the erasure of much contemporary feminism, but also runs the risk of 'lead[ing] to a politics marked by moralism, defeatism and conservatism'.[40] Activists in the UK have described their frustration at the dogged claim that young women aren't political in vivid terms, with one activist noting she was 'frantically waving the feminist flag, jumping up and down, blowing a whistle, tearing my hair out'.[41] Many Irish feminists empathise with this sense of invisibility, especially when the 'modern-day-lack-of-interest-in-feminism' story is trotted out yet again at women's conferences, in the media, or in academic fora. As Cork Feminista's Linda Kelly writes, 'for me, the problem isn't that there are no young feminists, the problem is that the myth has been propagated to the point where it is now accepted as fact. The result is devastating – a generation of excited and passionate activists is slowly being made to feel invisible'.[42]

The constant repetition of the claim that young women are apolitical and anti-feminist, has resulted in the claim's assumed status as self-evident truth, when in fact, it bears no correlation with empirical accounts of contemporary feminism. Sara Ahmed calls this the 'stickiness' of affect,[43] which in Ireland means that young women become automatically associated with anti-feminism, or indeed, with a superficiality that falls short of 'real' feminism. For, the story of feminist loss asserts either the complete disavowal of feminism by young women, or the inadequacy of their version of feminism, which, according to the storyteller, doesn't count as feminism at all.[44] The affective, emotional clinging to these clearly misleading interpretations of young women's relationship to feminism thus functions through a truism that is repeated continuously, and that clouds any potential alternative understanding of young women and feminism. And yet, there must be something deeper to the affective story of feminist loss than mere repetition. Should the emotional trauma caused by feminist loss not be healed by the obvious resurgence of feminism in recent years? Is repetition really so powerful as to dissuade feminists from recognising other feminists?

Let me further explore this idea of loss and trauma by drawing upon Toni Morrison's famous novel, *Beloved*. Set in post-American Civil War America, Morrison tells the story of the runaway slave Sethe, who comes to be haunted by what she believes to be the ghost of her dead daughter, Beloved. Beloved had been the only one of four children Sethe managed to kill when under threat of being returned to her slave owner, as she tried to 'put [her] babies where they'd be safe'.[45] Now settled with her second daughter, Denver, in Cincinnati, another escapee from the plantation, Paul D., arrives and relates the horrors of his escape, which hitherto he had dealt with by shutting his memories away in a tobacco box. Paul D. sets out to begin a new life with Sethe and Denver, who are largely ostracised from their community, and he drives out the baby ghost they had already become used to at their house, 124 Bluestone Road. Then, a young woman shows up at 124, and it gradually transpires that she is Beloved, the adult version of the baby ghost banished by Paul D. Overjoyed, and eager to (re)live her relationship with Beloved, Sethe showers her with motherly love. Ultimately, though, the mother-daughter dynamic is destructive, as it is driven by guilt on Sethe's side, who eventually even forgoes food, and greed by Beloved, who laps up everything Sethe gives her, becoming evermore demanding.

While Sethe views Beloved's return as an opportunity to be the mother she couldn't originally be, the trauma of killing and subsequently losing Beloved, is re-enacted rather than undone. This time, however, Denver is cut off from her mother and her sister, since Sethe and Beloved are obsessed with each other. As the story unfolds, we are told about Sethe's own mother, who kept her as the only child of a black man, while getting rid of the babies of white men who raped her during the journey into slavery from Africa to the Americas. The repressed memory of her mother's likely subsequent escape and hanging evokes in Sethe unease, as she perceives this as an act of abandonment. On philosopher Shannon Sullivan's reading, Sethe tries to interrupt 'the cycle of deathly violence in which her family is caught' but merely reinforces this through 'the very same violent acts'. Hence, 'Beloved is the phantasmic embodiment of a secret about her grandmother that was her mother's psychic burden and that has been handed down through the generations'.[46]

Beloved is, however, also a symbol of slavery, of the cruelty inflicted on 'sixty million and more'[47] slaves and their kin, and constitutes the original trauma endured by Sethe's mother, and through the generations, by Sethe and her children. Slavery is responsible for the degradation and litany of violence Sethe's family have been subject to over the years. Slavery is also ultimately responsible for the violent re-enactment of trauma that results in Beloved's death, and Denver's metaphorical death. It is intimately bound with a wilful repression of memory, as trauma is denied in a bid to continue, and to intercept the violence that has characterised their lives. And yet, it is precisely this repression that results in the painful re-enactment of violence, despite Sethe's best intentions, and despite her knowledge of a collective consciousness of trauma, which cannot be suppressed.

Describing Sweet Home, the plantation she escaped from, as a place that would continue even if it were erased from the earth, Sethe explains to Denver that such places can be seen, including by those who weren't there. She says:

> Someday you will be walking down the road and you hear something or see something going on. So clear. And you think

it's you thinking it up. A thought picture. But no. It's when you bump into a rememory that belongs to somebody else. Where I was before I came here, that place is real. It's never going away…The picture is still there and what's more, if you go there – you who never was there – … and stand in the place where it was, it will happen again; it will be there for you, waiting for you … That's how come I had to get all my children out. No matter what.[48]

Denver, then, who never was at Sweet Home, knows it and understands it through her 'rememory' of others. Hence, ghosts like Beloved, continue to haunt through the traumatic rememories of those subject to the primordial trauma of slavery. As Marianne Hirsch explains, 'rememory is neither memory nor forgetting, but memory combined with (the threat of) repetition … Rememory is Morrison's attempt to re-conceive the memory of slavery, finding a way to remember, and to do so *differently*, what an entire culture has been trying to repress'.[49]

I believe that many of Morrison's lessons on memory, rememory, trauma and loss, can be applied to the feminist context. Just as rememory of slavery is 'a way to remember…what an entire culture has been trying to repress', it can be said that women hold a rememory of the primal trauma that is patriarchy. While our culture has always sought to repress this through powerful anti-feminist backlash movements, post-feminist ideology and misogyny, there have been those, who recognise the continuous violence and trauma caused by patriarchy throughout the generations. As feminists we are aware of the cruelties and exclusions – those instances of sexism that surface as hauntings of an ever-present yet repressed and denied patriarchal trauma. Given what has been said about the story of feminist loss and affect, it is now possible to interpret this in terms of the emotional impact our culture's denial of patriarchy (and hence of the need for feminism) has.

The power of anti-feminist and sexist machinery and discourse can seem overwhelming in our society, where powerful positions are predominantly held by elite men, and where feminism continues to be marginalised and undermined. Feminists are right to challenge this, and to question, in particular, women's rejection of feminism. For, as Morrison highlights, trauma is not specific to one generation, but infects and spreads even to those who may not have experienced earlier, specific instances of violence.[50] All women, then, are subject to re-memories, to hauntings of patriarchy, as we continue to struggle with primordial patriarchal trauma and oppressive systems based on gender, but also on class, race, sexual orientation, and other markers of difference.[51]

Sadly, those attached to the feminist story of loss have primarily directed their feelings of anger and grief at women's denial of patriarchy at young women. This, in turn, results in a denial of young feminists – an erasure that is not dissimilar to the killing of Beloved and the detachment from Denver. While I do not wish to assert that tellers of the story of feminist loss unconsciously re-enact violence done to all women through patriarchy, it is nonetheless true that the rejection of young women's feminism and their resultant invisibility reflects exactly the same kind of invalidating we know and expect from patriarchal discourses. Regardless, then, of the unconscious or rational motivation for repeating the narrative of feminism lost, its repetition results in the very circumstance giving rise to trauma and loss in the storyteller in the first place. Ironically, the denial of rememory to young women, their assumed inability to partake in the collective consciousness of the primal trauma of patriarchy, is established and reinforced by people mourning disengagement with feminism and non-recognition of patriarchy.

Unless this pattern is interrupted and young women are recognised for the feminism they espouse, tellers of the story of feminist loss will continue to experience grief, rather than seeing their trauma redressed. Feminists must, therefore, 'remember, and ... do so differently' the stories we tell each other about feminism itself. We must remember and retell the stories of a feminism recently reinvigorated, of new techniques and tools for activism, of alliances formed, of campaigns successfully and painstakingly fought – in short, of contemporary feminist theoretical work and practice undertaken to counter primordial patriarchal trauma. Then the perceived trauma of a lost feminism can be displaced by the recognition of younger feminists, perhaps ultimately resulting in even more vibrant feminist movements in Ireland.

CONCLUSION

This chapter has focused on storytelling as a means of conceptualising feminism in Ireland. It has done so by establishing the need for feminist storytelling in the wider context of women's exclusion from the multitude of stories we term 'history'; in the context of the affective stories feminists tell each other about feminism; and in the context of my personal experience with the Irish Feminist Network. In no way do I wish to claim that my particular story takes precedence over others, nor do I believe that young feminists and young feminist organisations are above reproach or criticism. However, given that the power of Toni Morrison's rememory lies in one's capacity 'to tell, to refine and tell again',[52] I hope to have added a new and different story to the store of existing tales with which to remember this particular moment in time, and to have suggested a way of dealing with feminist trauma and the persistence of loss to allow for increased visibility of younger feminists.

Being mindful of the affective implications of my own writing, it should be noted that the foregoing should be read as a critical, but constructive treatment of a phenomenon in contemporary women's movements in Ireland. I do not wish to feed into the construction of 'bad' or 'good' feminist subjects. Generational divisions, if interpreted through Reger's 'political generations', are arguably less pronounced in the contemporary Irish context, and my analysis should not be understood as an instance of the reactive 'matricide' variety of disidentification, which may itself be seen as the corollary to the killing of daughters in Morrison's novel. Attachment to feminist stories of loss is cross-generational, although the narrative constructs younger women in a particular way. By theorising this attachment with rememory, I've tried to offer a way of understanding, and from there, disrupting the erasure of feminists tasked with carrying feminism into the future.

NOTES

1   Virginia Woolf, *A Room of One's Own & Three Guineas* (London, Vintage, 1996), p. 42.

2   *Ibid.*, p. 43.

3   I'm drawing upon Clare Hemmings' and Jonathan Dean's work on feminist stories and affect here, see 'Telling feminist stories', *Feminist Theory*, Vol. 6, 2005, pp 115–139; and Jonathan Dean, 'On the march or on the margins? Affirmations and erasures of feminist activism in the UK', *European Journal of Women's Studies*, Vol. 19, 2012, pp 315–329. My thanks are due to Dr Pauline Cullen (NUI Maynooth) for introducing me to this work.

4   Sadly such organisations have not always themselves adopted the label 'feminist'. For more, see Linda Connolly, *The Irish Women's Movement: From Revolution to Devolution* (Dublin, Lilliput Press, 2003); and my interview with Mamo McDonald in this volume.

5   Social scientists may, for example, refer to 'political opportunity structure' or 'resource mobilisation' as explanatory factors in

assessment of social movements. See Sidney Tarrow, *Power in Movement: Social Movements and Contentious Politics* (Cambridge, Cambridge University Press, 2011); and John D. McCarthy and Mayer N. Zald, 'Resource Mobilisation and Social Movements: A Partial Theory', *The American Journal of Sociology*, Vol. 82, No. 6, May 1977, pp 1212–1241.

6   I'm adopting Ailbhe Smyth's terminology here, see 'Women's Movement in the Republic of Ireland 1970–1990' in *Irish Women's Studies Reader*, edited by Ailbhe Smyth (Dublin, Attic Press, 1993), p. 249.

7   The wave metaphor in the Irish context is further probed in P. Cullen and C. Fischer, 'Conceptualising Generational Dynamics in Feminist Movements: Political Generations, Waves and Affective Economies', *Sociology Compass*, forthcoming.

8   See Barbara Findlen, *Listen Up: Voices from the Next Feminist Generation* (Seattle, Seal Press, 1995); or Rebecca Walker, *To Be Real: Telling the Truth and Changing the Face of Feminism* (New York, Anchor Books, 1995).

9   The second wave tale is well captured by Catherine Orr's interpretation, which holds that the 'construction of feminism as cultish flattens what I (or anyone else who has studied feminist histories) know to be a very complex and contradictory social movement into a few shorthand caricatures … Unfortunately, third wave texts are replete with this kind of characterization of the second wave. Essay after essay adds another chapter to a history of forgetting. The image of the monolithic, ideal, "mainstream" feminism against which these young women battle is rarely examined *as a representation*; rather, it almost always is accepted as "real". As a result, the contradictions that are navigated never seem to have historical precedents'. Catherine M. Orr, 'Charting the Currents of the Third Wave', *Hypatia*, Vol. 12, No. 3, 1997, p. 31.

10   Jonathan Dean, 'Who's Afraid of Third Wave Feminism', *International Feminist Journal of Politics*, Vol. 11, No. 3, 2009, pp 334–352.

11   Silla Roy, 'Melancholic politics and the politics of melancholia: The India women's movement', *Feminist Theory*, Vol. 10, No. 3, pp 341–357 and Dean, 'On the march or on the margins?'

12   *Op. cit.*, p. 120.

13   This hostility is born out by feminist work on a host of issues structured by the power of a historically theocratic racist,

classist, sexist state. See, for example, Ronit Lentin, 'A Woman Died: Abortion and the Politics of Birth in Ireland', *Feminist Review*, No. 105, 2013, pp 130–136.

14   Jo Reger, *Everywhere and Nowhere: Contemporary Feminism in the United States* (New York, Oxford University Press, 2012); see also P. Cullen and C. Fischer, 'Conceptualising Generational Dynamics in Feminist Movements: Political Generations, Waves and Affective Economies', *Sociology Compass*, forthcoming.

15   P. Cullen, 'Gendered Dynamics in a Strategic Action Field: A Case Study of The Irish Women's Movement', Working paper for the research cluster on Globalisation, Identities and Global Practice in the Department of Sociology at the National University of Ireland Maynooth, 2013.

16   Dean, 'On the march or on the margins?', p. 315.

17   Notably, this need not necessarily be a generational difference. Even younger women may adopt this narrative, although it does, of course, describe young women in a certain way.

18   See Susan McKay, 'Feminism Now', *The Irish Times*, 17/10/2012, available online at http://www.irishtimes.com/news/feminism-now-1.553554?page=2; see also McKay's contribution to this volume.

19   See, for example, Eddie Molloy, 'Cultural renewal required to restore value systems', *The Irish Times*, 26/06/2012.

20   For an analysis of the gendered nature of Ireland's crisis, see Mary Murphy, 'Gender, Governance and the Irish Crisis', Tasc, May 2012, available online here: http://www.tascnet.ie/upload/file/MurphyGenderGovernance.pdf.

21   I use the term 'younger' loosely here to roughly denote any woman under the age of forty. As a case in point against a strong interpretation of the wave metaphor, I myself do not neatly fall into a specific wave, having just missed the third wave in the 1990s, and now classing myself as somewhat along the older end of the spectrum of younger feminist activists.

22   These can be accessed on the Irish Feminist Network's YouTube channel here: http://www.youtube.com/user/IrishFemNetwork?feature=watch

23   Details here: http://www.irishfeministnetwork.org/the-coordinators.html

24   Irish Feminist Network, *Strategic Plan 2011–2013*, September 2011, available online at: http://www.irishfeministnetwork.org/

uploads/8/4/9/1/8491921/irish_feminist_network-__strategic_pl
an_2011__2013.pdf

25 For more on equality budgeting, and the campaign's demands,
    see Irish Feminist Network & Equality Budgeting Campaign,
    'Equality Budgeting in Ireland: An Information Booklet',
    available online at: http://equalitybudgeting.ie/wp-content/
    uploads/2012/11/EQUALITY-BOOKLET_high-res.pdf

26 See here for a list of member organisations:
    http://equalitybudgeting.ie/index.php/about-2/ In addition, the
    Irish Feminist Network ran a training programme for young
    women activists from April–June 2013, and many of these have
    also become Equality Budgeting Campaign members.

27 The budgetary process in Ireland is controlled by the 'Economic
    Management Council', which is made up of the two Finance
    ministers, and leader and deputy leader of the country. There is
    limited input from civil society, the legislature, and even
    members of the cabinet. For further details see C. Fischer,
    'Ireland should implement 'equality budgeting' to protect
    society's most vulnerable', *The Journal*, 09/06/2013, available
    online at: http://www.thejournal.ie/readme/column-ireland-
    should-implement-equality-budgeting-to-protect-societys-most-
    vulnerable-940196-Jun2013/

28 See http://www.turnofftheredlight.ie/ and http://www.abortion
    rightscampaign.ie/

29 See chapters by Anthea McTeirnan and Ivana Bacik in this
    volume.

30 See C. Fischer, 'The IFN's First Conference: Feminist Activism
    in Ireland', Irish Feminist Network Blog, 12/07/2012,
    http://www.irishfeministnetwork.org/1/post/2012/07/the-ifns-
    first-conference-feminist-activism-in-ireland.html

31 For seminar presentations, see http://equalitybudgeting.ie/inde
    x.php/news-3/

32 See http://www.irishfeministnetwork.org/2/post/2012/03/cake-
    biscuits-and-action-on-x-letter-writing-with-the-ifn.html

33 See http://www.irishfeministnetwork.org/2/post/2012/03/would
    -you-like- to-screen-miss-representation.html

34 See http://www.irishfeministnetwork.org/publications.html

35 Caroline Crawford, 'First furious farmers, then skipping Santas
    – it's all in a day's protesting for the Taoiseach', *Irish
    Independent*, 18/12/2012, available at: http://www.independ

ent.ie/irish-news/first-furious-farmers-th en-skipping-santas-its-all-in-a-days-protesting-for-the-taoiseac h-28948867.html

36   See http://www.irishfeministnetwork.org/2/post/2012/06/join-the-ifn-in-thedublin-pride-parade-30th-june-2012.html

37   See NWCI, 'News from NWCI's AGM: Motions Passed', http://www.nwci.ie/news/newsflash/2013/06/26/news-from-nwcis-agm-motions-passed/

38   We've had articles written about us, or have contributed original articles to publications such as the *Guardian*, *The Irish Times*, *The Journal*, *The Irish Examiner*, Ms. Magazine Blog, Politico, and *Image* magazine.

39   See Anna Carey, 'From the X Case to Pussy Riot: why I'm still a feminist, 20 years on', *The Irish Times*, 04/09/2012, http://www.irishtimes.com/life-and-style/people/from-the-x-case-to-pussy-riot-why-i-m-still-a-feminist-20-years-on-1.525993?page=1

40   Dean, 'On the march or on the margins?', p. 316.

41   Laura Woodhouse, as quoted in Dean, 'On the march or on the margins?', p. 322.

42   Linda Kelly, 'Where are all the y.oung feminists?', *Village Magazine*, 30/05/2012 available online at http://www.villagemag azine.ie/index.php/2012/05/where-are-all-the-young-feminists/

43   Sara Ahmed, *The Cultural Politics of Emotion* (London, Routledge, 2004).

44   As Kelly notes, 'for whatever reason, be it that something is not clearly labeled as "feminist" or because it doesn't happen in a physical room, it is often dismissed' – *op. cit.*

45   Toni Morrison, *Beloved* (London, Vintage Books, 2005), p. 193.

46   Shannon Sullivan, *Revealing Whiteness: The Unconscious Habits of Racial Privilege* (Bloomington, Indiana University Press, 2006), p. 112.

47   Morrison dedicates *Beloved* to these 'sixty million and more'.

48   Morrison, *Beloved*, pp 43–44.

49   Marianne Hirsch, 'Maternity and Rememory: Toni Morrison's Beloved' in *Motherhood and Representation* edited by Donna Bassin, Margaret Honey and Meryle Kaplan (Yale, Yale University Press, 1994), p. 96.

50   Violence against women is, of course, a feature of all patriarchal societies, past or contemporary. According to Women's Aid, one in five women in Ireland will experience violence from an

intimate partner throughout their lives – see 'Annual Report, 2012', p. 4.

51 While one may question the corollary between the oppressive systems of slavery/white supremacy and patriarchy, I think that the concept of 'rememory' can be utilised to theorise both. Of course, oppression is also intersectional, with systems based on race, gender, and other markers of difference, inter-functioning in complex ways.

52 Morrison, *Beloved*, p. 116.

Contemporary Feminism in Northern Ireland: From Deep Roots to Fresh Shoots

Kellie Turtle

In very recent times, a new period of feminist mobilisation has become evident in Northern Ireland.[1] Younger activists influenced by those spearheading national and international developments in the feminist movement, are working alongside those who have safely carried the legacy of women's activism from a period of deep division and conflict into more settled times. This chapter attempts to analyse the emerging trajectory of the movement, firstly by putting it in its historical context and examining the nature of the unique foundation on which today's activists are building. Primary evidence in the form of interview data gathered in 2009 will then bring into focus the experiences of women who experienced the professionalisation of women's organisation and will capture the energy for change that was emerging at that time. Finally, interviews with activists in 2012, three years after the establishment of new grassroots networks and contentious feminist protest, will highlight the movement's priorities and point towards future directions.

Belfast Feminist Network members Emma Copland, Louise Kennedy and Jessica Samoy Plunkett at the One Billion Rising dance flashmob on 14 February 2013 at Stormont Castle © Jessica Samoy Plunkett

In writing this chapter as an activist myself, I am conscious of Fiona McKay's suggestion that much of the literature on the feminist movement in the UK and Ireland is 'under-theorised, comprising personal testimony, historical accounts and prescriptive analyses'.[2] However, the approach I employ will be underpinned by a critical analysis of the journey of Northern Ireland's women's movement, and the application of relevant aspects of both social movement and feminist theory, in order to locate my account within the broader literature on contemporary feminist movements.

A Strong Foundation

Women's activism in Northern Ireland has deep and influential roots. In a city built on the labour of women in the linen mills and factories throughout the 19th and early 20th century, the contribution of Belfast trade union women like Winifred Carney and Betty Sinclair gave women a prominent place in social justice movements. The development of the second wave feminist movement in the North in the late 1960s has been well documented by key activists like Marie-Therese McGivern, Lynda Edgerton, Oonagh Marron and others, whose accounts are recorded in publications such as the *Field Day Anthology of Irish Writing*.[3] Through this work a picture emerges of a movement that was initiated by women angered by the poor quality of life in many communities in Northern Ireland, where living standards appeared to be lower than in the rest of the UK. Marie-Therese McGivern, writing in 1980 draws attention to the extreme levels of deprivation including, 'some of the worst housing in Western Europe', 'unemployment [of] over 50%' and 'one family in three now liv[ing] near or below the poverty line'.[4] This resulted in a movement that was 'much more representative of working-class women than elsewhere'[5] as, for many, 'what women felt were the main concerns of feminism ... were simply regarded as irrelevant to the everyday ordeal of ensuring life went on'.[6]

However, a different analysis of the birth of the women's movement would suggest that the efforts of university-educated middle-class women led to the first attempts to bring a feminist analysis to Northern Ireland's political and cultural status quo and draw women together into a collective movement. Eileen Evason highlights the formation of the Queen's University Women's Liberation Group in 1973 as an important precursor to the Northern Ireland Women's Rights Movement which went on to achieve important policy gains, set up the first women's centre, and gain influence through its wide-ranging work with other groups and networks.[7] As campaigning and women's centres flourished in the 1980s and early '90s, women from all strata of society worked to challenge issues of inequality that impacted on all women, with an acknowledgement that for many in deprived communities the impact was most pronounced. While these collective goals may have been feminist in nature, it is not assumed that they were decided upon from an exclusively feminist ideology, but rather as a practical response to the 'extent of oppression the individual woman suffered within her home'.[8]

The influence of the civil rights movement on the mobilisation of women in Northern Ireland was also significant. In fact, by the time the Northern Ireland Civil Rights Association was formed in 1967 to tackle discriminatory housing and employment policies overseen by the majority Unionist local government councils, women had been organising to protest these injustices from as far back as 1959. The groundwork done by women like Angela McCrystal, Patricia McCluskey and Brid Rodgers through the protest actions and political campaigning of the Homeless Citizens League, and later the Campaign for Social Justice, was an attempt to speak up for the 'thousands of working class Catholic women ... struggling to raise their families in woefully over-crowded, expensive and often unsanitary private houses and flats' due to preferential treatment for Protestant families seeking public housing.[9] The combined oppression of patriarchy and sectarianism meant these women appeared to bear the brunt of the injustices of that period in Northern Irish history. Subsequently, a relationship deepened between feminism and nationalism and pressure from within their own communities made it difficult for Protestant women to get involved in joint campaigns.

However, with the proliferation of women's centres in both Catholic and Protestant working class communities across Northern Ireland, new opportunities arose for women to become involved in cross-community activities that pre-dated any formal peace-building and remained largely undocumented. Networks like the Women's Information Group created neutral spaces for women from the centres to meet, forge a sense of identity as women, and work towards collective goals.[10] When particular women's centres were threatened with closure due to the withdrawal of funding, women from all communities protested and the momentum around such events led to the development of networks such as the Women's Support Network and the Women's Education Project, now the Women's Resource and Development Agency.

A MOVEMENT IN ABEYANCE:
THE EXPERIENCE OF WOMEN'S ORGANISATIONS FROM 1999–2009
The development of the women's movement since the Belfast (Good Friday) Agreement in 1998 has not been extensively mapped. One thing that is clear is that European Peace funding has brought a new stability and formalisation to all civil society groups, including those that seek to address the particular needs of women. The networks formed in the 1980s by way of mobilising women to engage in collective goals, have become key agencies in what is now a professional women's sector, campaigning for resources for the groups they represent and providing expert knowledge to policy makers

required to address gender as part of their equality agenda. At the local community level of women's centres, again an increase in resources, although at times unstable, has led to expansion in terms of the number of groups acting on behalf of women and the range of services they provide. State feminism has also been apparent in the formation of a gender equality unit in the Office of the First Minister and Deputy First Minister (OFMDFM) and the requirement on the departments of the Stormont government to report on the gender equality impact of all policy. In addition to this relatively mainstream work, single issue campaigns have persisted on issues such as violence against women and reproductive rights. With the continuing disparity between abortion rights for women in Northern Ireland and their counterparts in the rest of the UK, the Family Planning Association (fpani) and grassroots activists like Alliance for Choice have sustained a meaningful challenge through protest action, lobbying and pursuit of a judicial review of current law and practice.[11]

A number of social movement theorists in the last two decades have examined the professionalisation of women's movements, with the shift from mass mobilisation to social movement organisations (SMOs) and the development of state feminist structures in the form of women's policy machinery.[12] The commonly held model of cycles or waves of protest in conceptualising feminism as a social movement has mainly focused on the events that occur during cycles of peak activity. However, work that examines the periods in between can tell us much about how a movement is sustained over time through less obvious activities such as 'the survival of activist networks, sustaining a repertoire of goals and tactics and promoting a collective identity'.[13] Linda Connolly applies this approach to her study of the women's movement in Ireland since the 19th century as she describes how a small group of women activists were able to 'hold a movement in abeyance until shifting political conditions facilitate[d] the emergence of a more mass-based challenge'.[14] It is this same concept of abeyance that Grey and Sawer employ in their edited volume *Women's Movements: Flourishing or in Abeyance?*,[15] which uses a series of case studies to explore whether current directions represent a period of abeyance or a permanent redefining of the women's movement.

I gathered interview data in 2009 from eight participants obtained through purposive sampling,[16] to allow for analysis of these questions from the perspective of key women's movement actors in Northern Ireland, who are involved through their roles in political life, women's organisations or activist networks. Their descriptions of the movement's structures, activities and dynamics at that time support the model of abeyance as an accurate description of the holding pattern that characterised the women's movement throughout a decade of devolution.

The picture painted of the mainstream women's sector in the 2009 data was a disputed one, with some participants focusing on the gains made for women in marginalised communities, while others expressed frustration at the constricted repertoires and 'fractures and divisions' present in the formalised, state-approved organisations.[17] This is exemplified through these conflicting accounts from two women's centre managers:

> It's really, really good to meet with the Women's Centres Regional Partnership and talk to women from all over the province and hear what they are doing and tell them what you are doing ... good for information sharing and just as a support ... times when we're coming to a funding crisis, we get support from each other.

> We don't know what our shared value base is anymore because a number of centres employed men but didn't discuss the impact it would have on other groups and on collective

action ... women's centres in Belfast haven't had a full meeting since.

While the role of local women's centres in achieving gains for the most vulnerable women in society was recognised as important and highly effective, all participants raised concerns about the narrowed focus of women's activism when organisations are under constant pressure financially. For example:

> The women's sector is so choked by the daily demands of trying to fundraise and keep their heads above water that it's hard to see the bigger picture.

The role of the women's sector in Northern Ireland echoes the analysis of studies in other regions, such as work on feminist NGOs in Eastern Europe, which 'mostly work to provide social services to women at the apparent neglect of advocating for broader social changes that would benefit women and increase their rights and status'.[18] However, participants also discussed the influence of high level activist networks, such as the Women's Ad Hoc Policy Group,[19] that are engaged in institutional rather than public advocacy.[20] They consistently spoke about this group in positive terms as an inclusive space where 'everyone has an equal voice' and described it as a 'powerful force' in lobbying and assisting government to develop gender equality policy and strategy.

As well as examining current movement structures and dynamics, a final test applied to the 2009 data was to look for the presence of both internal and external conditions that suggest future mobilisation with a return to contentious protest is likely to happen. Participants pointed toward the growth of new activist networks outside the structure of the mainstream sector as evidence that a desire to re-establish collective feminist identity was emerging. For example:

What we have now ... it isn't working and it is going to collapse ... we are aligning ourselves more with like-minded groups ... I think it's starting to happen ... we should be choosing our own leadership ... it should be from the bottom up' (Women's Centre Manager speaking about the establishment of the 'Reclaim the Agenda' group).[21]

In addition to the presence of internal demand for mobilisation, there was also evidence that participants were experiencing an inhospitable political and cultural climate, which had worsened since devolution was re-established in 2007.[22] The women's sector had developed a 'pragmatic' mode of engagement with little room for confrontational tactics, and participants identified reproductive rights as the issue least likely to garner any political support despite evidence of some cultural liberalisation in that area.[23] In summary, participants in the 2009 interviews were divided on the prospect of a future wave of feminist mobilisation in Northern Ireland. While some suggested the current practice of 'chipping away' would bring long-term success, others claimed a new phase of activism was both necessary and inevitable.

FRESH SHOOTS OF MOBILISATION

In the years that have followed, both the obvious growth of new grassroots activist networks and the increasing evidence of contentious feminist protest have provided an answer to some of the outstanding questions posed by the 2009 interviewees. Authors working in the arena of popular feminist literature and journalism, rather than feminist academics, have driven the conversation and provided the most relevant analysis of emerging feminist communities. Online publications, blogs, and social media have also become important sites of debate and provide a platform for activism that allows for a dynamic analysis of the momentum that is currently transforming the feminist landscape. Two texts published in 2010, Kat Banyard's *The Equality Illusion: The Truth About Women and Men Today* and Catherine Redfern and Kristin Aune's *Reclaiming the F Word: The New Feminist Movement*, brought the work of a new generation of British activists into sharp focus and triggered even more growth with grassroots feminist networks being established across the UK within a few months, as well as in Belfast, Dublin, Galway and Cork.

The influence of these authors and activists has captured the attention of young women facing the political and social realities of enduring gender inequality, institutionalised sexism and cultural misogyny. While the internal and external abeyance conditions present in the previous decade suggested some potential for a new phase of mobilisation, the connection of emerging activists to a national and transnational movement through the vehicle of the internet has helped make that a reality. Another important trigger has been the combination of economic hardship with regressive government policy and contracting civil society space that is putting vulnerable women at even greater risk of marginalisation.[24] The engagement of new, younger activists has therefore developed in parallel with a refocusing of the abeyance SMOs that has seen those seeking a return to shared feminist values and repertoires of action beginning to mobilise in new ways.

For example, in early 2010 individuals connected to the mainstream women's sector through their professional roles created a network called Reclaim the Agenda (RTA) which aims to bring together individual women and women's organisations to progress women's social, economic, political and cultural equality. RTA is organised without the use of social media, has no website or public profile and operates a women-only policy and non-hierarchical structure. The group has been responsible for organising direct action protests in relation to economic policy such as welfare reform, as well as raising the profile of International Women's Day through organising a festival of events to mark the centenary celebrations in 2011. Developing in parallel over the same period of time, the Belfast Feminist Network (BFN) provides an alternative space for feminist discussion and organising, facilitated by women who have no previous experience within women's organisations or women's sector structures. The group depends heavily on online social networking for the purpose of advertising events, campaigning and engaging a wider audience beyond those who would traditionally identify as feminist. While there is no hierarchy, the group does not operate a women-only policy and a small number of men are both visible and involved in the organising of actions and campaigns.

There is an obvious generational divide between these two groups, although both enjoy some diversity in terms of the age and background of participants. RTA retains many abeyance characteristics in its structure and modes of action. For example, it has been able to harness the influence of state feminist actors, secured through the pragmatic approach of women's sector organisations, to obtain state funding for some activities while at the same time engaging in contentious protest and grassroots mobilisation. BFN is more easily identifiable as a contemporary activist network, in terms of dynamics, structure, and a discourse shaped by an analysis of the intersectionality of women's multiple identities. The influence of the internet is also a marked difference as BFN's use of social networking is both central to their local organising and has afforded opportunities for connecting with transnational movement objectives.

However, despite the different roots of these two activist networks and their differing spheres of influence and modes of operation, recently both the membership and the activities of the groups have become increasingly aligned. The opportunities each group affords the other in expanding their repertoires of action have been noted, given the effective infrastructure RTA can access and the autonomy from any state support that BFN enjoys. This alignment of values and increased cooperation has been evident in recent protest actions regarding reproductive rights, welfare reform and violence against women. It appears that the process of continuity and change that Taylor argued sustained linkages between the first and second waves of feminist mobilisation, could be applied to the current movement dynamics in Northern Ireland as new activist networks engage with the established abeyance organisations, albeit with their own priorities and approaches.[25]

The remainder of this chapter will discuss the dimensions of this phase of the feminist movement in Northern Ireland through the experiences of two activists who participated in semi-structured interviews conducted in November 2012. Both participants are involved with BFN. While one interviewee (Participant A) had no previous experience of feminist activism prior to joining BFN in 2012, the other (Participant B) is also active with RTA and worked for 10 years in the women's sector. She has therefore experienced the changes in the movement from inside the abeyance structures. Participant A is in her late 20s and Participant B is in her late 30s. Examining both perspectives side by side will allow for an analysis that reflects both the continuity with previous cycles of mobilisation and the extent to which the feminist movement is becoming redefined by new priorities and movement dynamics. Both participants were selected through purposive sampling, and their interview data is not necessarily representative of the wider movement's participants. However, this method is intended to offer a closer analysis of the current state of the feminist movement, from the perspective of a 'typical' activist.

ANALYSIS OF CURRENT ACTIVIST EXPERIENCES (2010–2013)

Participants were encouraged to discuss their observations about the feminist activist networks they are currently engaged with, as well as their own feminist goals and values. The evidence has been categorised into the following themes: activist space and structures; state feminism; social class and intersectionality; and sexual and reproductive rights. These themes represent the key priorities identified by both participants in relation to current movement dynamics and goals.

ACTIVIST SPACE AND STRUCTURES

Given the difficulties faced by the second wave organisations attempting to build a cohesive feminist movement in a context of religious and political division escalated by periods of intense violence, it is important to note that this is no longer experienced as a significant challenge. Both participants specified diversity and inclusivity as characteristics of both BFN and RTA that they value highly. Whereas in previous years, a politically mixed space may have been threatening or contentious, Participant A described the activist space at BFN as 'safe, because it is so diverse politically so there's an expectation that we will talk openly and all views will be respected'. Participant B described BFN as 'a broad church where people come together to work on issues and politics fall into line behind that'. She noted the approach of RTA in also prioritising 'issues first' but highlighted division, 'duplication' and a 'lack of willingness to work together' from other grassroots groups working on feminist issues outside of these networks. She attributed this to 'possible sectarianism' but felt that a desire to 'own' issues is a more prevalent cause. Participant A described her experience of feminism intersecting with her socialist political identity:

> I have friends in various socialist networks, have spoken at socialist conferences and made good contacts. But there are divisions in that movement ... broad-left politics, etc ... so I feel comfortable saying that first and foremost I identify with the feminist movement.

As well as the need for a unique feminist space in terms of ideology and priority goals, both participants highlighted an appreciation of networks that adhere to feminist values and structure. Participant B noted that a focus on non-hierarchical organising is 'overdue' following a departure from this model when the women's sector professionalised in the 1990s. Participant A described her experience of BFN as providing a dynamic that is 'raw, positive and progressive' and noted that 'I have learned so much from others, about feminism and about myself ... I wasn't expecting that'. Both made specific reference to the new activist space being carved out online, citing the benefits as the energy and democratic participation these methods of organising encourage:

> Social media gives things a real boost in terms of building broad campaigns that everyone can contribute to ... some people are shy, or young or can't make it to meetings but they are still able to contribute.

> I love the instant solidarity on the blogs and on Twitter. You can engage a lot of people very quickly, and it's great for using humour to highlight the absurdity of some of the sexism we're dealing with.

Both interviewees commented on the differing approaches to men in the feminist movement taken by RTA and BFN. Participant B was sympathetic to the reasons for advocating women-only spaces due to her experience within the women's movement over the last decade. However, she stated that she feels comfortable working alongside men on feminist issues, choosing to view them as important allies who can 'lend their voice ... so people can't say 'oh that's just something the women get upset about' ... it can have a powerful effect'. Participant A felt that generational differences in experiences of gender inequality in public and private spaces may account for the different policies of the two groups, stating; 'women my age are more used to men who actually get it ... because we've benefited from the work of previous generations so there are more young men who understand from their mothers why this is important'.

STATE FEMINISM

While Northern Ireland enjoys extremely limited state feminist machinery within government, a strong relationship has developed between political institutions and the lead agencies within the women's sector, who assume a state feminist role in ensuring women's representation through the inclusion of their interests in decision-making processes.[26] As Shireen Hassim points out in her study of the contemporary South African women's movement, while democratisation would appear to be a change in political opportunity structure that should favour women's movements, this is not always the case, and 'transitions should not always be seen as enhancing women's access to power'.[27] She notes the example of Central and Eastern Europe, where women benefited less from democratisation than men because of 'a far greater hostility to feminism'[28] in these new political structures. This resonates strongly with women's experiences of the socially conservative, religiously motivated ideologies and policies of most parties in the power-sharing structure in Northern Ireland, and highlights the challenges faced by state feminists in progressing a gender equality agenda. Participant B described her experiences of working within formal state feminist SMOs as 'frustrating' and suggested that 'the women's sector has become an industry, the outputs of which have proven that the model doesn't work'. She noted the dissatisfaction with the sector that drove the formation of RTA, particularly the focus on 'chasing funding' for women's services rather than engaging in political analysis as to why services are needed in the first place.

Participant A saw the emerging activist networks as a reaction to 'complete political stagnation' within Northern Ireland and therefore questioned the methods of state feminist organisations, since the politicians they seek to influence are 'disgraceful' and 'dominated by right wing Christian men who make a point of not addressing women's issues'. She acknowledged the value of having a strong women's sector however, focusing on the infrastructure they provide for women's representation, and saw opportunity in a supportive but 'slightly removed' relationship between these formal organisations and new activist networks:

> The relationship needs to continue I think. They see the passion and creativity we have and they are glad there are more young women getting involved with the same fire they had. We can get away with stuff they can't but they make a point of supporting us from a distance.

Both participants discussed the importance of cultural rather than political activism as a vehicle for achieving long term change that the professional women's sector currently does not prioritise. For example, Participant B expressed her frustration that the campaigns of women's SMOs continue to focus on 'changing laws, when we know that isn't enough' and she highlighted the role that new activist networks are playing in driving cultural feminism that is contentious and radical:

> Activism looks very different from the 1970s, it's not always a good thing taking to the streets as there's always the danger of being misconstrued. You need to be more strategic than that – interact with the media, don't let them dictate the conversation.

Participant A also recounted her experience of making a short film with BFN on the subject of rape prevention and victim blaming that, 'has had a big impact … it might seem subtle but it's challenging the other messages that people consume'.

Rape Culture poster © Emma Campbell, Belfast Feminist Network

Closely linked to the current divergence of grassroots groups from the activities and tactics of state feminist organisations, is a sense that there has been a failure to develop a feminist analysis of inequality and oppression that engages women from all social classes. A key achievement of the second wave women's movement in Northern Ireland was to secure the long-term existence of a strong network of women's centres, with training, education and childcare facilities, located in communities most acutely affected by poverty and the legacy of 'the troubles'. However, as Participant B pointed out:

> Women came out the other end of these services with no understanding of what they were even doing in a women's centre in the first place. The leaders had that understanding but it didn't trickle down. There needs to be feminist education, an induction about why women's centres are here. I don't think it's hard to do and I think women will respond to it ... one of the aims of RTA could be to put the politics back in the women's centre.

Molyneaux's distinction between women's movements that prioritise 'practical gender needs' and those that prioritise 'strategic gender interests' helps to articulate the current tension between the abeyance organisations of the women's sector and the new wave of mobilisation of grassroots activists.[29] The experience of Northern Ireland presents a challenging paradox in that despite the women's movement having been 'much more representative of working-class women than elsewhere',[30] the prioritisation of 'practical gender needs' has potentially hindered the development of a feminist discourse that engages these women in activism towards 'strategic gender interests'.

In addition to the efforts of RTA to inject a more contentious feminist politics into the service provision model of the women's sector, the dissatisfaction of younger activists involved with BFN reflects the growing popularity of 'intersectional' analyses within many contemporary feminist movements. Since the concept was first developed by feminist theorists in the 1980s,[31] largely to address the interrelationships of gender, race and social class, it has had considerable influence on the methodologies of international human rights bodies and the development of gender mainstreaming in international and domestic policy development.[32] More recently however, 'intersectional' has become shorthand for 'good' feminist activism, with the feminist blogosphere, if not the bookshelves, bursting with praise for those who embrace this approach and disdain for those who don't.[33] The discourse of 'privilege' and 'multiplicity' increasingly dominates the theoretical basis underpinning new grassroots movements. For many, this represents an attempt to fill in the gaps left by the previous wave of the feminist movement, which, as Participant B suggested 'didn't link issues together enough', and to overcome the divisive identity politics that crippled earlier phases of mobilisation.

In the case of BFN, this extends beyond the socialist class analysis favoured by both interview participants, to include explicit commitments in the group's vision statement to prioritise 'equal rights for LGB&T people', 'the intersection of sexism and ageism' and 'the simultaneous inequalities experienced by disabled women', although race is not given specific attention.[34] As an active member with BFN myself, I would describe the commitment to intersectionality in this context as a safeguarding mechanism against which we must constantly check our blindness to the marginalisation of women whose identities and experiences we have failed to represent.

SEXUAL AND REPRODUCTIVE RIGHTS

When asked to discuss the issues they are most motivated to challenge, it was immediately clear from both participants that issues relating to sexual and reproductive rights were central to many of their concerns. Participant A discussed her personal experiences of repressive sexual stereotyping on two different levels. Firstly, the impact of growing up in a 'patriarchal environment and a catholic education' that devalued and shamed expressions of female sexuality led her to rebel against the traditional gender role into which she felt forced. Later, her experience of sexual assault and an abusive relationship 'prompted thoughts about the prevailing attitudes to women and how our sexuality is taken for granted'. As a result, she is passionate about tackling 'the hypersexualisation of women in the media' and makes clear links between this issue and women's experiences of sexual violence.

Likewise, Participant B highlighted sexual violence, domestic violence and 'misogyny everywhere in our culture' as key issues and also expressed her frustration at the slow pace of women's sexual liberation:

> It's been 50 years since feminist consciousness-raising groups had women taking responsibility for their own orgasm but still we aren't open enough about sex ... just because it's more mainstream now to get your boobs out in magazines doesn't mean we are any further on in owning our sexuality.

These priorities are reflected in the campaigns and activities of BFN and a number of emerging activist networks around the UK and Ireland attracting the participation of younger feminists. The focus of many groups on tackling the sexual objectification proliferated through the sex industry and mainstream popular culture has drawn criticism for reflecting a middle class bias. However, Participant B felt these issues have a universal significance stating, 'it affects all women ... look at the link with domestic violence – that's happening across the board'. It is perhaps the commitment of both BFN and

RTA to maintain a 'broad church' approach without any hierarchical leadership that has allowed these networks to avoid the pigeon-holing that other groups are experiencing.[35] For example, whilst UK Feminista, a network that has heavily influenced the development of BFN, has a clear position on the legislation of the sex industry, campaigns on a platform of criminalising the purchase of sex, and refuses to engage with pro-sex worker organisations, BFN has accepted that a range of opinions exist within its membership and has given a platform to all of these at different times. This can be seen as an attempt to address the challenge of achieving consensus whilst maintaining openness. Third-wave feminist theorists have examined how women are expected to 'negotiate the often contradictory desires for both gender equality and sexual liberation',[36] a dilemma that is problematised by the extent to which our desires and choices are socially constructed.

Participant B also outlined her long-term commitment to the campaign for abortion rights, having engaged in direct action, education, and domestic and international lobbying. She describes this as an issue of 'social justice ... because women with money to travel have choice, it's the poorer women who suffer' and locates it within her wider concerns regarding the impact of poverty on women, compounded by the burden of caring responsibilities. This approach to the issue of abortion rights was echoed by Participant A, who discussed it alongside her anger that 'the same politicians who want to restrict women's reproductive choices also want to take away the welfare support they and their families depend on'. This resonates strongly with an emerging rhetoric of 'reproductive justice', such as that described by Kimala Price in her work on the challenge being posed by women of colour activists in the US to the individualistic paradigm of the pro-choice movement. Their framework also demands an intersectional analysis that acknowledges the need for 'gaining legal rights, lobbying and electoral politics' but 'recognises the importance of linking reproductive health and rights to other social justice issues'.[37]

Actions on this issue in Northern Ireland in the last year have included two mass rallies, a welcoming party and extensive media engagement on the opening of the Marie Stopes facility in Belfast, pro-choice contingents in both the Pride Festival and May Day parades, candlelight vigils following the death of Savita Halappanavar, performances of a 'pro-voice' play recounting the experiences of women denied abortions in Northern Ireland, films and photographic exhibitions focused on women's journeys to Great Britain, the roll-out of a community based education programme facilitating women's learning about their reproductive rights, numerous letters published in the editorials of all the mainstream newspapers, and articles in socialist, communist and anarchist publications.[38] It is clear that the growing grassroots challenge to the political stalemate on abortion is significantly defining this phase of feminist mobilisation and the relative silence of the mainstream women's sector on the issue has the potential to render them out of touch and unable to fully articulate the priorities of an active and developing women's movement.

CONCLUSION

Contentious feminist protest, whether on the streets, on the airwaves or online, has accelerated at an extremely rapid pace in the last few years. The current phase of mobilisation may not look like the mass movement of previous cycles, but is likely to be engaging the participation and support of as many, if not more people given the reach of social media and the focus on demanding cultural as well as legislative change. The current discourse and movement goals have undoubtedly been influenced by developments both in the UK and Ireland, as well as further afield. However, the particular political and social context of Northern Ireland, and the activist space women have historically occupied here, has shaped the contemporary movement in a unique way. The movement continuity provided by abeyance organisations has been hugely effective at maintaining a shared feminist identity and collective goals, while the energy from both within those abeyance SMOs and from outside them to strengthen that shared identity and redefine the goals, has driven a resurgence of mobilisation. What this looks like in the future will depend on the ability of such groups to work together, to maintain the diverse representation and credibility established in previous phases of the movement, and to build on this with a renewed assertiveness in presenting a feminist challenge to power.

International Women's Day rally: photographer Sean Harkin

In February 2013 BFN organised a local action as part of the global 'One Billion Rising' campaign, during which activists were supported online to call women onto the streets in dance flash mobs and demand and end to violence against women. This has been the most widely supported event organised by BFN as a relatively new group facilitated by a new generation of young activists. It drew support from all sections of the women's sector through partnership with RTA and Women's Aid, as well as trade unions, women's centres and unaffiliated individuals. In total, over 300 women participated in an action that contained elements of the repertoires of both abeyance and emerging networks, including engagement with political representatives coupled with grassroots mobilisation through social media. The potential for partnership this experience suggests is promising, but will undoubtedly be tested through activities that are more politically contentious than violence against women or depend on more confrontational tactics. While the emerging activist groups are committed to a practical application of intersectionality, if they manage to maintain an open, inclusive and yet cohesive movement, they must surely acknowledge that they inherited their ability to do so from the learning of the previous generation of activists who attempted it under much more difficult circumstances.

NOTES

1   The analysis in this chapter will be limited to Northern Ireland given the different political climates and the very particular movement trajectory that emerged in this jurisdiction.

2   Fiona McKay 'The state of women's movement/s in Britain: Ambiguity, complexity and challenges from the periphery', in *Women's Movements: Flourishing or in Abeyance?*, edited by S. Grey and M. Sawer (London, Routledge, 2008), p. 18.

3   Monica McWilliams, 'Women and Political Activism in Northern Ireland', in *Field Day Anthology of Irish Writing Vol. V:*

Irish Women's Writing and Traditions, edited by Angela Bourke *et al*, (Cork, Cork University Press, 2002), pp 374–411.

4   M.T. McGivern, 'Abortion in Ireland' in *Scarlett Woman* (11 June 1980) and 'Women and Political Activism in Northern Ireland', in *Field Day Anthology of Irish Writing Vol. V: Irish Women's Writing and Traditions*, edited by Bourke *et al* (Cork, Cork University Press, 2002), p. 391.

5   McWilliams, *Ibid*, p. 375.

6   Joanna McMinn and Margaret Ward, 'Belfast Women Against all the Odds', in *Personally Speaking: Women's Thoughts on Women's Issues*, edited by Liz Steiner-Scott (Dublin, Attic Press, 1985), p. 191.

7   Eileen Evason, *Against the Grain: The Contemporary Women's Movement in Northern Ireland* (Dublin, Attic Press, 1991).

8   Margaret Ward, 'The Women's Movement in the north of Ireland: Twenty years on', in *Ireland's Histories: Aspects of State, Society and Ideology*, edited by S. Hutton and P. Stewart (London, Routledge, 1991), p. 151.

9   Catherine B. Shannon, 'Women in Northern Ireland', in *Chattel, Servant or Citizen. Women's Status in Church, State and Society*, edited by Mary O'Dowd and Sabine Wichert (Belfast, Queens University, 1993), p. 239.

10   McMinn and Ward, 'Belfast Women Against all the Odds', pp 189–200.

11   Ruth Fletcher, 'Abortion Needs or Abortion Rights? Claiming State Accountability for Women's Reproductive Welfare: Family Planning Association of Northern Ireland v. Minister for Health, Social Services and Public Safety', *Feminist Legal Studies* 13 (2005) pp 123–134.

12   N. Matthews, 'Feminist Clashes with the State: Tactical Choices by State-funded Rape Crisis Centres', in *Feminist Organisations: The Harvest of the New Women's Movement*, edited by Martin M Feree and Patricia Y Martin (Philadelphia, Temple University Press, 1995), pp 291–305; A. Mazur and D. McBride, 'State Feminism since the 1980s: From Loose Notion to Operationalized Concept', *Politics & Gender* 3 (2007), pp 501–513.

13   Verta Taylor, 'Sources of continuity in social movements: The women's movement in abeyance', in *American Sociological Review*, 54 (1989) p. 772.

14 Linda Connolly, 'The Irish Women's Movement: From Revolution to Devolution' (Basingstoke, Palgrave, 2008), p. 77.

15 Sandra Grey and Martin Sawer (eds), *Women's Movements: Flourishing or in abeyance?* (London, Routledge, 2008).

16 This process involves selecting those participants who are considered most relevant to the purpose of the study. It is a non-probability method that prioritises in-depth qualitative analysis of an issue over drawing generalisations.

17 Connolly uses the word repertoires to describe the types of collective actions associated with a social movement.

18 Katja M. Guenther, 'The Possibilities and Pitfalls of NGO Feminism: Insights from Postsocialist Eastern Europe', *Signs: Journal of Women in Culture and Society,* 36 (2011), p. 863.

19 This is an informal group that meets regularly and is comprised of a diverse range of organisations, individuals and trade unions, who are concerned with influencing relevant government policies with the aim of promoting gender equality.

20 Sabine Lang, 'Between Institutional and Public Advocacy: Transnational Women's Networks in the European Union', (paper presented at the European Consortium for Political Research 5th General Conference, Potsdam Universität, 10–12 September 2009).

21 Reclaim the Agenda is an activist network established by women working within women's organisations that will be explored in more detail later in the chapter.

22 Prior to this, under direct rule from Westminster, those advocating for women's rights and gender equality would have been presenting their demands to the UK Parliament and engaging with the Secretary of State for Northern Ireland and the Northern Ireland Office. In 2007 the NI Assembly was re-established and most areas of governance transferred to the NI Executive at Stormont.

23 'Abortion comments out of step with NI' UTV News Online, published 29 August 2012, http://www.u.tv/news/Abortion-comments-out-of-step-with-NI/e3757deb-0fb6-41ee-996e-7f0564b863f5.

24 Women's Resource and Development Agency, 'The Northern Ireland Economy: Women on the Edge?' accessed Jan 2013 http://www.wrda.net/Documents/The%20NI%20Economy%20-%20Women%20on%20the%20Edge%20Report.pdf.

25 Taylor, 'Sources of continuity in social movements', pp 761–775.

26 Joni Lovenduski (ed.), *State Feminism and Political Representation* (Cambridge, Cambridge University Press, 2005).

27 S. Hassim, 'Voices, Hierarchies and Spaces: Reconfiguring the Women's Movement in Democratic South Africa', accessed Feb 2013. http://ccs.ukzn.ac.za/files/hassim%20womens%20moveme nt%20rr.pdf, 9.

28 *Ibid*, 9.

29 Maxine Molyneux, 'Mobilization without emancipation? Women's interests, the state and revolution in Nicaragua', *Feminist Studies* 11(1985), pp 227–254.

30 McWilliams, 'Women and Political Activism in Northern Ireland', p. 375.

31 Kimberle W. Crenshaw, 'Demarginalizing the Intersection of Race and Sex: A Black Feminist Critique of Antidiscrimination Doctrine, Feminist Theory and Antiracist Politics' in *University of Chicago Legal Forum*, 140 (1989), pp 139–167.

32 Nira Yuval-Davis, 'Intersectionality and Feminist Politics', *European Journal of Women's Studies,* 13 (2006), pp 193–209.

33 Bim Adewumne, 'What the Girls spat on Twitter tells us about feminism', *Guardian Comment is Free,* 8 October 2012 http://www.guardian.co.uk/commentisfree/2012/oct/08/girls-twitter-feminism-caitlin-moran.

34 'Vision and Aims', Belfast Feminist Network http://belfastfeministnetwork.wordpress.com/vision-and-aims/ accessed Jan 2013.

35 Carrie Hamilton, 'Enough middle-class feminism', *Guardian Comment is Free,* 24 March 2010. http://www.guardian.co.uk/commentisfree/2010/mar/24/middle -class-feminism-politics

36 R.C. Snyder-Hall, 'Women's Choices and the Future of Feminism', *Perspectives on Politics* 8 (2010), 247–253.

37 Kimala Price, 'What is Reproductive Justice?: How Women of Color Activists Are Redefining the Pro-Choice Paradigm', *Meridians: Feminism, Race, Transnationalism,* 10 (2010), 42–65.

38 For more on Savita Halappanvar, see 'Woman "denied a termination" dies in hospital', *Irish Times,* 14 November 2012, http://www.irishtimes.com/newspaper/frontpage/2012/1114/122 4326575203.html.

TRANS RIGHTS IN IRELAND:
A FEMINIST ISSUE

Leslie Sherlock

THE IRISH TRANSGENDER LANDSCAPE:
HISTORY AND ACTIVISM

Irish trans historical records, like written trans histories the world over, are patchy and incomplete. Trans people, like many other groups who do not fit societal norms, have been written out of history and had their stories erased. It is widely said that one of the world's first known female-to-male trans people to take testosterone and transition was Michael Dillon from County Meath, born in 1915.

Irish trans experiences remain largely undocumented until the 1990s, the Celtic Tiger economic boom, when dressing groups, a transvestite hotline, the Gemini 'dressing club' and websites facilitating support, dressing services and dating were set up.[1] Irish trans medical services at this stage were rumoured to have been limited to 'backstreet castrations' for trans women. In 1993, Dr. Lydia Foy's request that her birth certificate be amended to reflect her female gender was refused.[2] In 1997 she began her battle for the legal recognition of her gender by applying to the Irish government for a correction of the gender marker on her birth certificate – a battle she is still fighting today.

Transgender Equality Network Ireland (TENI), initially named Transsexual Equality Network Ireland, began slowly as a membership-based voluntary group working for trans rights and support around the year 2000, set up by members of the community in Cork and Limerick. A trans email listserve, Irish-T, also began in 2000. The Celtic Tiger's influx of immigration brought new additions to Ireland's trans tapestry, including the group 'Pink Philippines'. In 2005 TENI began operating in a more organised way, and a few more websites were established, such as Tranniehaven as a social site. The 'T' was beginning to be discussed and considered for inclusion within a few Irish LGBT or 'gay' groups, including online groups.[3] Leading the way in Irish trans inclusion were Dublin's LGBT Resource Centre (OutHouse), Ireland's LGBT Youth Services (BeLonG To) and some select LGBT societies on Irish University campuses. In 2005 TENI, in collaboration with OutHouse, began Ireland's first trans peer support group.

Success came to the trans movement in those early years through the building of grassroots support networks and completion of some project-based initiatives. Alongside these successes, however, came some power struggles, personality clashes and differences in opinion which have unfortunately also been characteristic of feminist, LGBT and other grassroots community movements. These dilemmas consumed much time and energy, and caused division within the community. Debates centred on full inclusion of all trans identities versus a sole focus on transsexual[4] experiences or those identifying as having 'Gender Identity Disorder (GID)',[5] as well as on differing opinions in relation to the trans movement's connection to the 'gay' community. 'Break off' groups formed: Gender Identity Disorder Ireland (GIDI) and Gender Identity Support Ireland (GISI), both of which continue to operate from their respective different perspectives.

The then voluntary-run TENI carried forward setting up a support group in Cork, completing some project-based initiatives and giving talks to the Gardaí (Irish police force) and health services, as well as university groups. Participation in a government-funded Transgender Medical Symposium and production of an information leaflet for General Practitioners in 2008 brought some limited visibility to the organisation, though TENI still lacked resources and capacity to fully capitalise on this, or to assist in education on adding the T into existing LGBT work. In 2008, TENI applied for and subsequently received three years worth of core funding through Atlantic Philanthropies' Human Rights strand of work, alongside the LGBT initiative, LGBT Diversity. This funding aimed to improve the situation for some of Ireland's most marginalised members of the LGBT community, namely those in rural areas and transgender people. With this core funding, TENI was able to establish itself as a legal entity, to hire a small staff and to lease a premises.

By 2009, TENI was operating as a legal entity and carrying forth a programme of work that aimed to accomplish results in the core areas of Support, Education, Advocacy, Capacity Building and Organisational Development. Also in 2009, TENI hosted Ireland's first transgender conference, 'Transforming Attitudes', which brought researchers, politicians and legal analysts from Ireland and abroad together to discuss the devastating state of trans rights in Ireland and to contemplate advocacy strategies for legal gender recognition. Since 2009, TENI has been instrumental in facilitating increased inclusion of transgender experiences within Ireland's LGBT tapestry. 'Transgender' has become a word that is increasingly recognised, and transgender experiences have been more widely covered by the media and discussed within society. TENI completed its Atlantic Philanthropies programme of work and found some successes in discussions with politicians, and also with health services, and in identifying funding streams that have allowed it to continue operating. In 2012, TENI hosted the European Transgender Council, bringing Ireland to the table in a more prominent way within the European transgender rights movements and communities.

IRISH TRANS RESEARCH

Transgender identities and experiences are diverse. Due to the enormous stigma related to trans experiences, it is impossible to quantify how many people identify as transgender in Ireland. Invisibility and lack of rights and recognition hide the realities of trans people's lives, with much LGBT research failing to include statistics on trans experiences. Many efforts mistakenly conflate gender identity, gender roles and sexual orientation. When a questionnaire asks whether a respondent identifies as L, G, B or T, it has the effect of erasing the experiences of trans people who also identify as lesbian, gay or bisexual, as well as erasing the experiences of those trans people who do not identify with the trans label (perhaps considering themselves as simply having a trans history). LGBT research also often fails to reach the myriad of trans people who, for a variety of reasons, do not affiliate or feel a sense of belonging within the LGBT community.

In 2009, TENI published *Transphobia in Ireland*, a literature-based report, which collated relevant policy and societal issues.[6] The report identified three broad themes that most seriously impact upon trans people: institutionalised transphobia, hate crime reporting and monitoring, and trans discrimination.[7] Also in 2009, *Supporting LGBT Lives* was published. This is the most comprehensive study to date carried out on the lives of LGBT people in Ireland and is fully inclusive of trans identities.[8] Among the trans-specific findings in the study, the majority of trans participants (40/46) reported having felt depressed at some point in their lives. 44% of transgender participants had self-harmed at some point in their lives, 11% of whom had self harmed in the previous 12 months.[9] Over a quarter of those who identified as transgender indicated that they had attempted suicide at least once, most of whom had tried to take their lives on more than one occasion.[10]

Martine Cuypers, Dublin Pride, June 2011 © Transgender Equality Network Ireland (TENI), photographer Louise Hannon

Isolation, fear, stigma, physical violence and family rejection contribute to depression, anxiety, self-harm, suicide and substance misuse rates amongst the trans population. On a more positive note, *Supporting LGBT Lives* found that most LGBT people develop mental health 'resilience' through acceptance and support from family, friends, community organisations and services, and positive experiences at school or work.[11] In 2012, TENI participated in a UK and Ireland-based research project that looked at transgender health. The survey findings have yet to be published, however, preliminary data is in line with the *Supporting LGBT Lives* findings. The survey has a sole trans focus, much greater sample size, and details other elements of mental health, such as access to services. Increased research into this area is vital for progressing the trans rights movement in Ireland.

CHALLENGES FACED BY TRANS PEOPLE IN IRELAND
INSTITUTIONALISED TRANSPHOBIA

When government, legal or social practices encourage, tolerate, or support discrimination against transgender people by denying civil, political and social rights, institutionalised transphobia is evident. Trans people in Ireland face various forms of injustice and are subject to shaming, harassment, discrimination, and violence in addition to denial of legal rights and equal protections – a lack of recognition on every level.[12]

Ireland lacks sufficient, essential, dedicated and specialised trans health services – surgeons, postoperative care, endocrinologists, psychiatrists, therapists, and a designated gender specialist. There is no defined treatment path for transition-related care, leaving the confusing process to be maneuvered by the individual. The lack of trans-aware service providers can further perpetuate discrimination simply through ignorance. Trans people may face legal and institutional difficulties from negative stereotypes and mispronouning to overt discrimination and social exclusion. In nearly any institutional setting, facilities such as toilets, changing rooms and athletic teams are gendered within a rigid binary system. While some trans people are comfortable using gendered services, many feel unsafe or are unsure as to whether policies are inclusive. Many others prefer 'unisex' or non-gendered spaces where available.

Many service providers are unaware that not everyone identifies with the sex assigned at birth, and can easily make incorrect assumptions about a person's gender identity and preferred pronoun. With education and awareness, though, it is not difficult to simply treat a person with respect – regardless of gender identity. Our world is, in many ways, split by rigid and stereotypical gender divides, and the gendered nature of society can cause particular difficulty to trans individuals, especially those who are young people and/or are not 'out'.

Employment is another area of difficulty. Oftentimes a trans person will be dismissed, or constructively dismissed, upon 'coming out' in the workplace, as many employers do not know how to sensitively support this process. Unemployment rates amongst trans people remain high, as many trans people meet transphobic discrimination when attempting to secure employment. For those trans people in employment, the workplace is not always a friendly and welcoming place, but with some diversity training and transgender inclusive policies, trans employees can be included in a respectful manner as part of a workplace team.[13]

TRANS DISCRIMINATION AND EQUALITY LEGISLATION
The Equality Tribunal is a quasi-judicial body established for the purpose of investigating complaints under the Employment Equality Act and the Equal Status Act. The

gender ground protection in the Equality legislation prohibits discrimination in the provision of goods and services, accommodation and education, and in the workplace. There are no protections from discrimination regarding functions of the State that are not defined as a service, and these are not open to challenge by way of the Equal Status Act. The key challenge in making a complaint is that trans people must effectively 'come out'. The decision in the 2011 Louise Hannon case proved that transsexual people,[14] specifically, can be protected under the gender ground of the Equal Status Acts, yet trans people remain unprotected from discrimination as a separate and distinct category.[15] Countries like Sweden have introduced a separate anti-discrimination ground for 'gender identity and expression', which protects an array of differently gendered individuals from this type of transphobia.[16]

HATE CRIME MONITORING AND REPORTING

The more personal and individual level manifestations of transphobia are harassment, bullying and hate crime. Lack of hate crime data in Ireland does not reflect an absence of such motivated crimes, but rather demonstrates that they are under-reported (TENI, 2009). Trans people are not specifically protected by hate crime legislation in Ireland and the full extent of transphobic crimes are unknown because the Gardaí do not collect data on such incidents (TENI, 2009). Experience or expectations of being received with hostility, being dismissed or disrespected and the absence of a mechanism to recognise and record the specific motive of an incident increases vulnerability for trans people. It is clear why few people report incidents. Transphobic violence, therefore, remains invisible to the Gardaí, law and policy makers, politicians and wider Irish society.

In jurisdictions where records are kept, statistics for transphobic hate crimes and trans murders are incredibly high.[17] Lack of education and rampant misunderstanding in society about trans lives and experiences perpetuate stereotypes that trans people represent the 'ultimate deception', and this notion is reproduced in mainstream films and jokes. As there is no specific hate crime legislation to protect LGBT people in Ireland, transphobic attacks have not been monitored or tried as such. In response to this, TENI launched, in 2013, their Stop Transphobia and Discrimination (STAD) campaign. STAD is a community-based hate crime monitoring effort, aiming to map discrimination based on gender identity or gender expression throughout Ireland that aims to address the need to track transphobic attacks.[18]

Vanessa Lacey, Stop Trans* Pathologisation Protest, October 2012 © Transgender Equality Network Ireland (TENI), photographer Louise Hannon

LEGAL GENDER RECOGNITION

The lack of legal gender recognition, in the form of a birth certificate, has surfaced as a crisis issue for many trans people in Ireland. Current lack of recognition renders Irish law incompatible with obligations of European human rights legal precedents. In 2013, Ireland remains one of the only countries in Europe that fails to afford legal recognition to transgender people.

Dr. Lydia Foy began challenging the Irish government in 1997 to obtain a birth certificate appropriately reflecting her gender. Since the European Court of Human Rights case, Goodwin v. UK in 2002, the European Convention on Human Rights has guaranteed the rights of transsexual people to have their gender recognised and to be able to marry someone of a different gender.[19] Upon appeal, in 2007 the High Court delivered a landmark judgment ruling which asserted that by denying Dr. Foy the right to alter her name and sex on her birth certificate under the Civil Registration Act 2004, the State is in breach of Article 8 of the European Convention on Human Rights.

In 2007, the Council of Europe Commissioner for Human Rights, Thomas Hammarberg, visited Ireland and recommended a change in the law so that transgender people can obtain a birth certificate reflecting their gender. In 2009 he published a viewpoint mentioning the Foy case specifically, and demanding immediate granting of full and unconditional human rights for trans people in Ireland.[20] In 2010, the Irish Government announced its intentions to legislate for Gender Recognition, and sought input into this process. In 2011, the government-appointed Gender Recognition Advisory Group (GRAG) presented their long-awaited report to Minister for Social Protection, Joan Burton, outlining recommendations and criteria for a scheme to allow transgender people to apply for legal recognition in the form of gender change on their birth certificates. The GRAG recommendations were strongly opposed by trans individuals, NGOs and human rights groups who engaged in communication and lobbying to protest the gender recognition 'evidentiary criteria' recommended by the GRAG, as well as the ongoing delays in implementing legislation. Finally, in 2013, Joan Burton published Heads of the Gender Recognition Bill. Frustratingly, the Heads of Bill reproduce much of the exclusive and disrespectful requirements and discourse found in the GRAG report.

While the introduction of transgender legal recognition into Irish law is something to be celebrated, the evidentiary criteria proposed are discriminatory, oppressive and unrealistic. The GRAG's 2011 report articulated offensive viewpoints by labelling transgender people 'lonely, distressed, passive', and making recommendations which de-humanise transgender experiences. Unfortunately, despite years of activism, education, and lobbying from the transgender community, the Department of Social Protection did not adequately engage trans people in their process, and Joan Burton's 2013 Heads of Bill largely ignore both the experiences and perspectives of transgender people, and international best practice and trans human rights norms.

The Heads of Bill propose requiring that applicants for gender recognition submit a collection of 'evidence' as a prerequisite. They propose requiring a statement from the applicant's primary physician confirming that the person has transitioned/is transitioning to their acquired gender. There are no policies regulating access to transition-related treatment in Ireland, but current practice necessitates fulfilment of mental disorder diagnostic criteria as set out by the Diagnostic and Statistical Manual of Mental Disorders (DSM) of the American Psychiatric Association. Diagnostic criteria strictly rely on binary understandings of gender and explicitly exclude intersex individuals from diagnosis.[21]

All of this is in addition to the stigma, both internalised and externalised, that can result from being required to undergo mental illness diagnosis to access medical services and legal rights. Until the 1970s, homosexuality was classified as a mental disorder. The implication was that being gay, in and of itself, implied impairments to judgement, stability and capability. Today this classification seems absurd. Instead of a diagnosable mental disorder, being lesbian, gay or bisexual (LGB) is now seen as an aspect of identity which is self-determined. There are emerging movements to reject medicalised and pathologising models, preferring a social model which simply sees trans as a self-determined identity. Not everyone feels they were 'born this way', with many coming to a trans identity well into adulthood. Simultaneously, growing numbers of young people are identifying with, and requiring support in, their identities from an early age. There are as many different ways to be trans as there are ways to be human, and medical models will never be able to do this justice. Imagine if homosexuality was still considered a mental disorder, and in order to access Ireland's civil partnership legislation, partners would be required to submit diagnoses as 'evidence' prior to relationship recognition. Outrage would ensue – it would feel like the dark ages. Many trans people feel that *they* are the experts on their experiences, and procedures for accessing legal rights should reflect this. 'Coming out' as trans is no small undertaking and, like declaring a gay identity, it is not taken lightly by transgender people. Many trans people resent the fact that members of the medical profession are seen as the 'real experts', in addition to serving as the gatekeepers of trans lives.

Perhaps the most widely criticised requirement within the Heads of Bill is that an applicant must be single. The requirement is callous and ignorant of the reality that many transgender people are in loving relationships. Unique complications arise with the Irish divorce requirements of four years' separation and no prospect of reconciliation. For the trans person with a family, this choice is impossible. Transgender families are uniquely disadvantaged, coupling the lack of same-sex marriage recognition and gender recognition with a unique set of social stigmas. Some trans relationships, although straight, cannot enjoy the privileges of marriage, while other trans relationships and families struggle with losing societal respect and recognition upon a gender transition. The requirement that an applicant be single effectively obliges one to choose between exercising one's right to be married or one's right to gender recognition, and can also infringe on the rights of a supportive spouse. It is ironic how, in Ireland, we have come full circle with the divorce issue. During the 1980s and 1990s activists, including many feminists, fought to change the Constitution, which prohibited dissolution of a marriage. Today transgender people may be forced to divorce. The Irish Constitution's special protection of marriage seems not to be extended to one of the nation's most marginalised groups.

The Heads of Bill's proposed requirement that an applicant be over the age of 18 is incredibly problematic. Not allowing a mechanism for gender recognition until an applicant reaches 18 years of age is out of touch with the lived realities of young trans people in Ireland today. LGBTQ people in Ireland are coming out, to themselves and to others, at younger and younger ages. Many trans people do not identify with the sex assigned at birth from an early age. With the age of medical consent set at age 16 in Ireland, it is ignorant and unrealistic to make young people wait until age 18 to have their gender recognised. This puts young trans people into jeopardy with lack of recognition in schooling, giving many young people no choice but to leave school early.[22]

It is now more than 20 years since Lydia Foy first asked to have her birth certificate amended. Irish transgender people have waited too long for this basic human right. Throughout Europe, there has been a movement away from requirements such as mental illness diagnosis and forced divorce. As Ireland is one of the last countries in Europe to implement Gender Recognition Legislation, this is a key opportunity to implement good practice. Respectful legislation would rely on a transgender person's self-determination of their identity, rather than medical opinion. Realistic legislation would recognise that transgender people have relationships and families, just like any other segment of the population, and would protect these families. Minister Burton will leave a legacy with this legislation, and it appears as though she may be remembered for oppressing Ireland's transgender population and ignoring the rights of intersex people, rather than for grasping the opportunity to lead Europe by taking a stance for transgender human rights.

PATHOLOGISATION AND HEALTH SERVICES

Medical services for transgender people in Ireland are dismal. There is no defined treatment path through the Health Service Executive (HSE) for transition, though this is something that TENI is currently addressing through initiating collaborations and education with the HSE. What's worse is the dearth of medical professionals with transgender expertise. Gender reassignment surgery is not available in Ireland. Individuals wishing to have surgery must pay privately abroad, or apply for the Treatment Abroad Scheme, often waiting several years. If going the public route, transgender people often have to rely on the hope that they will encounter a GP and local area psychiatrist who is understanding and willing to accommodate, even if they do not have transgender experience or expertise. Many trans people have met transphobia from their physicians, and unfortunately this includes the physicians who are considered 'trans experts' as well as those who are unfamiliar with trans experiences.[23]

The extreme levels of discrimination and social isolation that transgender people experience worldwide is widely documented, and high rates of self harm and suicidality often stem from the intolerance transgender individuals face.[24] Although not every trans person desires or is able to undergo medical procedures, such as hormones and surgery, for those who wish to physically transition in this way surgery is not only medically necessary, for many transgender people it is literally lifesaving. It is inconsistent for the Gender Recognition Heads of Bill to require medical interventions within its evidentiary criteria while such services are in many ways inaccessible. The dearth of medical professionals with expertise in transgender healthcare in the Irish context must urgently be addressed.

MEDIA COVERAGE OF TRANS ISSUES

Trans people experience widespread discrimination, and obstacles in accessing health services contribute to their marginalisation. The media often compounds this situation by presenting sensationalised stories about transgender experiences, often focusing on one specific type of trans narrative, most prominently the older transgender woman who is 'suffering' and lonely. While statistics of mental health difficulties are high within the trans population, this is undeniably due to stigma, isolation and social marginalisation. One side effect of the increased capacity of the Irish trans advocacy movement and the recent government-level discourse on trans rights has been an increase in visibility of trans issues within the Irish media.

While much of this coverage has been respectful, and trans media discourses in Ireland have come a long way in just a short time, there has unfortunately also been an increase in transphobic media discourses and there is still a body of work to be accomplished in this realm. The media rarely reflects trans experiences as diverse, and trans people as leading happy and fulfilled lives. It is time for Irish society to stop ignoring the insidious ways that transphobia continues to be disguised as humour, and to stand in solidarity with trans people.

FEMINISM AND TRANSGENDER
HISTORIC DISCOURSES

Feminism does not have a flawless history or reputation when it comes to supporting trans rights and realities. Janice Raymond was infamously at the fore of the tirade against trans people in the name of feminism with her 1979 *Transsexual Empire* in which she constructs transsexuality as the 'rape' of women and the 'female form'.[25] Sheila Jefferies believes that womanhood is not 'in the head', but comes from being born embodied female. Germaine Greer has insisted that 'other delusions may be challenged, but not a man's delusion that he is female'.[26] Each of these positions downgrades or erases the reality of trans experiences. The primary arguments anti-trans feminists have used to argue against transgender inclusion insist that transgender people simply do not exist, are delusional or, worse, violently encroaching on the position of women. This type of thinking inspired an era of struggle and discord for all varieties of trans people when it came to 'women-only' spaces, feminist organising, and feminist theoretical discourse.[27] Trans-feminine individuals were seen as attempting to bring 'male privilege' into feminist spaces, and were always already 'failed women'. Trans-masculine people, on the other hand, were seen as traitors who were attempting to join the patriarchy rather than assisting in solidarity with its dismantling. What these discourses left unscrutinised, was the ways in which trans people were actively demonised and excluded from feminism before ever being given a chance to make their case, and before ever being considered as quite possibly battling the same power structures and systems of oppression.

It is not hard to see how trans people, and particularly trans women, could feel disenfranchised by feminism more broadly, or feel apprehensive about trans-feminist alliances after reading this historical account. As long as there are strands of feminism that speak out against trans inclusion (and yes, this is an ongoing reality) trans people will be sceptical of feminism, and feminists might feel hesitant to take a stand for trans rights. It is long overdue for feminism, in its broadest sense, to understand once and for all that trans people are not the enemy, and in fact that many trans people are feminists and many feminists identify as trans. All types of feminisms need to see how trans people are embedded within the struggles as cisgender women and girls – and are arguably experiencing these oppressions most poignantly.[28] Any exclusion of trans women that may take place at the hands of cisgender women could easily be likened to the other types of stigma and oppression that have historically taken place between women, both within and outside of the feminist movement – the othering of women of colour, single mothers or lesbians, for example. For many feminists, any 'debate' about trans inclusion relates to the arguments on gender essentialism versus social construction. For the gender essentialists, trans realities throw a theoretical wrench into the equation, but the essentialist argument is becoming increasingly outdated as intersex experiences become more widely discussed, and as we learn more about the biological 'naturalness' of ambiguous genitals and sex assignments at birth.[29] Many scholars have called on feminist theory, and particularly radical feminist schools of thought, to re-evaluate their historical stances on transgender realities.[30]

Underlying some of the discord that the feminist and transgender movements have grappled with, is the notion that the feminist struggle is a personal *and* political one, whereas trans movements are often seen as solely personal. The extremities to which law, policy and societal practices have introduced, enforced and institutionalised transphobia are only beginning to be discovered, whereas a feminist analysis of legal, economic and societal structures has long been established. While the feminist political analysis is ongoing, in that the oppression seems not to have changed, but rather to have shape-shifted in recent years and decades, a transgender political analysis is in its infancy. With the differing breadth of discourses available, it is easy to see how the struggles may appear to have less in common than they actually do.

Solidarity between the movements requires a socio-political analysis which sees gender as more nuanced than just a binary notion of men and women. Anytime a feminist asks 'where are the women?' or 'how might this affect women?' we need also to ask 'where are the trans people?' and 'how will this issue affect trans experiences?'. If women are the oppressed gender category when situated in relation to men in a binary system, it follows that those who sit outside of the binary system or whose inclusion within the categories 'men' and 'women' has been debated would experience further marginalisation and oppression by a hierarchical gender system. Every time a gender analysis is completed that looks only at women and men, trans experiences are erased. Each time a survey is conducted which gives only two gender options, an opportunity to investigate the presence of and impact on trans realities is missed. As feminists, it is our obligation to do better. We have a responsibility to look at gender oppression more comprehensively. We must still evaluate the privileged position of cisgender men, but thereby also evaluate gender oppression as occurring intersectionally for everyone outside of this gender privilege paradigm. Those who are the lowest positioned within the gender hierarchy are arguably those whose position within the seemingly socially obligatory two-gender-binary system is always already contested and 'othered'.

As with feminist movements, trans activism is rooted in personal, political and social realities and struggles. Hegemonic cis-masculinity and violent policing of gender norms are the common oppressors to both groups, and their struggles simultaneously have striking similarities and critical differences. While historical feminist movements in Ireland fight for equal pay, lone parent rights, and bodily autonomy, trans movements battle extreme levels of unemployment, lack of access to medical services, and lack of legal gender recognition (that is, for the political acknowledgement that trans people exist). All women's bodies are policed and scrutinised by the media and society, and it could be argued that trans women's bodies are the most policed of all. Society looks for cues of masculinity in all women, and women are scrutinised and demonised when they are seen to be transgressing gender norms. Sexism, heterosexism and cissexism run in parallel, each privileging the power positioning of the cisgender male, and 'othering' anyone situated outside of this experience.[31] Intersectionality of identities plays a similar role for trans people as it does for cisgender women. Those who live outside of the norm because of their class, race, ethnicity, religion, dis/ability, family status, marital status, membership of the Traveller community, and so on, are all exponentially disenfranchised by these same hierarchies of privilege. When working intersectionally, it is important to always be mindful, aware and responsive to the ways in which trans and feminist identities intertwine and intersect with other aspects of identities that may contain similar histories of struggle and exclusion.

IRISH FEMINISM AND TRANS ACTIVISM

Today there are many feminist groups and spaces that have wholeheartedly taken on the task of trans inclusion and have joined in the fight for trans rights. Many trans people are feminists and many feminists are trans people, and of course they are not mutually exclusive categories. Especially in the Irish context, it is not uncommon to see a strikingly similar crowd in attendance at a pro-choice rally one day, and a trans awareness activity the following day. Many international feminist websites, blogs and organisations have implemented trans inclusive policies and maintain trans aware discourses, learning to check cisnormative thinking at every turn. Ireland is no exception.[32] Several feminist groups made submissions to the Gender Recognition Advisory Group process. Feminist groups also comprised much of the crowd at the October 2012 Dublin transgender 'Rally for Recognition', which marked the International Day of Action for Trans Depathologisation and called on Minister Joan Burton to implement inclusive and respectful gender recognition without delay. TENI's core group of volunteers mostly either came to trans activism through feminist movements, or became involved in feminism as a result of participation in trans rights activities. Many Irish grassroots feminist groups have actively taken on the task of learning about trans issues and experiences, integrating the fights for this cause within their remits. Increasingly, Gender Studies and Women's Studies coursework in Ireland is trans-aware and trans-inclusive, educating future cohorts of trans-feminist activists and scholars. Of course, though, trans and feminist activism have not melded perfectly in Ireland, and we could always do better.

One unfortunate example of room for improvement was demonstrated by Nell McCafferty, arguably one of Ireland's most well-known feminists. Along with the numerous, various feminist groups in attendance at the October 2012 Dublin transgender 'Rally for Recognition', McCafferty was present, but she clearly and loudly made it known that she was not there in support of trans rights. Instead, she came to heckle the activists, to argue against trans inclusion in LGBT movements, and to quite simply question the validity of trans people and trans experiences. She was unpleasant, persistent, and verbally attacked a number of trans people and activists at the rally and in the pub afterwards. Examples such as these highlight the ways in which both the trans and feminist movements could benefit from a more concerted, express and direct dialogue and collaboration.

Perhaps one of the most obvious topics with which the feminist and trans movements in Ireland could easily align, is access to medical procedures and bodily autonomy. The reproductive rights movement, and particularly the ongoing battle to implement safe and legal access to abortion in Ireland, is about the right to choose. The likeness between the abortion rights movement and the struggle for access to trans related surgeries and hormones without necessitating a mental disorder diagnosis seems uncanny. A simple 'my body, my choice' placard could easily be used at rallies for both causes.

In order for trans inclusion to be meaningful, it must be integral to a movement, and not just an 'add-on'. Although trans inclusion within feminist groups is a start, it cannot be a case of letting one trans person into feminist groups as a token, and asking that person to represent and educate everyone else on trans issues and experiences. Although feminist support at trans rallies and within trans activism is a start, feminists should not just turn up as a once off, without following the ethos of trans awareness and inclusion through all policies and positions taken by the feminist group in question. It must also not be the case that trans people are made to do the inclusion work, or that inclusion is put off until trans people join all of the feminist spheres. In order for trans people to join feminist causes, it must be made clear that the trans education work is ongoing and that spaces are welcoming to people of all genders.

Making trans issues central and integral within feminist discourses requires a rethinking of cisgender and binary gender norms and structures within society. These norms remain taken-for-granted by many cisgender feminists who have never had to consider them. Gender norms assume that everyone identifies with the sex assigned to them at birth, and that however we 'read' a person's gender, certain physical cues will tell us their gender identity. It is rare, for example, to see a 'round of pronouns' along with names when doing introductions in feminist spaces, yet this is one of the key elements to facilitating a trans-inclusive and trans-positive space. 'Women-only' spaces have been a historic issue of difficulty for trans feminists when it is not made clear that these spaces are for 'all women' or for 'women and all varieties of trans people'. Holding separatist spaces for cisgender women is discriminatory and ignorant of cisgender privilege.

While reflection on trans inclusion is increasing within community spaces, discussions within grassroots organisations and in online blogs and articles, the key players within the feminist movements (the large organisations and those feminists with international power and popularity) have not yet taken public stances on the cisnormativity of feminist movements.[33] Trans acceptance is one thing, but an active and ongoing critique of cisnormativity is quite another. Core feminist issues, such as sexual violence, employment inequalities, access to healthcare and media representation, to name but a few, are the same key areas of work for the trans movement. Every time a feminist movement fails to consider and include a trans analysis and perspective, cisgender feminists assert their privilege in a way which actively contributes to the marginalisation and exclusion of trans realities. Reframing activism in relation to all of these struggles in a way that integrally critiques the cisgender norms that widely inform discourse on these topics will benefit everyone. If feminism is a movement to end sexism, the movement will lose meaning lest our definition of sexism is not extended to include heterosexism and cissexism. I argue that it is not feminism if it is trans-exclusive or cisnormative, it is not feminism if it is not inclusive and intersectional. A trans aware feminism brings feminist movements up to date, and repositions feminist discourses with a more accurate focus on the real oppression of gender norms and hierarchies.

NOTES

1   Much of the information in this section is from informal conversations with Philippa Ryder, an early trans activist.
2   TENI, 'Introduction to Recognition', accessed 5/7/2013 at http://www.teni.ie/page.aspx?contentid=586
3   LGBT stands for Lesbian, Gay, Bisexual and Transgender (LGBT)
4   A person who identifies within the male/female binary notion of gender, and who identifies with the gender other than that which was assigned at birth. This includes trans men and trans women.
5   A mental illness diagnosis as classified by the Diagnostic and Statistical Manual of Mental Disorders (DSM) of the American

Psychiatric Association. This classification has been associated with transsexual experiences prior to Version 5 of the DSM, which changed the diagnosis to the more broadly encompassing Gender Dysphoria (GD).

6   Transgender Equality Network Ireland (TENI) *Transphobia in Ireland*, Dublin, 2009.

7   Transphobia is the fear, dislike or hatred of people who are transgender or challenge conventional binary gender categories of male and female.

8   P. Mayock, Bryan, A., Carr, N. and Kitching, K. *Supporting LGBT Lives: A Study of the Mental Health and Well-Being of Lesbian, Gay, Bisexual and Transgender People*, National Office of Suicide Prevention, GLEN and BeLonG To Youth Service, 2009.

9   Mayock *et al* 2009, p. 87.

10 Mayock *et al* 2009, p. 95.

11 Mayock *et al* 2009, pp 23–24.

12 TENI, 2009, p. 15.

13 See also Stephen Whittle, Lewis Turner, Ryan Combs, and Stephenne Rhodes. 'Transgender EuroStudy: *Legal Survey and Focus on the Transgender Experience of Health Care* (Brussels, ILGA-Europe, 2008), p. 17.

14 Transsexual is one of a number of different identities within the transgender umbrella. A transsexual person fits within the gender binary and is seen as transitioning from one gender to the other, such as is the case with trans women and trans men. When legislation protects transsexual people, it is unclear whether or not all varieties of trans people are included.

15 Tanya Ni Mhuirthile, 'Louise Hannon at the Equality Tribunal', accessed 06.07.2013 at http://humanrights.ie/gender-sexuality-and-the-law/guest-post-a-step-towards-the-protection-of-the-rights-of-transgender-people/

16 Diskriminerings Ombudsmannen (DO). *Gender Identity and Gender Expression*, 2009 http://www.do.se/Documents/sprak/english/gender%20identity%20and%20gender%20expression%20tillganglig%20(2).pdf

17 See Transrespect Versus Transphobia, accessed 06.07.2013 at http://www.transrespect-transphobia.org/en_US/tvt-project/tmm-results/march-2013.htm

18 More information at http://www.teni.ie/page.aspx?contentid=771

19 Whittle *et al*, 2008, p. 18.

20 See Michael Farrell online at http://humanrights.ie/
    announcements/guest-contribution-farrell-on-foy-case/

21 Intersex is an umbrella term for a variety of identities and/or
    conditions where a person's anatomy does not conform
    perfectly to expected biological norms for either gender.

22 Mayock, *et al*, 2009, p. 68.

23 Whittle, *et al*, 2008, p. 60.

24 See also Transgender Europe, www.tgeu.org

25 Janice G. Raymond, *Transsexual Empire: The Making of the She-
    Male* (Teachers College Press, 1994), p. 104.

26 Germaine Greer, 'Caster Semenya sex row: What makes a
    woman?' (20 August 2009) http://www.theguardian
    .com/sport/2009/aug/20/germaine-greer-caster-semenya

27 Julia Serano, *Whipping Girl: A Transsexual Woman on Sexism and
    the Scapegoating of Femininity* (Seal Press, 2009).

28 A cisgender person is somebody whose identity and experience
    of gender corresponds with the sex assigned to them at birth. In
    other words, a non-transgender person.

29 See also Anne Faust-Sterling, *Sexing the Body: Gender Politics and
    the Construction of Sexuality* (Basic Books, 2000).

30 See Eleanor MacDonald, 'Critical Identities: Rethinking
    Feminism Through Transgender Politics' in *Atlantis* 23 (1998) 1;
    Kate Bornstein, *Gender Outlaw: On Men, Women, and the Rest of
    Us* (London, Routledge, 1994); Patrick Califia, *Sex Changes: The
    Politics of Transgenderism* (Cleis Press, 1997); and Serano, 2009.

31 *Sexism* is prejudice or discrimination against people who are not
    cisgender males. It is rooted in the privilege and power
    afforded to cisgender males by the patriarchy. Sexism works in
    tandem with other bases of discrimination and oppression, and
    can be overt or covert, personal, structural or societal.
    Heterosexism is prejudice or discrimination against people who
    break the heteronorm, based on a belief that heterosexuality is
    the only correct sexual orientation. Heterosexism is a system of
    negative attitudes and bias in favour of heterosexuality, based
    on the assumption that heterosexuality is the norm and is
    superior to all other sexual orientations. Heterosexism can be
    overt or covert, personal, structural or societal.
    Cissexism is prejudice or discrimination against people who
    break the cisgender norm or who are not cisgender, based on a
    belief that cisgenderism is the only correct gender identity and

that being transgender is divergent. Cissexism can be overt or covert, personal, structural or societal.

32 The cisgender norm dictates that there are fundamental differences between discreet categories of men and women, that all people must fit within this two binary gender system, and that all people identify with the sex assigned to them at birth. Cisnormativity sees gender as fixed, biological and binary, and erases the possibility of being born with a body or having/developing a gender identity which transgresses these sex/gender rules. The cisgender norm works in tandem with the heteronorm to create an environment which breeds homophobia and transphobia, and functions with other norms to award advantages to those which fit within normative hierarchical identity systems.

33 See also http://feministsfightingtransphobia.wordpress.com /about/

Afterword

IRISH FEMINISMS: PAST, PRESENT AND FUTURE:
100 YEARS AND BEYOND

Mary McAuliffe

Irish Feminisms: Past, Present and Future introduces the
reader to some of the diversity of thought among feminist
activists, scholars and academics in the last one hundred
years. Influenced by the scholarship and activism of
women like Mary Cullen and Margaret Mac Curtain, the
academics and activists in this edited collection have
contributed a multiplicity of histories, ideas and stories
from the various waves of Irish feminisms. From the first
wave women who battled to find their place in a
conservative, patriarchal, misogynist society to the second
wave feminists who battled a conservative, patriarchal,
misogynist culture to the third and indeed fourth wave
feminists who continue to battle a society replete with
sexism, snapshots of feminist activism in each wave are
produced here.

As each of these waves crested, women in Ireland often experienced the backlash of a society determined to control, regulate and contain unruly females, these 'unmanageable revolutionaries' who, time and again, raised their heads above the parapet. The dead hand of respectability, that dominant ideology of the twentieth century, was often felt by women who dared to raise an oppositional voice to the dominant patriarchal culture. Whether it was by legislating women out of the workplace or by confining them in institutions such as Mother and Baby Homes or Magdalen Laundries until the later twentieth century, Irish women were often treated as dangerous and diseased, and contaminating to the body politic, to society and to the nation if they were perceived to behave contrary to the code of respectability.

Irish women resisted this ideology of respectability in many ways over the last one hundred years. Those women who fought for a republic in the 1916 Rising and the War of Independence expected a full and equal role in the new State. This was the guarantee given to them in the Proclamation of 1916. The backlash came swiftly. As Keogh has noted, a 'Gaelic Utopia did not arise from the ashes of 1916, 1919 or 1923'.[1] Especially for Irish women, there was to be no egalitarian Utopia.

This new Ireland was an under-industrialised, rural, agricultural state recovering from years of war, with low employment and high emigration. The first government of Cumann na nGaedhael was socially conservative and ideologically wedded to traditional Catholic values. Successive governments would continue to be socially conservative, especially in the area of women's rights. One government even fell in 1951 partly as a result of an attempt to introduce the Mother and Child Scheme. Part of the Scheme was a plan to provide free medical care for all expectant mothers and their children up to the age of 16.

This was opposed by the Irish Medical Association as an attempt to introduced socialised medical care, and by the Roman Catholic Church hierarchy, as an attempt to interfere with the rights of the family and provide women with gynaecological care and information which might not be in line with Catholic principles. A letter from the Bishop of Ferns, James Staunton, on the issue stated that

> education in regard to motherhood includes instruction in regards to sex relations, chastity and marriage ... we regard with greatest apprehension the proposal to give to local medical officers the right to tell Catholic girls and women how they should behave in regard to this sphere of conduct at once so delicate and sacred.[2]

Theses Catholic principles that Bishop Staunton and others, secular and religious, held so dear, were fundamental to the positioning of Irish women in the home, to the control of their fertility and to the regulation of their sexuality through the first six to seven decades of a post-colonial Ireland. Despite the campaigns of the maternalist feminists of the Irish Countrywomen's Association and the Irish Housewives' Association through the 1940s to 1960s, and grassroots organising by the second wave feminists of the Irish Women's Liberation Movement and Irishwomen United in the 1970s, women were still being sent to Mother and Baby Homes and Magdalen Laundries until the 1990s.

In this volume, academics and activists have documented some of the ways in which the discourses of respectability and domesticity, the legislative attempts to limit women's access to work, the regulation of female sexuality and the control of female fertility were resisted. Motherhood was dominant, but only legitimate motherhood within the confines of church-sanctified marriage. Illegitimate motherhood was seen as deserving of the most stringent of punishments, including incarceration in institutions of penance, prayer and work.

Female sexuality was only for reproductive purposes, any self-determined expression of sexuality was sinful and a threat to society and to Irish Catholic identity. As with illegitimate motherhood, perceived unbridled and unregulated expressions of female sexuality had to be contained, in carceral institutions like Magdalen Laundries where penance and hard physical labour were presumed to mortify the body and save the soul.

As Ireland modernised through the later twentieth century, new ideas, at odds with the inward-looking, moralising, respectable, misogynist society began to filter through the culture. Influences from the civil rights movements in the United States, feminism in the UK and the USA, the student movements in Europe, as well as the relaxing of censorship and the opening up of more of the country to TV, especially British TV, began, as Gibbons wrote, to 'disengage the family from the cycle of inhibition, authority and conservatism in which it had been traditionally enclosed'.[3] As the family, in which the woman was centrally and ideologically positioned by Irish society, began to loosen from these bonds of traditionalism, women began to break free.

If the 1970s was the era of campaigns for women's rights, women's access to the workplace and equal pay, as well as women's access to contraceptives, the 1980s was the era of the politics of the body. As Inglis has noted, the 'economic recession [of the 1980s] coincided with the emergence of a new strident Catholic morality'.[4] Since the 1970s, contraceptives had been available from pharmacies to married couples with a doctor's prescription, however a campaign to make them more widely available 'initiated a church-led moral panic about promiscuity, infidelity and liberal individualism'.[5] In 1983 abortion, which had been illegal under the Offences Against the Person Act (1861), was now made unconstitutional when the 8th Amendment to the Constitution was passed by over a 53% majority of the electorate.[6] This Amendment to the Irish Constitution still stands, as do Articles 41.2.1 and 41.2.2 which position women within the home.

Despite the advances achieved by feminist activists, the constitutional position of women is still dictated by the ideology of domesticity and Catholic moral thinking. Through the 1980s the backlash to the gains of the feminists of the 1970s continued: in 1984 Eileen Flynn was fired from her teaching post for being pregnant and unmarried, a condition deemed incompatible with the Catholic ethos of the school in which she taught. Earlier, in 1984, a 15-year-old girl, Ann Lovett, and her newborn baby died in a grotto in Granard and later that same year, in Kerry, an unmarried mother, Joanne Hayes, would be accused of giving birth to and killing twins, despite the fact that blood samples showed she could not have been the mother of both babies. What happened in the Kerry Babies Case, and indeed to Ann Lovett in Granard, 'has to be understood in the context of the Catholic church's [and the Catholic state's ongoing] monopoly over morality, [and] its obsession with sexual morality'.[8]

Throughout the later part of the twentieth century Irish women continued to fight against the forces of state and church to achieve rights and freedoms. The several referenda on abortion, on divorce, campaigns for the rights of single mothers, deserted wives, battles for changes in the law on domestic violence, sexual abuse and rape, as well as the campaigns for self-determined sexuality and control of fertility were some of the many battles fought, some won, some continuing into the present day.

The election of Mary Robinson as President of Ireland in 1990 was a major symbolic turning point in the campaign for equal citizenship, a Presidency she dedicated to 'Mná na hÉireann' (the Women of Ireland). Despite this break-through election however, traditional Ireland did not release its grip on women's lives and bodies easily. In 1992 the state used the law to prevent a 14-year-old pregnant rape victim from leaving Ireland with her parents to obtain an abortion. This was the 'X' case, which brought the issue of reproductive rights back on the agenda. Another referendum ensued which allowed women the right to travel and the right to information as well as allowing suicide as a reason for termination, while continuing to protect the equal right to life of the woman and the unborn.

The 'hard graft' of feminist activism continued into the twenty-first century, where new challenges arose and old unfinished battles continued. Political representation of women in our national institutions of government continues to be abysmal, although the introduction of gender quotas should help begin to correct that. Violence against women continues to be a major problem, and institutional responses to a rape culture, which insists, still, on victim-blaming are slow to change. Lack of attention to issues of childcare and the failure to legislate for state-regulated and funded childcare centres (first demanded by IWU in the 1970s) were serious failures in the years of the Celtic Tiger. Despite extensive lobbying by the National Women's Council of Ireland and other women's organisations the Irish government saw fit to invest many hundreds of millions in consultant reports on sports facilities and new prisons which never materialised rather than in building a country-wide network of regulated crèches. This reflected the ongoing lack of acceptance of gender as a central issue in deciding social and economic policy. Despite many advances in women's access to education and the workplace, in women's right to self-determined sexuality and reproductive rights, in legislation protecting women against violence and rape, in protections for single and working parents, there are still issues which make Ireland a country where women are not full and equal citizens. Some of these issues, of migrant women, trans women, working class women, rural women are reflected in this volume.

What of Irish feminism into the future? Many of the issues which were raised at the Irish Feminist Network conference in 2012, and which are further enlarged on in this collection, continue to be pressing. Reproductive rights, in particular the laws which resulted in the tragic death of Savita Halappanavar, have galvanised a new generation of activists joining experienced feminists who have been campaigning on this for years. Each generation is talking with and learning from the other. New campaign platforms are being used and adapted, from online zines to social media (Facebook, Twitter, blogs), as well as the continued use of time-honoured platforms of protest, such as marches and direct action activities. Discussions about allies, in particular the role of men in feminist activism, are as lively as ever. Newer issues like the relationship of feminism with trans activism, the difficulties faced by migrant women, especially those in direct provision, the growing, vile and sexualised harassment of women and, in particular feminist activists on online fora, the sexualisation of young girls, are but a few of the challenges facing Irish feminists into the future. Whatever shape or shapes it may take, Irish feminism, multi-faceted, vigorous and necessary, will, no doubt, be around for the next one hundred years.

NOTES

1 Dermot Keogh, *Twentieth-Century Ireland: Nation and State* (New York, Palgrave 1995), p. 35.

2 Angela Bourke *et al*, *The Field Day Anthology of Irish Writing: Irish Women's Writing and Traditions, Vol 5* (Cork, Cork University Press, 2002), pp 170–171.

3 Luke Gibbons, *Transformations in Irish Culture* (Cork, Cork University Press, 1996), p. 65.

4 Tom Inglis, 'Sexual Transgression and Scapegoats: A Case Study from Modern Ireland', *Sexualities*, 2002, Vol. 5, No. 5, p. 7.

5 Inglis, 'Sexual Transgression and Scapegoats', p. 7.

6 The Eight Amendment to the Constitution reads: 'The State acknowledges the right to life of the unborn and, with due regard to the equal right to life of the mother, guarantees in its laws to respect, and, as far as practicable, by its laws to defend and vindicate that right'.

7 Article 41.2: '1 In particular, the State recognises that by her life within the home, woman gives to the State a support without which the common good cannot be achieved.' And '2 The State shall, therefore, endeavour to ensure that mothers shall not be obliged by economic necessity to engage in labour to the neglect of their duties in the home'.

8 Inglis, 'Sexual Transgression and Scapegoats', p. 18.

Senator IVANA BACIK is Reid Professor of Criminal Law at Trinity College Dublin, and a barrister. She is a Labour Party Senator for Dublin University (elected 2007 and re-elected 2011). Ivana has written extensively on criminal law, criminology, human rights and related matters, and has a record of campaigning on civil liberties and feminist issues. Her publications include *Kicking and Screaming: Dragging Ireland into the Twenty-First Century* (O'Brien Press, 2004).

CLARA FISCHER is a Newton International Fellow of the British Academy at the Gender Institute, London School of Economics and Political Science, and a UCD Women's Studies Research Associate. Her work is interdisciplinary, spanning the broad fields of philosophy, political science, gender studies, and Irish studies. She specialises in feminist theory, and is the author of *Gendered Readings of Change: A Feminist-Pragmatist Approach*. Outside of the academy, Clara has worked as a researcher in the NGO sector and in the Oireachtas, and is involved in several social justice campaigns. She was a coordinator of the Irish Feminist Network from July 2011–October 2013.

GRAINNE HEALY is a long-time feminist activist, former chairwoman of the National Women's Council of Ireland (NWCI) and vice president of European Women's Lobby (EWL). Grainne was a community sector appointee to The Women's Health Council, The Equality Authority and the National Economic and Social Forum. Acting as Chairwoman of the European Observatory on Violence Against Women for ten years, Grainne has led many organisations working for social justice over the last three decades. She is currently Chairwoman of Marriage

Equality, the organisation seeking access to civil marriage for same-sex couples in Ireland. She co-authored with M. O'Connor, 'The Links Between Prostitution and Sex Trafficking: A Briefing Handbook' (EWL 2006) and is currently completing a PhD exploring the meanings of civil partnership for same-sex couples in Ireland at Dublin City University.

MARY MCAULIFFE holds a PhD from the School of History and Humanities, Trinity College, Dublin. She currently lectures on the UCD Women's Studies programmes at UCD. Her research interests include gender and Irish history, memory and history, oral history and military history. Her latest publication was a re-issue, with new introduction, of the mid-19th century travelogue by Frances Taylor, *Irish Homes and Irish Hearts* (UCD Press Classics Series, 2013). She is past President of the Women's History Association of Ireland (2011–2014) and a committee member of the Irish Association of Professional Historians.

CLAIRE MCGING currently lectures political geography at the National University of Ireland, Maynooth. A former Irish Research Council Postgraduate Scholar, her research centres mainly on the relationships between sex, gender and electoral politics on the island of Ireland. She has published on women and politics nationally and internationally, and regularly discusses this topic in the media.

SUSAN MCKAY is a writer. She was a founder of the Belfast Rape Crisis Centre and has written extensively about feminist issues. Her books include *Sophia's Story* (Gill and MacMillan 1998), and *Without Fear: 25 Years of the Dublin Rape Crisis Centre* (New Island 2005). She was CEO of the National Women's Council of Ireland from 2009–2012.

ANTHEA MCTEIRNAN is a journalist with *The Irish Times*, the former chair of the Irish Family Planning Association, a member of the National Women's Council's advisory group on reproductive rights and a campaigner on equality issues. She worked with the late Michael Solomons on his biographical polemic *Pro Life? The Irish Question* (Lilliput Press 1992). She is also the mother of two sons.

SALOME MBUGUA has over 20 years' experience of working with disadvantaged and under-represented groups especially women, children, and youth in Kenya, Uganda and Ireland. She is the founder of AkiDwA, the African and Migrant Women's Network Ireland, and is currently its CEO. Salome has served on the board of the Equality Authority, HSE Health Intercultural Strategy Advisory Group, and is currently an advisory and monitoring member of the National Action Plan on UN Resolution 1325 on women in armed conflict with the Department of Foreign Affairs. She serves on the board of the Black European Women's Council based in Vienna and the European Network of Migrant Women based in Brussels. Salome has a master's degree in Equality Studies and a certificate in Women's Studies from University College Dublin.

LESLIE SHERLOCK is a gender and sexuality educator, activist and researcher. She is completing her PhD in Trinity College Dublin's Children's Research Centre, in which she uses a queer and feminist perspective to examine narratives of good and inclusive practice in sexuality education from Ireland and Sweden. Leslie's activist and educational interests include sex education, trans* experiences, sexual health, feminism, hetero/cis-normativity, queerness and empowerment. Leslie regularly lectures in university settings and delivers trainings in colleges, workplaces and community groups.

AILBHE SMYTH is an activist and academic who has been involved in feminist, LGBT, and radical politics for a long time. She was the founding director of the Women's Education, Research and Resource Centre (WERRC) and head of Women's Studies at UCD from 1990 until 2006 when she left the university to work with community groups and organisations. She has lectured and written extensively about women, politics and culture in contemporary Ireland.

KELLIE TURTLE is an organiser with Belfast Feminist Network which she co-founded in 2010. She is involved in grassroots activism, campaigning and public awareness raising around feminist issues. Kellie obtained her MA in Gender and Society from Queen's University Belfast in 2009.

From 2005 until her retirement in December 2013 Dr. MARGARET WARD was the Director of the Women's Resource and Development Agency, a regional organisation for women, based in Belfast. She has also worked as an academic at Bath Spa University and the University of the West of England. She is a feminist historian, whose first book *Unmanageable Revolutionaries: Women and Irish Nationalism* (1983) was a pioneering study that continues to be influential. Dr. Ward is a Trustee of Museums Northern Ireland and a board member of Libraries Northern Ireland and is currently a Visiting Fellow in the School of History and Anthropology at Queen's University, Belfast.

INDEX

ABC case, 131, 140–142, 162–164

Abortion 10, 77, 131–133, 141, 143, 147–165, 219, 229, 244, 332, 333

Abortion Act (1967), 151

Abortion Rights Campaign, 259

Action on X, 261

Affect and Emotion (in feminism), 21, 105, 251–273

Anti-Amendment Campaign, 74, 137

Anti-Discrimination Pay Act (1974), 95

Ahern, Bertie, 203, 206

Ahmed, Sara, 262

AIM, 72

Alliance for a No Vote, 161

AkiDwA, 12, 218, 217–227

All Party Oireachtas Committee on the Constitution, 161

Anglo-Irish Treaty (1922), 48

Associated Country Women of the World Conference, 114–115

Association for Deserted and Alone Parents, 72

Asylum system, 220, 228–231
  Women in, 222, 228–231, 232

Athlone Families Together, 230

Atlantic Philanthropies, 242, 306

Auberting, Rosine, 85

Bacik, Ivana, 12, 21, 147–168

Banda, Joyce, 218

Banshee, 92, 97–98, 100

Banúlacht, 221

Bean na hEireann, 27, 28

Behan, Niall, 140

Belfast Feminist Network, 276–301

Bell, Elizabeth, 31

Bellos, Linda, 122

BeLong To, 304

Beloved, 263–267

Bennett, Louie, 35, 39, 42

Bergin, Joan, 247

Black Association of Women Step Out, 233

Boland, Eavan, 9

Boxer, Marilyn, 13

Braiden, Olive, 242

Browne, Kathleen, 51, 55, 63, 64, 65, 66, 67, 68

Burton, Joan, 312, 313, 316, 322

Butler, Josephine, 25

Byers, Margaret, 23, 25

Carson, Edward, 35, 36

Casement, Sir Roger, 55

Catholic Church, influence of, 25, 49, 51, 61, 62, 68, 91, 113, 130, 147, 240, 331, 333